Stories of
Plants and Trees

Selected Authors

Forgotten Classics Family Library
Libraries of Hope

Stories of Plants and Trees

Selected Authors

Plants and Their Children, by Mrs. William Star Dana, New York: American Book Company, (1896).

The Garden of Earth, by Agnes Giberne, London: Society for Presenting Christiona Knowledge, (1921).

The Story of a Thousand-Year Pine, by Otis A. Mills, Boston: Houghton Mifflin Company, (1909).

Libraries of Hope, Inc.
Appomattox, Virginia 24522

Website www.librariesofhope.com
Email: librariesofhope@gmail.com

Printed in the United States of America

CONTENTS

PLANTS

AND THEIR CHILDREN

BY

MRS. WILLIAM STARR DANA
AUTHOR OF "HOW TO KNOW THE WILD FLOWERS"

ILLUSTRATED BY

ALICE JOSEPHINE SMITH

PREFACE

A CHILD'S reading book, it seems to me, should secure for the child three things, — practice in the art of reading, amusement, and instruction. Whether my little book is fitted to attain this threefold object, others must decide; but in laying it before the public, let me urge careful attention to a few suggestions.

1. As the book is arranged so as to begin with the opening of the school year and to follow it to its close. the interest of pupils will be increased by reading the different chapters during the seasons to which they refer.

2. The teacher should exercise judgment as to the omission of any chapter or group of chapters which may seem beyond· the comprehension of the class. With a little care, such an omission may nearly always be made without injury to the usefulness of the rest of the book.

3. Specimens of the objects described, when these can be found in the locality, should always be on exhibition in the schoolroom. Whenever possible, the children themselves should collect and handle these specimens. If for any reason this collection by the children cannot be accomplished, the teacher should not fail to anticipate the readings, and to provide the objects mentioned.

By the observance of these simple and practicable suggestions, it is believed that, while the children are being trained in the art of reading, their powers of observation and of reasoning will be devel-

3

oped, and that they will be inspired with a lifelong interest in nature. The child's mind is peculiarly alive to the charm of nature when she is studied in detail, and through her it can be trained to observe accurately and to reason logically.

Through the neglect of nature study, the wits of the country child lose just the sharpening they most need, to say nothing of a stimulus and delight which can ill be spared by one whose mental life is apt to be monotonous.

The wits of the city child may secure in other ways the sharpening so essential to success in life: yet the training afforded by a logical study of plants, and the pleasure which such a study, rightly directed, is sure to yield, are as invaluable to him as to his country cousin.

Experience having proved to my keenest satisfaction that almost invariably children can be interested in stories of plants and *their* children, to the children of the land I offer this little book, in the earnest hope that its pages may lead at least some few of them to find in life a new joy and a deeper meaning.

The aid derived from many sources in the preparation of " Plants and their Children " is heartily acknowledged; but more especially I wish to extend my thanks to Messrs. Holt & Co. for their courtesy in allowing the reproduction of several cuts from their valuable and interesting publication, " The Natural History of Plants," translated from the German of Kerner von Marilaun.

PLANTS AND THEIR CHILDREN

PART I — FRUITS AND SEEDS

IN THE ORCHARD

IS there a nicer place in which to play than an old apple orchard? Once under those favorite trees whose branches sweep the ground, you are quite shut off from the great, troublesome, outside world. And how happy and safe you feel in that green world of your own! — a world just made for children, a world of grass and leaves and birds and flowers, where lessons and grown-up people alike have no part.

In the lightly swinging branches you find prancing horses, and on many a mad ride they carry you. The

5

larger ones are steep paths leading up mountain sides. Great chasms yawn beneath you. Here only the daring, the cool-headed, may hope to be successful and reach the highest points without danger to their bones.

Out here the girls bring their dolls, and play house. Nothing can make a more interesting or a more surprising house than an apple tree, its rooms are so many and of such curious shapes. Then, too, the seats in these rooms are far more comfortable than the chairs used by ordinary people in everyday houses. The doings of the Robin family are overlooked by its windows. One is amazed to see how many fat worms Mother Robin manages to pop down the yawning baby throats, and wonders how baby robins ever live to grow up.

From these windows you watch the first flying lesson ; and you laugh to see the little cowards cling to the branch close by, paying little heed to their parents' noisy indignation. All the same, you wish that you too might suddenly grow a pair of wings, and join the little class, and learn to do the one thing that seems even more delightful than tree climbing.

That you children long to be out of the schoolroom this minute, out in the orchard so full of possibilities, I do not wonder a bit. But as the big people have decided that from now on for some months you must spend much of your time with lesson books, I have a plan to propose.

What do you say to trying to bring something of the outdoor places that we love into the schoolroom, which we do not love as much as we should if lessons were always taught in the right way ?

Now let us pretend — and even grown-up people, who can do difficult sums, and answer questions in history and geography better than children, cannot "pretend" one half so well — now let us pretend that we are about to spend the morning in the orchard.

Here we go, out of the schoolroom into the air and sunshine, along the road, up the hill, till we reach the stone wall beyond which lies our orchard.

Ah! it is good to get into the cool of the dear, friendly trees. And just now, more than ever, they seem friendly to you boys and girls; for they are heavy with apples, — beautiful red and golden apples, that tempt you to clamber up into the green sea of leaves above.

Now let us "pretend" that you have had your fill, and are ready to gather quietly about me on the long grass. But first, please, one of you bring me an apple. Let it be well-grown and rounded, with a rosy, sun-burned cheek; for, as we are to spend some little time with this apple, the more perfect it is in shape, the richer in color, the sounder all the way through, the better. It is good to be as much as possible with

FIG. 1

things that are beautiful and wholesome and hearty, even though they are only apples.

Here we have (Fig. 1) a fine specimen. What do you know, any of you, about this apple? Perhaps this seems a strange question. But when we see something that is fine and beautiful, is it strange that we wish to know its history? If I see a man or a woman who seems to me all that a man or woman should be; if he or she is fine-looking and fine-acting, straight and strong, and beautiful and kind, and brave and generous, — I ask, "Who is he? Where does she come from? What have they done?"

Of course, a fine apple is not so interesting as a fine man or woman, or as a fine boy or girl. Still there is much of interest to learn even about an apple.

None of you seems anxious to tell the apple's story, so I shall have to start you with some questions.

Do you remember playing in this same orchard last spring?

Yes, you have not forgotten those Saturdays in May. The trees were all pink and white with apple blossoms. The air was sweet with fragrance, and full of the voices of birds, and of bees that were bustling about from flower to flower. No, indeed! you have not forgotten those happy mornings. What is more, you never will. They are among the things that will stay by you, and be a rest and help to you all your lives. I wish there were no child living that might not carry with him always the memory of May days in an apple orchard.

How has it come about, do you suppose, that these trees which in May were covered with flowers are now heavy with apples?

Can any of you children answer this riddle? How have these great apples managed to take the place of the delicate apple blossoms?

There are some children who keep their eyes open, and really see what is going on about them, instead of acting as if they were quite blind; and perhaps some such child will say, "Oh, yes! I know how it happened.

I have seen it all," and will be able to tell the whole story at once.

I should like very much to meet that boy or girl, and I should like to take a country walk with him or her; for there are so few children, or grown people either, who use both their eyes to see with, and the brain which lies back of their eyes to think and question with, that it is a rare treat to meet and to go about with one of them.

But I should be almost as much pleased to meet the child who says, "Well, I know that first the blossoms come. Early in May they make the orchard so nice to play in. But in a few days they begin to fall. Their little white leaves come dropping down like snowflakes; and soon after, if you climb out along the branches and look close, where there was a blossom before, you find now a little green thing something like a knob (Fig. 2). This tiny knob keeps growing bigger and bigger, and then you see that it is a baby apple. As the weeks go by, the little apple grows into a big one; and at last the green begins to fade away, and the red and yellow to come. One day you find the great grown apple all ripe, and ready to eat. But I never could see just what made it come like that, such a big, heavy apple from such a little flower, and I always wondered about it."

Now, if we wonder about the things we see, we are on the right road. The child who first "sees" what is happening around him, and then "wonders" and asks questions, is sure to be good company to other people and to himself. (And as one spends more time with

Fig. 2

himself than with any one else, he is lucky if he finds himself a pleasant companion.) Such a child has not lost the use of his eyes, as so many of us seem to have done. And when the little brain is full of questions, it bids fair to become a big brain, which may answer some day the questions the world is asking.

Before I tell you just how the big apple managed to take the place of the pretty, delicate flower, let us take a good look at this flower.

But in September apple flowers are not to be had for the asking. Not one is to be found on all these

FIG. 3

trees. So just now we must use the picture instead. And when May comes, your teacher will bring you a branch bearing the beautiful blossoms; or, better still, perhaps she will take you out into the orchard itself, and you can go over this chapter again with the lovely living flowers before you.

Now, as you look at this picture of the apple flower (Fig. 3), you see a circle made up of five pretty leaves. Sometimes these are white; again they are pink. And in the center what do you see? Why, there you see a quantity of odd-looking little things whose names you do not know. They look somewhat like small, rather crooked pins; for on the tips of most of them are objects which remind you of the head of a pin.

If you were looking at a real flower, you would see that these pin heads were little boxes filled with a yellow dust which comes off upon one's fingers; and so for the present we will call them "dust boxes."

But besides these pins — later we shall learn their real names — besides these pins with dust boxes, we find some others which are without any such boxes. The shape of these reminds us a little of the pegs or pins we use in the game of tenpins. If we looked at them very closely, we should see that there were five of them, but that these five were joined below into one piece.

Now suppose we take the apple blossom and pull off all its pretty white flower leaves, and all the pins with dust boxes, what will be left?

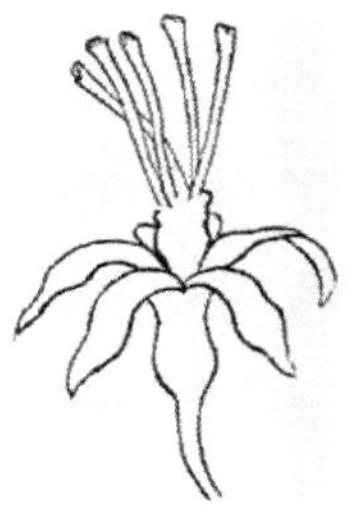

FIG. 4

This picture (Fig. 4) shows you just what is left. You see what looks like a little cup or vase. The upper part of this is cut into five pieces, which are rolled back. In the picture one of these pieces is almost out of sight. In the real blossom these pieces look like little green leaves. And set into this cup is the lower, united part of those pins which have no dust boxes on top.

I fancy that you are better acquainted with the apple blossom than ever before, never mind how many mornings you may have spent in the sweet-smelling, pink and white orchard. You know just what goes to make up each separate flower, for all the many hundreds of blossoms are made on the one plan.

And only now are you ready to hear what happened to make the apple take the place of the blossom.

THE STORY OF THE BEE

THIS is what happened. And it is a true story.

One morning last May a bee set out among the flowers on a honey hunt.

Perhaps it would be more true to say that the bee set out to hunt for the sweet stuff of which honey is made; for while this sweet stuff is still in the flower cup it is not honey, any more than the wheat growing in the field is bread. The wheat becomes bread later, after it has been cut and gathered and threshed and ground, and brought into the kitchen and there changed into bread; and the sweet stuff becomes honey only after the bees have carried it home and worked it.

As the bee left home this particular morning, it made up its mind that it would devote itself to the apple blossoms; for did you know that when a bee goes flower visiting, usually it gives all its attention to one kind of flower till it has finished that special round of visits?

So off the bee flew; and in a few moments it saw hundreds of little pink and white handkerchiefs waving at it from the apple orchard.

What do you suppose these were, these gay little handkerchiefs? They were the flower leaves of the apple blossoms. I call them handkerchiefs, because, just as boys and girls sometimes wave their handkerchiefs when they wish to signal other boys and girls, so the apple tree uses its gay flower leaves to attract the attention of the bee, and persuade it to visit the flowers. Of course, really, they are not handkerchiefs at all. They would hardly be large enough for any but fairy noses, would they?

When the bee saw so many bright handkerchiefs waving it welcome, along it hurried; for it knew this was a signal that material for honey making was at hand. Another minute, and it had settled upon a freshly opened flower, and was eagerly stealing the precious sweet.

You children know, that, when you are given permission to go to the closet for a piece of candy or cake, you are not apt to set about it very gently. You are in too much of a hurry for that. Often you come very near knocking everything over, in your haste to get hold of what you want.

And bees are quite as greedy as any boy or girl could be. So our friend dived right into the pretty flower, brushing rudely against the little dust boxes. These, being full to overflowing with golden dust, spilled their contents, and powdered the bee quite yellow.

Having made sure that nothing more was to be found

just there, off flew the dusty bee to the next blossom. Into this it pushed its way, and in so doing struck those pins which have no dust boxes; and upon their broad, flat tips fell some of the yellow dust grains with which its body was powdered.

Now there began to happen a strange thing.

But before I tell you more, I must stop one moment to remind you that these pins without dust boxes are joined below into one piece, and that this piece is set deep into the green cup which holds the rest of the flower (see Fig. 4); and I must tell you, that, if you should cut open this cup, you would find a number of little round objects looking like tiny green eggs.

The strange thing that began to happen was this : —

Soon after the yellow dust from the bee fell upon the flat tips of the pins without dust boxes, the little green objects deep within the green cup became full of life, and began to get larger. And not only this : the green cup also seemed to feel this new life; for it too grew bigger and bigger, and juicier and juicier, until it became the fine juicy apple we have before us this morning.

So now you understand a little of what happened to make the great apple take the place of the delicate blossom.

THE APPLE'S TREASURES

IF we lift our apple by its stem, it hangs in the same position as when growing on the tree (Fig. 5).

But the blossom whose place in the world is taken by this apple held its little head proudly in the air. So let us put the apple in the same position, and see what is left of the flower from which it has come (Fig. 6).

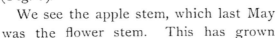

We see the apple stem, which last May was the flower stem. This has grown

FIG. 5

thick and strong enough to hold the apple fast to the tree till it ripens and is ready to drop.

The upper part of the stem you cannot see, because the apple has swelled downwards all about it, or upwards we should say, if it were still on the tree.

On the top of the apple, in a little hollow, we see some crumpled things which look like tiny withered leaves.

FIG. 6

You remember that when the bee left the yellow dust in the apple blossom, the green cup began to grow big and juicy, and to turn into the apple. And these little crumpled things are all that is left of the five green leaves into which the upper part of the cup was divided. These little leaves have been out in all kinds of weather for many weeks, so no wonder they look rather mussy and forlorn.

It is hard to realize that from the center of this now crumpled bunch grew the pretty apple blossom.

Now where are those tiny round things that were packed away inside the green cup?

Well, as that cup is now this apple, the chances are that they are still hidden safely away within it. So let us take a knife and cut the apple open.

FIG. 7

What do you find in its very heart? If you cut it through crosswise, you find five brown seeds packed as neatly as jewels in their case (Fig. 7); and if you cut it through lengthwise, you discover only two or three seeds (Fig. 8).

Probably I need not say to you that these seeds were once the little round things hidden within the green cup.

Some day I will tell you a great deal more about the wonderful golden dust which turns flowers into apples as easily

FIG. 8

as Cinderella's fairy godmother turned rats into ponies, and pumpkins into coaches.

But all this will come later. Just now I want to talk about something else.

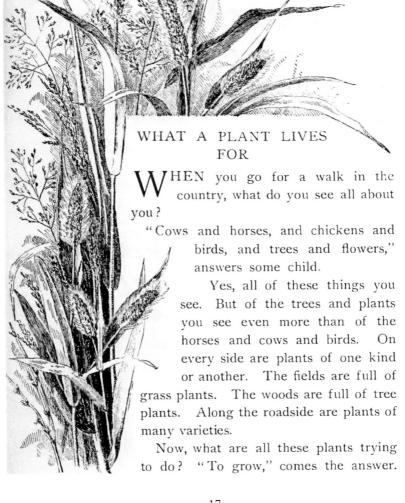

WHAT A PLANT LIVES FOR

WHEN you go for a walk in the country, what do you see all about you?

"Cows and horses, and chickens and birds, and trees and flowers," answers some child.

Yes, all of these things you see. But of the trees and plants you see even more than of the horses and cows and birds. On every side are plants of one kind or another. The fields are full of grass plants. The woods are full of tree plants. Along the roadside are plants of many varieties.

Now, what are all these plants trying to do? "To grow," comes the answer.

To grow big and strong enough to hold their own in the world. That is just what they are trying to do.

Then, too, they are trying to flower.

" But they don't all have flowers," objects one voice.

You are right. They do not all have flowers; but you would be surprised to know how many of them do. In fact, all of them except the ferns and mosses, and a few others, some of which you would hardly recognize as plants, — all of them, with these exceptions, flower at some time in their lives.

All the trees have flowers, and all the grasses (Figs. 9, 10); and all those plants which get so dusty along the roadside, and which you call " weeds," — each one of these has its own flower. This may be so small and dull-looking that you have never noticed it; and unless you look sharply, perhaps you never will. But all the same, it is a flower.

But there is one especial thing which is really the object of the plant's life. Now, who can tell me this: what is this object of a plant's life?

Do you know just what I mean by this question? I doubt it; but I will try to make it clear to you.

FIG. 9

If I see a boy stop his play, get his hat, and start down the street, I know that he has what we call " an object in view." There is some reason for what he is doing. And if I say to him, " What is the *object* of your walk?" I mean, " For what are you going down the street?" And if he answers, " I am going to get a pound of tea for my mother," I know that a pound of tea is the *object* of his walk.

18

So when I ask what is the *object* of a plant's life, I mean why does a plant send out roots in search of food, and a stem to carry this food upward, and leaves to drink in air and sunshine? What is the object of all this?

A great many people seem to think that the object of all plants with pretty flowers must be to give pleasure. But these people quite forget that hundreds and thousands of flowers live and die far away in the lonely forest, where no human eye ever sees them; that they so lived and died hundreds and thousands of years before there were any men and women, and boys and girls, upon the earth. And so, if they stopped long enough quietly to think about it, they would see for themselves that plants must have some other object in life than to give people pleasure.

Fig. 10

But now let us go back to the tree from which we took this apple, and see if we can find out its special object.

"Why, apples!" some of you exclaim. "Surely the object of an apple tree is to bear apples."

That is it exactly. An apple tree lives to bear apples.

And now why is an apple such an important thing? Why is it worth so much time and trouble? What is its use?

"It is good to eat," chime all the children in chorus.

Yes, so it is; but then, you must remember that once upon a time, apple trees, like all other plants and trees, grew in lonely places where there were no boys and girls to eat their fruit. So we must find some other answer.

Think for a moment, and then tell me what you find inside every apple.

"Apple seeds," one of you replies.

And what is the use of these apple seeds?

"Why, they make new apple trees!"

If this be so, if every apple holds some little seeds from which new apple trees may grow, does it not look as though an apple were useful and important because it yields seeds?

And what is true of the apple tree is true of other plants and trees. The plant lives to bear fruit. The fruit is that part of the plant which holds its seeds; and it is of importance for just this reason, that it holds the seeds from which come new plants.

———oo;o;oo———

THE WORLD WITHOUT PLANTS

WE have just learned that the fruit is important because it holds the plant's seeds; and we know that seeds are important because from them come the new plants for another year. Let us stop here one moment, and try to think what would happen if plants should stop having seeds, if there should be no new plants.

We all, and especially those of us who are children, carry about with us a little picture gallery of our very own. In this gallery are pictures of things which our real eyes have never seen, yet which we ourselves see quite as plainly as the objects which our eyes rest upon in the outside world. Some of these pictures are very beautiful. They show us things so wonderful and delightful and interesting, that at times we forget all about the real, outside things. Indeed, these pictures often seem to us more real than anything else in the world. And once in a great while we admire them so earnestly that we are able to make them come true; that is, *we turn our backs upon them*, and work so hard to bring them about, that at last what was only a picture becomes a reality.

Perhaps some of you children can step into this little gallery of your own, and see a picture of the great world as it would be if there should be no new plants.

This picture would show the world some hundreds of years from now; for, although some plants live only a short time, others (and usually these are trees) live hundreds of years.

But in the picture even the last tree has died away. Upon the earth there is not one green, growing thing. The sun beats down upon the bare, brown deserts. It seems to scorch and blister the rocky mountain sides. There are no cool shadows where one can lie on a summer afternoon; no dark, ferny nooks, such as children love, down by the stream. But, after all, that does not matter much, for there are no children to search out such hidden, secret spots.

"No children! Why, what has happened to them?"

Well, if *plants* should stop having children (for the little young plants that come up each year are just the

children of the big, grown-up plants), all other life —
the life of all grown people, and of all children, and of
all animals — would also come to an end.

Did you ever stop to think of this, — that your very
life depended upon these plants and trees? You know
that they are pretty to look at, and pleasant to play
about; but I doubt if you ever realized before, that to
them you owe your life.

Now let us see how this can be. What did you have
this morning for breakfast?

Bread and milk? Well, of what is the bread made?
Flour? Yes, and the flour is made from the seeds of
the wheat. If the wheat stopped having seeds, you
would stop having bread made from wheat seeds. That
is plain enough.

Then the milk, — where does that come from?

"That comes from the cows, and cows are not
plants," you say.

True, cows are not plants, but what would happen to
the cows if there were no plants? Do not cows live in
the green meadows, where all day long they munch the
grass plants? And would there be any green meadows
and all-day banquets, in years to come, if the grass did
not first flower, and then seed? So then, no grass, no
cows, and you would be without milk as well as without
bread for breakfast.

And so it is with all the rest of our food. We live on
either plants or animals. If there were no plants, there
would be no animals, for animals cannot live without
plants.

It is something like the house that Jack built, isn't it?

"We are the children that drink the milk, that comes from the cows, that eat the grass, that grows from the seeds in the meadow."

"If there were no seeds, there would be no grass to feed the cows that give us our milk for breakfast."

And so it is everywhere. Plants give us a kind of food that we must have, and that only they can give. They could get on well enough without animals. Indeed, for a long time they did so, many hundreds of years ago. But animals cannot live without plants.

I think you will now remember why seeds are of such great importance.

———∞o°∞∞———

HOW THE APPLE SHIELDS ITS YOUNG

SOME time ago you noticed that apple seeds were packed away within the apple as neatly as though they were precious jewels in their case.

When we see something done up very carefully, surrounded with cotton wool, laid in a beautiful box, and wrapped about with soft paper, we feel sure that the object of all this care is of value. Even the outside of such a package tells us that something precious lies within.

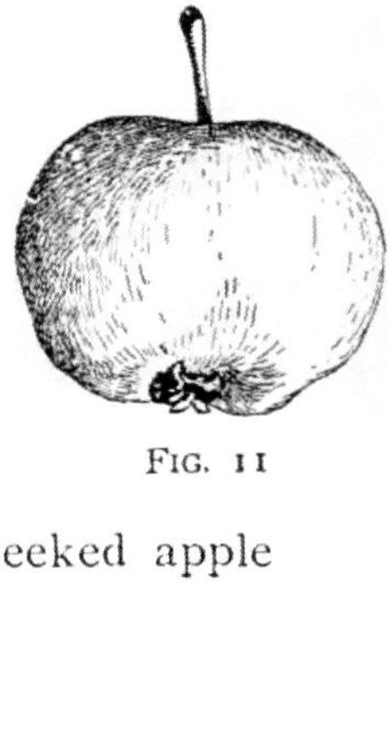

FIG. 11

But what precious jewels could be laid away more carefully than these apple seeds? And what jewel case could boast a more beautiful outside than this red-cheeked apple (Fig. 11)?

Pass it around. Note its lovely color, its delicate markings, its satin-like skin. For myself, I feel sure that I never have seen a jewel case one half so beautiful.

FIG. 12

Then cut it open and see how carefully the soft yet firm apple flesh is packed about the little seeds, keeping them safe from harm (Fig. 12).

But perhaps you think that anything so good to eat is not of much use as a protection. It takes you boys and girls about half a minute to swallow such a jewel case as this.

But here comes the interesting part of the story.

When you learn how well able this apple is to defend from harm its precious seeds, I think you will look upon it with new respect, and will own that it is not only a beautiful jewel case, but a safe one.

All seeds need care and wrapping-up till they are ripe; for if they fall to the ground before they are well grown, they will not be able to start new plants.

You know that you can tell whether an apple is ripe by looking at its seeds, for the fruit and its seeds ripen together. When the apple seeds are dark brown, then the apple is ready to be eaten.

But if, in order to find out whether an apple was ripe, you were obliged always to examine its seeds, you might destroy many apples and waste many young seeds before you found what you wished; so, in order to protect its young, the apple must tell you when it is ready to be eaten in some other way than by its seeds.

How does it do this? Why, it puts off its green coat,

and instead wears one of red or yellow; and from being hard to the touch, it becomes soft and yielding when you press it with your fingers. If not picked, then it falls upon the ground in order to show you that it is waiting for you; and when you bite into it, you find it juicy, and pleasant to the taste.

While eating such an apple as this, you can be sure that when you come to the inner part, which holds its seeds, you will find these brown, and ripe, and quite ready to be set free from the case which has held them so carefully all summer.

But how does the apple still further protect its young till they are ready to go out into the world?

Well, stop and think what happened one day last summer when you stole into the orchard and ate a quantity of green apples, the little seeds of which were far too white and young to be sent off by themselves.

In the first place, as soon as you began to climb the tree, had you chosen to stop and listen, you could almost have heard the green skins of those apples calling out to you, "Don't eat us, we're not ripe yet!"

And when you felt them with your fingers, they were hard to the touch; and this hardness said to you, "Don't eat us, we're not ripe yet!"

But all the same, you ate them; and the sour taste which puckered up your mouth said to you, "Stop eating us, we're not ripe yet!"

But you did not pay any attention to their warnings; and, though they spared no pains, those apples were not able to save their baby seeds from being wasted by your greediness.

But there was still one thing they could do to prevent your eating many more green apples, and wasting more half-ripe seeds. They could punish you so severely for having disobeyed their warnings, that you would not be likely very soon to do the same thing again.

And this is just what they did.

When feeling so ill and unhappy that summer night from all the unripe fruit you had been eating, perhaps you hardly realized that those apples were crying out to you, —

"You would not listen to us, and so we are punishing you by making you ill and uncomfortable. When you saw how green we were, we were begging you not to eat us till our young seeds were ripe. When you felt how hard we were, we were trying to make you understand that we were not ready for you yet. And, now that you *have* eaten us in spite of all that we did to save ourselves and our seeds, we are going to make you just as unhappy as we know how. Perhaps next time you will pay some heed to our warnings, and will leave us alone till we are ready to let our young ones go out into the world."

So after this when I show you an apple, and ask you what you know about it, I fancy you will have quite a story to tell, — a story that begins with one May day in the orchard, when a bee went flower visiting, and ends with the little brown seeds which you let fall upon the ground, when you had finished eating the rosy cheeks and juicy pulp of the apple seed case. And the apple's story is also the story of many other fruits.

SOME
COUSINS OF THE APPLE

THE pear (Fig. 13) is a near cousin of the apple.

But perhaps you did not know that plants and trees had cousins.

As you learn more and more about them, you will begin to feel that in many ways plants are very much like people.

Both the pear and the apple belong to the Rose family. They are cousins to all the garden roses, as well as to the lovely wild rose that you meet so often in summer along the roadside.

We know some families where the girls and boys look so much alike that we could guess they were brothers and sisters, even if we did not know that they all lived in the one house and had the one family name. If we look carefully at the plants we meet, at their leaves and flowers and fruits, and even at their stems and roots, often we may guess rightly which ones belong to the same family.

FIG. 13

27

If we place side by side an apple blossom and a pear blossom, we see that they are very like each other. Both have the green outside cup which above is cut into five little green leaves. Both have five white or pinkish flower leaves. Both have a good many pins with dust boxes, and from two to five of those pins without dust boxes.

If we place side by side a pear and an apple, we see in both cases that it is the green cup, grown big and juicy and ripe, which forms the delicious fruit.

If we cut these two fruits open lengthwise, we can see just how the pins without dust boxes are set into the green cup; and we can see that the lower, united part of these pins makes a little box which holds the seeds.

In the picture (Fig. 14) the shading shows you where

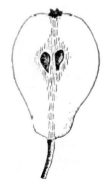

this seedbox ends, and the green cup, or what once was the green cup, begins. This is rather hard to understand, I know; but your teacher can make it clear to you with a real pear.

So it ought to surprise you no longer to learn that the apple and the pear are cousins.

Now, I want you to look at the picture at the head of this chapter. This is the wild rose, the flower from which the great Rose family takes its name.

FIG. 14

This rose is a much larger flower than either the apple or the pear blossom. Its flower leaves are deep pink. These bright flower leaves make gay handkerchiefs for signaling when the rose plant wishes to attract the attention of the bees.

But there are five of them, just as there are in the apple and the pear blossom; and there are the pins with dust boxes, — so many of them, in the rose, that it would take some time to count them all. And in the center are the pins which have seedboxes below; for these pins in the rose are quite separate one from another, and each one has its own little seedbox.

So, though different in some ways, in others the flower of the rose is very much like those of the apple and the pear.

FIG. 15

In this picture (Fig. 15) you see its fruit. This is called the "rose hip." When ripe, it turns bright red. In late summer you see the rosebushes covered with these pretty hips. At times this fruit does not look altogether unlike a tiny apple or pear; but if we cut it open lengthwise, we see that its inside arrangements are quite different.

The lower parts of the pins without dust boxes do not grow into one piece with the green cup (now the red cup), as in the apple and the pear. Instead, this cup (Fig. 16) is hollow. To its inner sides are fastened the little seedboxes, as you will see if you look carefully at the picture. This hollow case with its separate seedboxes shows you that the rose plant is not so closely related to the pear and the apple trees as these trees are to each other.

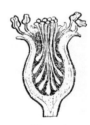

FIG. 16

DANA'S PLANTS. — 3

UNEATABLE FRUITS

PERHAPS one day you bit into the fruit of the rose, and found it sour and unpleasant to the taste. You may have forgotten that not long ago you learned a new meaning for the word " fruit." Possibly you still fancy that a fruit must be something good to eat. So many people have this idea, that once more I wish to make clear to you that *the fruit is the seed-holding part of the plant.*

Whether this part is good to eat or not, makes no difference as to its being a fruit.

The apple is a fruit, you remember, not because it is good to eat, but because it holds the seeds of the apple tree.

And for this same reason the pear is a fruit. It is the case in which is laid the seedbox of the pear tree. This case, when ripe, happens to be juicy and delicious; but it would be quite as much a fruit if it were dry and hard, and without taste.

And so the rose hip is a fruit, because it is the case which holds the little seedboxes of the rose flower.

What is the fruit of the milkweed ?

All country children know the milkweed plant, with its big bright leaves, and bunches of pink or red or purple flowers (Fig. 17). And you know the puffy pods that later split open, letting out a mass of brown, silky-tailed seeds. There! I have given the answer to my own question; for if the plant's fruit is the seed-holding part, then the milkweed's fruit must be this pod stuffed full of beautiful, fairy-like seeds.

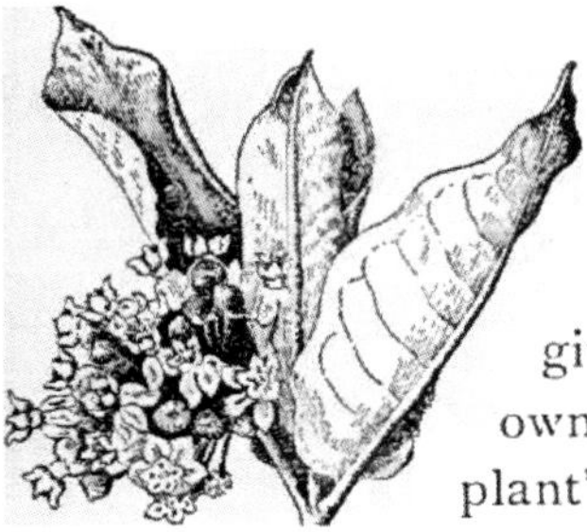

FIG. 17

FIG. 18

Then you know the burdock (Fig. 18) which grows along the country road. But perhaps you do not know that the fruit of this is the prickly burr which hooks itself to your clothes on your way to school. This burr (Fig. 19) is the case which holds the little seeds of the burdock, and so it must be its fruit.

FIG. 19

The fruit of the dandelion is the silvery puffball (Fig. 20) or "clock," by blowing at which you try to tell the time of day. If you pull off one of the feathery objects which go to make up the puffball, at its lower end you see a little dandelion seedbox (Fig. 21).

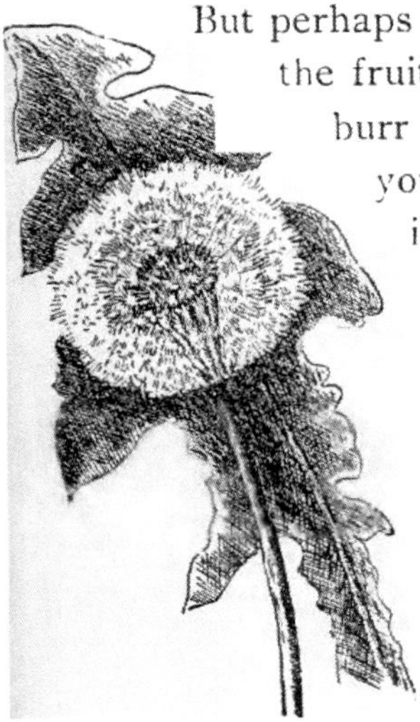

FIG. 20

And these fall days, along the roadsides and in the

31

FIG. 21

woods, everywhere you see fruits which you will hardly know as such unless you keep in mind the true meaning of the word.

Many of these I am sure you would not care to eat. The burr from the burdock would not make a pleasant mouthful. Neither would you like to breakfast on a milkweed pod. And a quantity of dandelion puffballs would hardly add to the enjoyment of your supper.

If you should tell your mother you had brought her some fruit, and should show her a basket of burrs and pods, she would think you were only joking, and perhaps a little foolish; and I dare say she would be greatly surprised to find you were using the word quite rightly.

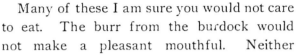

MORE COUSINS OF THE APPLE

FIG. 22

THE apple has three cousins, all of whom are very much alike. These cousins are the cherry, the plum, and the peach (Figs. 22, 23, 24). All three belong to the Rose family.

Have you ever noticed the great family likeness between these three fruits?

Look at them in the pictures. To be sure, they are of different sizes, but they are almost alike in shape.

32

And if you should cut them open lengthwise, right through the stony center, all three would look much like the next picture, which is taken from a peach (Fig. 25). All these fruits have the soft outer part which you find so pleasant to the taste.

FIG. 23

Within this, in all of them, is a hard object, which we call the stone or pit; and inside this stone or pit, in each case, lies the seed.

These next pictures show you two views of the flower of the cherry (Figs. 26, 27).

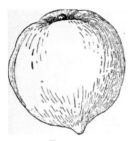

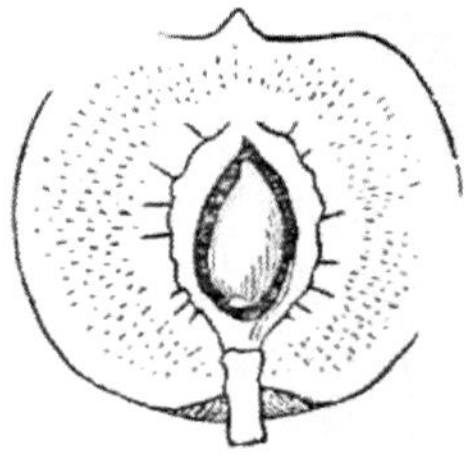

FIG. 24

Here you see a likeness to other members of the Rose family, to the blossoms of the apple and the pear.

You see that the green cup is cut into five little leaves (in the picture these are turned back and downward). You see also the

FIG. 25

five white flower leaves, and ever so many of the pins with dust boxes.

But you find only one of those pins without dust boxes; and this, as you now

FIG. 26

know, has a seedbox below.

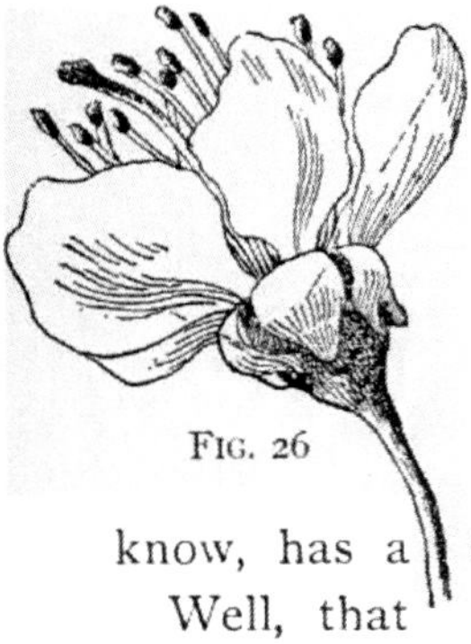

Well, that is all right. The cherry blossom has but one of these pins, and the flowers of the peach and of the plum have only one.

FIG. 27

33

Figure 28 shows you a cherry blossom cut open. Here you see plainly the single pin with a seedbox.

This seedbox with its case is what grows into the cherry. The white flower leaves, and the pins with dust boxes, fall away. In the cherry flower the green cup also disappears, instead of making the best part of the fruit, as it does with the apple and the pear. And

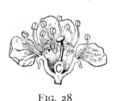

the upper part of the seedbox pin withers off; but the seedbox below grows juicy and ripe and red, at least its outer case does.

By the end of June you take out the long ladder and place it against the cherry tree.

FIG. 28

Seating yourself on one of its upper rungs, you swallow the outside of the shining little ball we call the cherry, letting the stony seedbox inside drop down upon the ground, where all ripe seeds belong.

The story of the plum and of the peach is almost the same as the story of the cherry. If you understand how the single seedbox of the cherry blossom turns into the cherry fruit, then you understand how the same thing happens with the single seedboxes of the plum and the peach blossom.

You know that in the flowers of the pear and the apple there were several of these pins without dust boxes; and although these were joined below into a single seedbox, this had separate compartments for the many seeds.

But the single seedboxes of the cherry, the plum, and the peach, have but one hollow. Usually in this hollow we find only one seed. So you see that these three fruits make a little group by themselves because of their great likeness to one another.

STILL MORE COUSINS

CHERRIES and plums we find growing wild in the woods and fields. While in many ways the wild trees are unlike those we grow in our orchards, yet, if you look closely at their flowers and fruits, you will find they answer generally to the descriptions you have been reading.

FIG. 29

Early in May, when the orchard is still gray and dreary, suddenly we notice that the upper branches of the cherry tree look as though a light snow had fallen. It seems as if the lovely blossoms had burst forth in an hour. One's heart gives a joyful jump. Summer is really coming. The flowers of May promise the fruit of June.

But when we find the blossoms of the wild cherry, it is several weeks later. Some of the little wood flowers have already come and gone. The trees are thick with leaves before we discover the fragrance of its slender, drooping clusters; for, though in other ways these blossoms are almost exactly like those of the cultivated cherry, they are much smaller, and grow differently on the branches.

This same difference in size and manner of growing you will find between the wild and the cultivated fruits. You country children know well the little chokecherries (Fig. 29) that are so pretty and so plentiful along the

lanes. These hang in bunches that remind you somewhat of the clusters of the currant. They are much
smaller than the market cherry; yet if you cut one
through, you will see that in make-up it is almost exactly like its big sister.

Those of you who live near the sea find wild beach
plums (Fig. 30) growing thickly along the sand hills.

These are hardly larger
than good-sized grapes;
yet if you cut them
open, you see that they
are really plums.

In our woods and
fields we do not find
any wild peaches. The
peach was brought to
us from far-away Persia.
Only in the garden and

FIG. 30

orchard do we meet its beautiful pink blossoms. To
see these growing naturally we must go to their Persian
home.

So, while we remember that the cherry, the plum,
and the peach belong to one little group because of
their likeness to one another, let us not forget that
the peach is one of the foreign members of the Rose
family.

IN THE WOODS

WHAT do you say this morning to going to the woods rather than to either garden or orchard?

Not that I am ready to take back anything I said at the beginning of this book about the delights of the orchard as a playground. For actual play I know of no better place. An apple tree is as good a horse as it is a house, as good a ship as it is a mountain. Other trees may be taller, finer to look at, more exciting to climb; but they do not know how to fit themselves to the need of the moment as does an apple tree.

But for anything besides play, the woods, the real woods, are even better than the orchard. The truth is, in the woods you have such a good time just living, that you hardly need to play; at least you do if you are made in the right way.

So now we are off for the woods. We have only to cross a field and climb a fence, and we are in the lane which leads where we wish to go.

Through the trees comes a golden light. This is made partly by the sunshine, but mostly by the leaves turned yellow. These yellow leaves mean that summer is over. It is in summer, when we are having our vacation, that the leaves work hardest; for leaves have work to do, as we shall learn later. But now they are taking a rest, and wearing their holiday colors.

Twisting in and out over the rails of the fence are clusters of berries which are very beautiful when you look at them closely. Each berry is an orange-colored case which opens so as to show a scarlet seedbox within (Fig. 31). A little earlier in the year you could not see this bright-colored seedbox. It is only a short time since the outer case opened and displayed its contents. These are the berries of the bittersweet. Last June you would hardly have noticed its little greenish flowers, and would have been surprised to learn that they could change into such gay fruit.

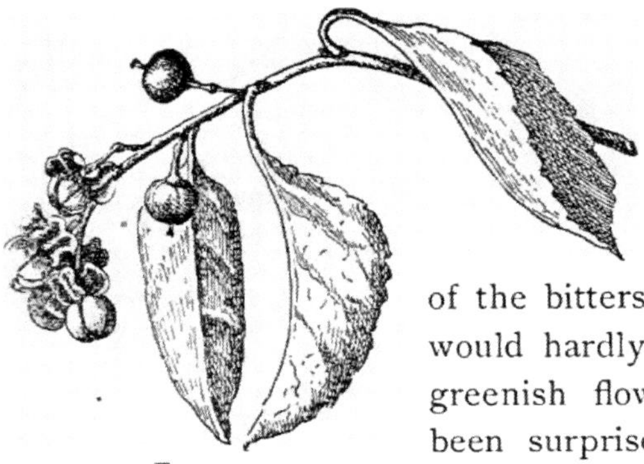

FIG. 31

Do you see a shrub close by covered with berries? These berries are dark blue. They grow on bright-red stalks. If we wait here long enough, it is likely that we shall see the birds alight upon some upper twig and make their dinner on the dogwood berries; for this is one of the Dogwood family, — the red-stalked dogwood, we call it (Fig. 32). When its berries turn a very dark blue, then the birds know they are ready to be eaten, just as we know the same thing by the rosy cheeks of the apple.

FIG. 32

You can be pretty sure that any fruit so gayly colored as to make us look at it twice, is trying to persuade some one — some boy or girl, or bird, or perhaps even some bear — to come and eat it.

You have not forgotten, I hope, why these fruits are so anxious to be eaten? You remember that when their seeds become ripe, and ready to make new plants, then they put on bright colors that say for them, "Come and eat us, for our little seeds want to get out of their prison!"

Once upon a time these seeds did not find their cozy seed cases a prison. So once upon a time the baby robins were content to stay safe in their nest. And once upon a time all the playground you needed was a little corner behind your mother's chair. But seeds, like birds and babies, outgrow their surroundings, and need more room.

Here is a tall shrub with bright-colored leaves, and clusters of dark red fruit that grow high above our heads (Fig. 33). It looks something like certain materials used in fancywork. This shrub is called the sumac; and if you pick and pull apart one of its fruit clusters, you find that it is made up of a quantity of seeds that are covered with little red hairs. There is nothing soft and juicy about the fruit of the sumac. Whether it is ever used as food by the birds, I do not know. I wish some child would make it his business to find out about this. Some of you are sure to live near a clump of sumacs. By watching them closely for a few weeks, you

FIG. 33

ought to discover if any birds feed upon their fruit.

If you do make any such discovery, I hope you will write a letter telling me of it; and then, if another edition of this book is published, I shall be able to tell other children more about the fruit of the sumac than I can tell you to-day.

There are many interesting things about plants yet to be found out ; and you children will find it far pleasanter to make your own discoveries, using your own bright eyes, than to read about the discoveries of other people. Every field, each bit of woods, the road we know so well leading from home to the schoolhouse, and even the city squares and parks, are full of interesting things that as yet we have never seen, even though we may have been over the ground a hundred times before.

Now let us leave the lane, and strike into the woods in search of new fruits. This morning we will look especially for those fruits which by their bright colors and pleasant looks seem to be calling out to whomsoever it may concern, "Come and eat us!"

Close at hand is one of our prettiest plants. Its leaves look as though they were trying to be in the height of the fall fashion, and to outdo even the trees in brightness of color. These leaves are set in circles about the slim stem. From the top of this grow some purple berries (Fig. 34).

This plant is the Indian cucumber root. If one of you boys will dig it up with your knife, you will find that

FIG. 34

its root is shaped a little like a cucumber. Though I have never made the experiment myself, I am told that it tastes something like the cucumber. It is possible, that, as its name suggests, it was used as food by the Indians. To hunt up the beginnings of plant names is often amusing. So many of these are Indian, that in our rambles through the woods we are constantly reminded of the days when the red man was finding his chief support in their plants and animals.

In June we find the flower of the Indian cucumber root. This is a little yellowish blossom, one of the Lily family. Small though it is, for one who knows something of botany it is easy to recognize it as a lily. Indeed, the look of the plant suggests the wood and meadow lilies. This is partly because of the way in which the leaves grow about its stem, much as they do in these other lilies.

Now look at the beautiful carpet which is spread beneath your feet. Here you will wish to step very lightly; for otherwise you might crush some of those bright red berries which are set thickly among the little white-veined leaves.

These are called "partridge berries," — a name given them because they are eaten by partridges. But the bare winter woods offer few tempting morsels for bird meals; and it seems likely that the nuthatch and snow-bird, the chickadee and winter wren, hail with delight these bright berries, and share with the partridges the welcome feast.

Please look closely at one of the berries in Fig. 35, and tell me whether you see anything unusual.

"There are two little holes on top."

Yes, that is just what I hoped you would notice. I

FIG. 35

do not know of any other berries in which you could find these two little holes; and as I do not believe it would be possible for you to guess what made these holes, I will tell you about them.

The flowers of the partridge vine always grow in twos. The seedboxes of these two flowers are joined in one. So when the flowers fade away, only the one seedbox is left. When this ripens, it becomes the partridge berry; and the two little holes show where the two flowers were fastened to the seedbox.

Try not to forget this, and early next July be sure to go to the woods and look for the little sister flowers. Perhaps their delicious fragrance will help you in your hunt for their hiding place. Then see for yourselves how the two blossoms have but one seedbox between them (Fig. 35).

42

Now, we must take care not to wet our feet, for the ground is getting damp. We are coming to that lovely spot where the brook winds beneath the hemlocks after making its leap down the rocks. What is that flaming red spot against the gray rock yonder?

As we draw nearer, we see that a quantity of scarlet berries are closely packed upon a thick stalk (Fig. 36).

Do you know the name of the plant which owns this flaming fruit?

If you were in these woods last May, at every turn you met one of those quaint little fellows we call "Jack-in-the-pulpit."

Jack himself, you remember, was hidden almost out of sight by his "pulpit." This pulpit was made of a leaf striped green or purple, or both; and this leaf curled about and above Jack (Fig. 37).

FIG. 36

After a time the pretty leaf pulpit faded away, and Jack was left standing all alone.

The lower part of Jack is covered with tiny flowers. After these had been properly dusted by the little flies (for flies, not bees, visit Jack), just as the apple blossom began to change into the apple, so these tiny flowers began to turn into bright berries.

While this was happening, Jack's upper part began to wither away; and at last all of it that was left was the queer little tail which you see at the top of the bunch of berries.

FIG. 37

It is said that the Indians boiled these berries, and then thought them very good to eat.

43

If we were lost in the woods, and obliged to live upon the plants about us, I dare say we should eat, and perhaps enjoy eating, many things which now

FIG. 38

seem quite impossible; but until this happens I advise you not to experiment with strange leaves and roots and berries. Every little while one reads of the death of some child as the result of eating a poisonous plant.

The next picture (Fig. 38) shows you the fruit of Solomon's seal. These dark-blue berries hang from beneath the leafy stem, just as the little flowers hung their yellow heads last May.

Next come the speckled red berries of the false Solomon's seal (Fig. 39), a big cousin of the smaller plant. As you see, this bears its fruit quite differently, all in a cluster at the upper part of the stem. These two plants seem to be great chums, constantly growing side by side.

We have been so busy and so happy that the morning has flown, and now we must be finding our way home to dinner; for, unlike

FIG. 39

the birds, we are not satisfied to dine on berries alone.

At almost every step we long to stop and look at some new plant in fruit; for, now that we have learned how to look for them, berries of different sorts seem thick on every side.

FIG. 40

Low at our feet are the red ones of the wintergreen (Fig. 40).

On taller plants grow the odd white ones, with blackish spots, of the white baneberry (Fig. 41), or the red ones of the red baneberry.

Still higher glisten the dark, glass-like clusters of the spikenard.

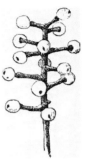

FIG. 41

Along the lane are glowing barberries (Fig. 42) and thorns bright with their "haws" (for the fruit of the thorn is called a "haw"). These look something like little apples.

Here, too, is the black alder, studded with its red, waxy beads. But we must hurry on, not stopping by the way. And you can be sure that those birds we hear chirruping above us are glad enough to be left to finish their dinner in peace.

FIG. 42

DANA'S PLANTS. — 4

WHY SEEDS TRAVEL

AT last I think we all understand that by the red of the apple, the purple of the plum, and the different colors worn by the berries we find in the woods, these plants are inviting us, and the birds also, to eat their fruit, and so release from prison their little seeds.

But what would happen, do you suppose, if no one should accept this invitation? What would become of their seeds if these pears and apples and berries were not eaten by boys and girls and birds?

Most of this question you can answer for yourselves.

If you leave the apple on the tree, after a time it falls off upon the ground ; and unless picked up, there it lies till it decays. In the orchard every fall you see apples decaying on the ground. In a little while the fleshy part disappears, and the little seeds are thus let out of prison without help.

But many plants are not satisfied to leave their seeds so near home. Why is this, do you suppose?

Well, this is quite a long story.

All plants of the same kind need just the same sort of food. If too many apple trees grow together, they soon use up all the apple-tree food in the neighborhood.

So if a seed is to grow into a strong, hearty, well-fed plant, it ought to begin life in some place not already full of plants in search of just the food that it needs for itself.

If a plant or tree makes its fruit so good to eat that some boy or girl or bird is likely to pick it, the chances are that it will be carried at least a short distance before its seeds are dropped upon the ground.

Once in a while a plant is rewarded for its pains by having its young carried thousands of miles.

Think how far from its home the peach has traveled. As I told you before, it comes to us from Persia.

Now, if the Persian peach tree had not made its fruit very juicy and delicious, it is not likely that any one would have taken the trouble to bring its seeds way over here to us.

But this peach being what it is, one of the most delicious of fruits, the tree was rewarded for its pains by having its children taken where they were petted, and made much of, and had things all their own way; for no other peach trees were on hand to do their best to crowd them out.

Then think of the little partridge berry. The fleshy part of this the birds eat and digest. But the little seeds pass unharmed from the bird's stomach to the earth, sometimes many miles from the woods where they were born.

What is true of the peach and of the partridge berry is true of many other fruits.

Without the help of man or bird or beast, these little seeds could at last get out of their seed cases; but without such help, often they could not get the start in life they need.

So it would seem as if a fruit's bright color and delicious flavor were saying to us not only, "Come and eat us and set our seeds free," but also, "and carry us far away, so that we may have a fair chance in the world."

SOME LITTLE TRAMPS

FIG. 43

WHEN I came home from that walk in the woods the other day, it took me some time to rid my clothes of many odd-looking little things, such as you see in the picture above (Fig. 43).

This round burr (Fig. 44) was one of the worst of my hangers-on. You know it quite well. It is the fruit of the burdock. Can some child tell me why I call this prickly burr a fruit?

Now let us look carefully at this seed case or fruit of the burdock.

FIG. 44

Instead of being smooth to the touch, like some other fruits we know, such as the apple and the pear, it is covered with stiff hooks. By these hooks it fastened itself so firmly to my clothes, that it was difficult to pull it off without making a tear.

Why does the burdock put its seeds into such a prickly case?

Please stop reading for a moment and try to answer this question.

Cudgel well your brains for the use of such a prickly seed case as that of the burdock plant.

48

PLANTS AND THEIR CHILDREN

Now I am hoping that one of you children will be able to think out some such answer as this: —

"Of course, the burdock plant doesn't want its seeds to fall on the piece of ground that has been used up already by other burdocks, any more than the partridge vine wishes to drop its seeds in the same little hollow where other partridge vines have eaten all the good food. As this burdock plant cannot make its seed case so bright and pretty, and good to eat, that the birds will carry it off, it must manage in some other way to send its seeds on their travels. And this is what it does: it covers the seed case with little hooks. When the seeds inside are quite ripe, this case breaks off very easily. So when the children come hunting berries, it hooks itself to their clothes, or else it catches in the hair of their dogs, or takes hold of the wool of grazing sheep, and gets carried quite a way before it is picked or rubbed off. When that happens, it is far enough from its old home to set up for itself."

I should indeed be pleased if one of you children could give me some such answer as that.

So you see this prickly seed case does just as much for its little charges as the juicy apple and velvety peach do for theirs.

And the same thing is true of all those other hooked, or barbed, or prickly little objects that I picked off my clothes the other day, and that cling to you when you take a walk in the fall woods.

They are all fruits. They are the ripe seed cases of the different plants.

But they are dull-looking, and often quite vexing,

instead of being pleasant to the sight and taste and touch.

This makes no difference, however, in their having things pretty much their own way. We do not in the least want to carry abroad these little torments, scattering far and wide their seeds, so that another year there will be more burrs and barbs and bristles than ever, to tear our clothes and worry our dogs; but they force us to do them this service, whether we will or no, and never stop to say " By your leave."

At every turn they are waiting for us. Where we climb the fence, and cross the fields, and break through the woods, we can almost fancy that we hear them whispering together, " Here they come! Now is our chance! "

They remind us of those lazy tramps that lie along the railway, getting on the trucks of passing trains, and stealing rides across the country.

These ugly hooked fruits have one great advantage over the pretty ones that are good to eat. They do not have to wait our pleasure. But when we are most busy and hurried, without a moment to loiter in the apple orchard or among the berry bushes, then, quite as well as, if not better than, during our leisure moments, they lay hold upon us with their tiny claws, and cling closely till we set to work to get rid of them. When we pick them off and fling them to the ground, we are doing just what they most wish.

FIG. 45 In this picture (Fig. 45) you see the seed case of the tick trefoil. This plant belongs to the Pea family; and its fruit is really a pod, something like that of the

garden pea. But when this pod of the tick trefoil is ripe, it splits into five little pieces. Each piece is a separate seed case. This is covered with hooked hairs, by means of which it fastens itself to our clothing and to the hair of animals, just as the burr of the burdock did. These little seed cases go by the name of "ticks."

FIG. 46

Here is the fruit of the stick-tight (Fig. 46). You see its two teeth that are so well fitted to weave themselves into either cloth or hair.

Fig. 47 shows you a strange and terrible fruit of this same class. It grows on an African plant, and may fasten itself so firmly into the hair of animals, that the attempt to get it out is almost hope- less. Sometimes an unfortu- nate lion will kill himself in his efforts to wrench this tormenting seed case from

FIG. 47

his skin. In his struggles he gets it into his mouth, and so dies.

I am glad to say we have nothing so terrifying as this among our hooked fruits.

Even if at times you are tempted to lose your patience with such impertinent little tramps as they are, I think you can hardly help admiring the clever way in which they manage to get a free ride.

51

SEED SAILBOATS

ON your way to school these fall days, often you notice certain white, silky things floating lazily through the air. Sometimes you catch one of these little objects, and blow it away again with a message to a friend. Or perhaps you wish upon it. At least, this is what I did as a child. Life in those days was full of these mysterious "wishes." A white horse, a hay cart, the first star, a wandering thistle down, — each promised the possible granting of one's most secret wish.

That the thistle down comes from the thistle plant, you know. But not all the silky things that look like fairy sailboats are thistle down, for many plants beside the thistle let loose these tiny air ships.

Have you ever wondered where they come from, what they are doing? Or do they seem to you so lazy, so drifting, so aimless, that you doubt if they are going anywhere in particular, or have really anything to do?

But by this time you have learned that plants have better reasons for their actions than you had dreamed before you began to pay them some attention. You

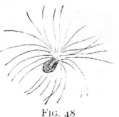

have discovered that they dress their flowers in gay colors so that the bees may be tempted to visit them and powder them with golden dust. You have learned that they make their fruits juicy and delicious so that boys and girls and

FIG. 48

birds may be persuaded to carry off their seeds; and the better you know them, the more certain you feel that they manage their affairs with much common sense, that they are not likely to take time and trouble for nothing.

So let us look closely at some of these air ships, and try to guess their errand.

I hope that some time ago you were told to get together as many different kinds as you could find, and to bring them here this morning.

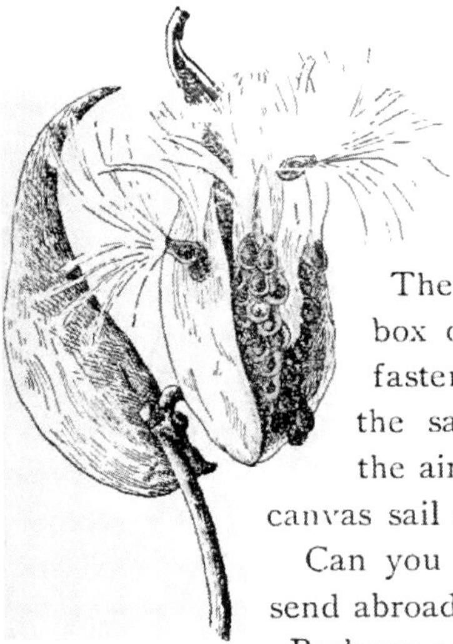

In this picture you see some of the air ships of the milkweed (Fig. 49).

The lower part of Fig. 48 is a seedbox of the milkweed. To this are fastened the silky threads which make the sail that carries the seed through the air with the least wind, just as the canvas sail carries the boat across the water.

Can you think of some other plants that send abroad seed sailboats?

FIG. 49

Perhaps some of you remember the beautiful pink or purple flowers which grew last summer in tall spikes along the road and up the moun-

53

tain side. These were borne upon a plant called sometimes fireweed and again willow herb (Fig. 50). The
first name was given to it because it grows freely
in places that have been laid waste by
fire. The latter one it owes to its
leaves, which look somewhat like
those of the willow.

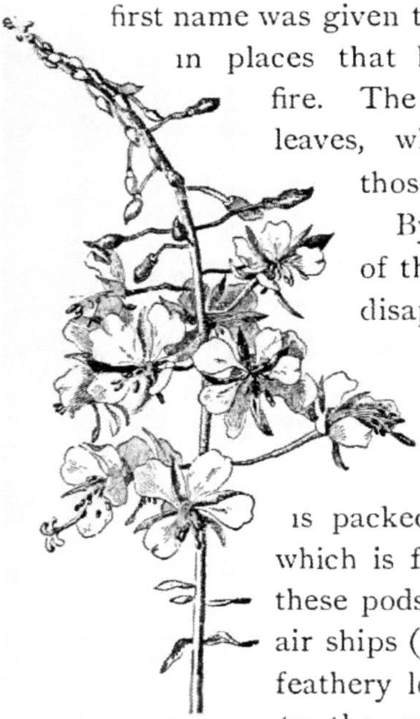

By the end of August most
of these beautiful blossoms had
disappeared, leaving in their
place the fruit. This fruit of
the fireweed or willow herb is
a long pod such as you see in
the picture (Fig. 51). This pod
is packed full of seeds, to each one of
which is fastened a silky sail. Finally all
these pods split open, letting out their little
air ships (Fig. 52), and giving a beautiful,
feathery look
to the great
patches in
which they are found.

Another plant which
launches
air ships is
the clema-
tis. In Au-
gust its
pretty white
blossoms

FIG. 51

FIG. 50

FIG. 52

FIG. 53

FIG. 54

clamber over the stone wall, and twist about the bushes

and trees, making the lanes very lovely. In the fall this climber is almost as pretty as in summer, for its fruit clusters (Fig. 53) are made of such long-tailed seeds as you see in Fig. 54. When these open, and float away with the first light wind, you can see how well their little sails are fitted to catch the breeze.

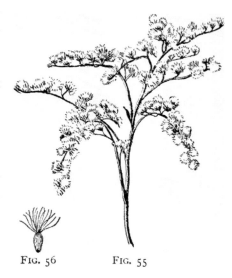

In October and November nearly every roadside is lined with clusters such as you see in the next picture, except that the picture cannot give their soft,

FIG. 56   FIG. 55

FIG. 57   FIG. 58

velvety look. These are the fruit clusters of the golden-rod (Fig. 55), made up of quantities of silky-tailed seeds such as you see above (Fig. 56).

And this is the fruit cluster of the aster (Fig. 57). Each little puffball is composed of many aster seeds (Fig. 58).

The pasture thistle is almost as beautiful in fruit as in flower. It swells up into a great silvery cushion, which finally vanishes in a cloud of floating thistle down.

And here is the fruit cluster of the dandelion (Fig. 59), and also a single seed sailboat (Fig. 60).

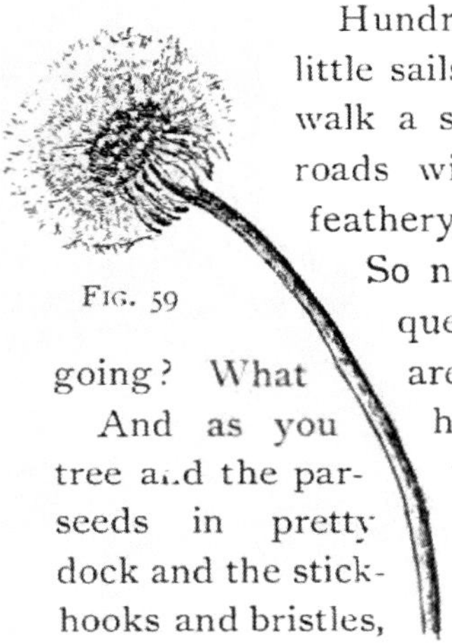

Hundreds of other plants attach these little sails to their seeds. You can hardly walk a step in the fall along the country roads without meeting these masses of feathery fruit made up of just such seeds.

So now we come back to our questions, "Where are they going? What are they doing?"

FIG. 59

And as you tree and the par- seeds in pretty dock and the stick- hooks and bristles,

FIG. 60

have learned why the apple tridge vine pack their cases, and why the bur- tight cover theirs with you ought to answer

these questions very easily. You found that those plants wished to send their little seeds abroad, so that they might get a better foothold in some piece of earth that was not used already by plants hungry for the very food that they most needed.

This is just what the thistle and milkweed and dande- lion and aster want for their seeds; and this is why they fasten them to little sails, and send them far away on a voyage of discovery.

FIG. 61

WINGED SEEDS

MANY of the trees also send their seeds on air voyages, in the hope of finding some piece of land that will give them a chance to grow into new, strong trees.

The seeds of the willow (Fig. 62) have silky white sails such as we have found already in the plants of the milkweed and willow herb; and the cotton-wood tree is so called because its tufted

FIG. 62

seeds remind one of the famous cotton seeds from which we get our cotton thread (Fig. 63).

There are other trees which use wings instead of sails when they send their seeds flying through the air.

FIG. 63

Here you have the winged fruits of the maple (Fig. 64). In summer you see these winged fruits hanging in clusters from the trees; and later in the year they are thickly scattered along the village street and in the city squares.

You can understand

FIG. 64

how easily the maple seeds inside these cases would be carried upon the breeze by their wings.

57

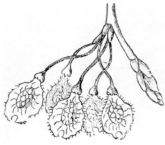

FIG. 65

FIG. 68

Each seed of the elm tree is winged nearly all the way round. The picture (Fig. 65) shows you a cluster of these as they look upon the tree.

Here is a bunch of the long-winged seeds of the ash (Fig. 66). Next comes a fruit cluster from the hop hornbeam (Fig. 67), and above is a single fruit (Fig. 68).

The seeds of the pine tree are hidden away in the pine cone (Fig. 69) you know so well, and those of the hemlock in the hemlock cone (Fig. 61). When they are quite ripe, they break away from these cones. In

FIG. 66

FIG. 69

so doing, each one carries with it a little piece of the cone, which acts as a wing to the seed (Fig. 70).

Nearly all of these seeds you can find for yourselves when you wander about the country. Indeed, if you have eyes that are good for anything, many of them you cannot help seeing. It is all very well to read about these plants and trees, and to look

FIG. 67

FIG. 70

58

at pictures of their flowers and fruits, and to have your teacher bring into the schoolroom specimens for examination. If this is all the city children can do (although even in the city one can do more than this), why, surely it is far better than nothing.

But best of all is it to go right into the woods and fields where these strange, interesting creatures are living, and to see for yourselves their manners and customs.

SHOOTING SEEDS

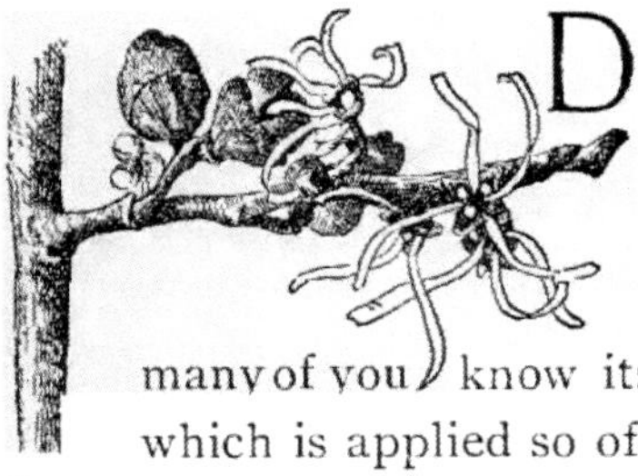

DOWN by the brook and along the sides of the mountain grows a tall shrub which is called the witch-hazel. I hope some of you know it by sight. I am sure that many of you know its name on account of the extract which is applied so often to bruises and burns.

Fig. 71 This picture (Fig. 71) shows you a witch-hazel branch bearing both flowers and fruit; for, unlike any other plant I know, the flower of the witch-hazel appears late in the fall, when its little nuts are almost ripe. These nuts come from the flowers of the previous year.

It is always to me a fresh surprise and delight to

come upon these golden blossoms when wandering through the fall woods.

Often the shrub has lost all its leaves before these appear. You almost feel as if the yellow flowers had made a mistake, and had come out six months ahead of time, fancying it to be April instead of October. In each little cluster grow several blossoms, with flower leaves so long and narrow that they look like waving yellow ribbons.

But to-day we wish chiefly to notice the fruit or nut of the witch-hazel.

Now, the question is, how does the witch-hazel manage to send the seeds which lie inside this nut out into the world? I think you will be surprised to learn just how it does this.

If you have a nut before you, you see for yourselves that this fruit is not bright-colored and juicy-looking, or apparently good to eat, and thus likely to tempt either boy or bird to carry it off; you see that it is not covered with hooks that can lay hold of your clothing, and so steal a ride; and you see that it has no silky sails to float it through the air, nor any wings to carry it upon the wind.

And so the witch-hazel, knowing that neither boy nor girl, nor bird nor beast nor wind, will come to the rescue of its little ones, is obliged to take matters into its own hands; and this is what it does. It forces open the ripe nut with such violence, that its little black seeds are sent rattling off into the air, and do not fall to the ground till they have traveled some distance from home. Really they are *shot* out into the world (Fig. 72).

PLANTS AND THEIR CHILDREN

If you wish to make sure that this is actually so, gather some of these nuts, and take them home with you. It will not be long before they begin to pop open, and shoot out their little seeds.

Did you ever hear of Thoreau? He was a man who left his friends and family to live by himself in the woods he so dearly loved. Here he grew to know each bird and beast, each flower and tree, almost as if they were his brothers and sisters. One day he took home with him some of these nuts, and later he wrote about them in his journal, —

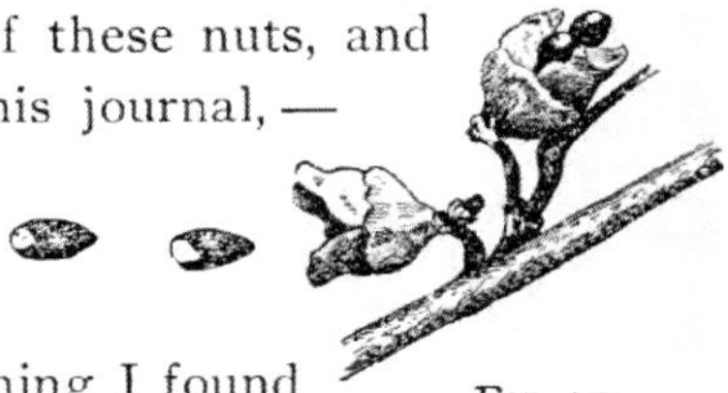

" Heard in the night a snapping sound, and the fall of some small body on the floor from time to time. In the morning I found it was produced by the witch-hazel nuts on my desk springing open and casting their seeds quite across my chamber."

FIG. 72

Now, I do not want any of you children to go off by yourselves to live in the woods; but I should like to think that you could learn to love these woods and their inmates with something of the love that Thoreau felt. And if you watch their ways with half the care that he did, some such love is sure to come.

Although the witch-hazel's rough way of dealing with its young is not very common among the plants, we find much the same thing done by the wild geranium, or crane's bill, and by the touch-me-not.

The wild geranium is the pretty purplish, or at times pink flower which blossoms along the roads and in the woods in May and early June.

DANA'S PLANTS. — 5

61

Its seedbox has five divisions. In fruit this seedbox tapers above into a long beak, which gives the plant

its name of "crane's bill." When the fruit is quite ripe, it splits away from the central part of this beak in five separate pieces, which spring upward so suddenly that the seeds are jerked out of the five cells, and flung upon the earth at a distance of several feet. The picture (Fig. 73) shows you how this is done. But a little search through the summer woods will bring you to the plant itself; and if you are patient, perhaps you will see how the wild geranium gets rid of its children. But though this habit may at

FIG. 73

first seem to you somewhat unmotherly, if you stop to think about it you will see that really the parent plant is doing its best for its little ones. If they should fall directly upon the ground beneath, their chances in life would be few. About plants, as about people, you must not make up your minds too quickly.

Another plant that all of you country children ought to know, is the touch-me-not, or jewelweed. Sometimes this is called "lady's eardrop," because its pretty, red-gold, jewel-like flowers remind us of the drops that once upon a time ladies wore in their ears. These flowers we find in summer in wet, woody places. In the fall the fruit appears. This fruit is a

FIG. 74

little pod (Fig. 74) which holds several seeds. When this pod is ripe, it bursts open and coils up with an elastic spring which sends these seeds also far from home (Fig. 75).

This performance of the touch-me-not you can easily see; for its name "touch-me-not" comes from the fact that if you touch too roughly one of its well-grown pods, this will spring open and jerk out its seeds in the way I have just described.

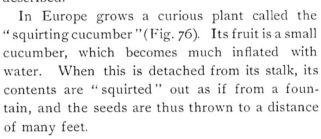

FIG. 75

FIG. 76

In Europe grows a curious plant called the "squirting cucumber" (Fig. 76). Its fruit is a small cucumber, which becomes much inflated with water. When this is detached from its stalk, its contents are "squirted" out as if from a fountain, and the seeds are thus thrown to a distance of many feet.

———oo⟩o⟨oo———

THE CHESTNUT AND OTHER SEEDS

A T the head of this chapter you see the fruit of the chestnut tree (Fig. 77).

What fine October days this picture brings to mind, — clear, cold mornings when we arm ourselves with baskets and a club, and go chestnuting.

FIG. 77

Usually the boys climb the tree, and shake the burrs rattle out their branches till the open contents. But sometimes a teasing cluster refuses to set loose its treasure. Then the club comes into play. If it strikes the great burrs, and raps out their fat chestnuts, a shout of joy follows.

What a delight it is to hunt in the long grass for the glossy brown beauties just after a sudden shower from above! No one speaks. All are bent low in breathless search.

I know of nothing much more perfect in its way than an open chestnut burr, still holding its two or three fine nuts. Its green, prickly outer covering makes a fine contrast to the velvety brown lining; and within this beautiful case the plump, shining nuts are laid with the daintiest care.

Perhaps the chestnut burr is even safer as a seed case than the apple. While its seeds (the chestnuts) are young and unripe, it does not stop to plead, " Pray, don't destroy my baby nuts!" but it seems to call out sternly, "Hands off!" and promptly punishes the boy or girl who disobeys this rough command.

But when the chestnut seeds are quite ripe, then it opens as wide as it knows how; and very tempting it looks as it unfolds its contents. A chestnut tree in October looks like one great invitation.

The acorn (Fig. 78), the seed of the oak tree, is pretty enough as a plaything, but less pleasing than the chestnut. Only the squirrel seems to find it fair eating.

FIG. 78   The trees which hide their seeds in nutshells contrive in different ways to send them abroad.

Many of these nuts are hoarded as winter food by the squirrels. Often in a moment of fright these little creatures drop them by the way. Again, they forget just where they deposited their hoard, ŏr for some other reason they leave it untouched. Thus many nuts are scattered, and live to change into trees.

Others may fall into the water, and float to distant shores. The cocoanut, for example, has been carried in this way for hundreds of miles. Its outer covering protects the seed from being soaked or hurt by water; and when at last it is washed upon some distant shore, it sends up a tall cocoanut tree.

———o○;◦;○o———

SOME STRANGE STORIES

WHEN I began to tell you children about the different ways in which plants send their young out into the world, I had no idea that I should take so much time, and cover so many pages with the subject. And now I realize that I have not told you one half, or one quarter, of all there is to tell.

You have learned that seeds are scattered abroad by animals that eat the bright cases in which they are packed, and by animals into whose hair or clothing they manage to fasten themselves.

You know that sometimes seeds are blown through the air by means of silky sails to which they are fastened, or else by their little wings.

You discovered that certain plants actually pushed their young from their cozy homes in no gentle fashion, much as a mother bird shoves her timid little ones from the edge of the nest.

And in the last chapter you read that occasionally seeds were floated by water to distant shores.

Now, these are the chief ways in which plants contrive to dispose of their seeds; but they are not the only ways. Before leaving the subject altogether, I will mention a few plants which use other contrivances.

This picture (Fig. 79) shows you the fruit of the poppy. Many of you know it well. In the fall you find in the garden these pretty seedboxes. They answer famously as pepper pots, if one chances to be playing house in the orchard.

Just below the top of the poppy seedbox the picture shows you a circle of little openings; and inside the seedbox are many poppy seeds (Fig. 80).

But how can seeds get out of these openings, do you suppose?

FIG. 79

If they were lower down, it would be an easy matter for the seeds to drop out, right on the ground. But perhaps it is well that this cannot happen. Did such a quantity of seeds fall upon one small bit of earth, they would have a poor chance for life.

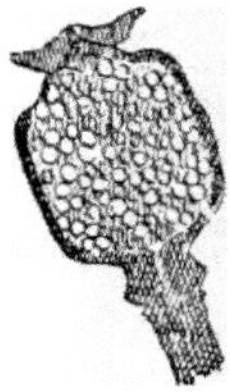

Well, then, you ask, must they wait patiently in the seedbox till some child comes along and pulls it off for a pepper pot?

No, they are not obliged to wait always for you children. This is fortunate for the poppy plants that are so unlucky as to live in lonely gardens where no children ever play.

FIG. 80

Then what *does* happen?

If you will go out into the garden the next windy fall day, you will see for yourselves. You will see the tall poppy plants swaying to and fro with every gust of wind; and you will see how the seedboxes are tossed from side to side, and that every now and then a very violent toss sends the little seeds tumbling head over heels out of the little openings just as effectively as if the wind too were playing house and using them as pepper pots.

When the seeds are let loose in this way, the tall poppy plants are swayed so far to one side, and the wind is blowing so hard, that they land upon the ground much farther from home than would have been the case had they fallen through openings cut in the lower part of the seedbox.

In the East grows a strange plant called the "rose of Jericho." Its fruit is a pod. When this plant is nearly ready to get rid of its seeds, what do you think it does? It lets go its hold upon the earth, curls itself up into a little ball, and is driven here and there by the wind. When it finds a nice damp place, it stops and uncurls itself; and the little pods split open, and drop their seeds on the earth.

Some plants bear fruits that look very much like insects. It is believed that sometimes these are taken for such, and snapped up by birds, and thus succeed in getting away from home.

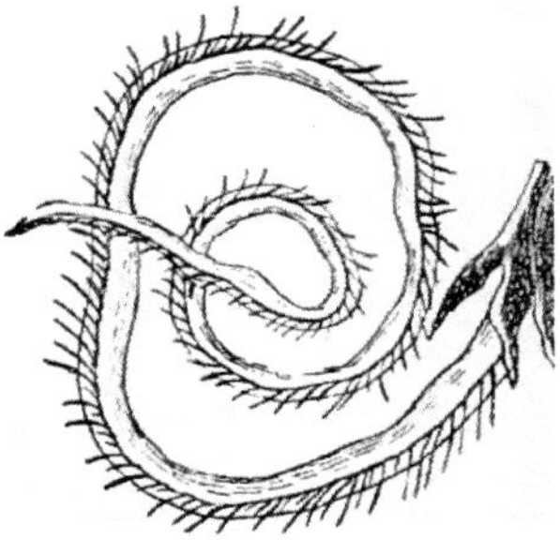

FIG. 81

This picture (Fig. 81) shows you a pod which, as it lies upon the ground, looks like a centiped.

Here you have a seed which is shaped and marked like a beetle (Fig. 82).

The next picture (Fig. 83) shows you a seed from the castor-oil plant. You can see that it

FIG. 82   might easily be mistaken for some insect.

Think how disappointed the bird must be, after having greedily snapped up and carried off one of these little objects, to discover that for all his pains   FIG. 83 he has secured nothing but a dry, tough pod or seed.

But if the mother plant really does any thinking at all, cannot you fancy how she chuckles with delight over the trick she has played, and the clever way in which she has started her young on its travels?

There is still another way in which birds help to scatter seeds. They alight in wet places, covering their little feet with mud. Now, a clot of mud may contain many different seeds; and for days this clot may stick to the bird's foot, and thus cause the seeds it holds to be carried for hundreds of miles.

Have you ever heard of Darwin? He was a great man who spent most of his life in studying plants and animals.

How many years do you suppose he was interested in the study of those long, brown worms which you find in quantities in the lawn and after heavy rains along the sidewalk? At intervals for forty-four years he studied these little creatures which you girls think ugly and uninteresting enough, although the boys know they make fine fish bait.

Well, Darwin once raised eighty-two plants from seeds contained in a clot of earth which was clinging to the leg of a partridge. So you can see that when a bird gets his feet wet, he may really be doing the world a service. And it is not likely that he takes cold himself.

Now, I want you children to see how many different ways you can recall in which plants scatter abroad their little seeds; and later I want you to go out into the garden, or into the woods, and see if you cannot discover many of the seeds about which you have been reading. But better still it would be if you could find others of which I have told you nothing.

I should like you to make a list of the different plants which you find in fruit, putting after each name a slight description of the way in which it gets rid of its seeds. This will not be a stupid task at all if you set your mind to it. It will give your walks a new pleasure, and it will bring to your school work something of the freshness and joy which belong to the woods.

PART II — YOUNG PLANTS

————∘∘⦂⊙⦂∘∘————

HOW THE BABY PLANT LIVES

WHEN these little seeds at last find a good resting place, what do you think happens to them? They grow into new plants, of course. But how does this come about? How does a seed turn into a plant?

I could hardly expect you to guess this, any more than I could have expected you to guess how the apple flower changes into the apple fruit. I will tell you a little about it; and then I hope your teacher will show you real seeds and real plants, and prove to you that what I have said is really so.

Of course, you believe already that I try to tell you the exact truth about all these things. But people far wiser than I have been mistaken in what they thought was true; and so it will be well for you to make sure, with your own eyes, that I am right in what I say.

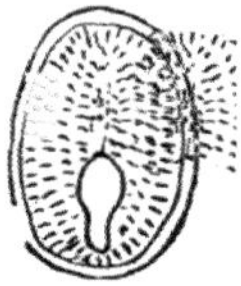

If you should cut in two the seed of that beautiful flower the garden peony, and should look at it very closely through a good magnifying glass, you would find a tiny object such as you see in the half seed shown in this picture (Fig. 84). Both your eyes

FIG. 84

70

and your glass need to be very good to show you that this little object is *a baby peony plant.* Fig. 85 gives the little plant as it would look if taken out of the seed.

Every ripe seed holds a baby plant; and to become a grown-up plant, it needs just what boy and girl babies need, — food and drink and air.

But shut up so tight in its seed shell, how can it get these?

Well, in this peony seed its food is close at hand. It is packed away inside the seed, all about the little plant.

FIG. 85

In the picture (Fig. 84), everything except the little white spot, which shows the plant, is baby food, — food that is all prepared to be eaten by a delicate little plant, and that is suited to its needs just as milk is suited to the needs of your little sister or brother.

The little leaves of the baby plant take in the food that is needed to make it grow fat and strong.

Now, how does the baby plant get water to drink?

I have asked your teacher to soak over night some peas that have been dried for planting, and to bring to school to-day a handful of these, and also a handful which have not been soaked. She will pass these about, and you can see how different the soaked ones are from the others. Those that have not been in the water look dried and wrinkled and old, almost dead in fact; while those which have been soaked are nearly twice as large. They look fat, and fresh, and full of life. Now, what has happened to them?

Why, all night long they have been sucking in water through tiny openings in the seed shell; and this water has so refreshed them, and so filled the wrinkled coats and swelled them out, that they look almost ready to burst.

So you see, do you not, how the water manages to get inside the seed so as to give the baby plant a drink?

Usually it is rather late in the year when seeds fall to the earth. During the winter the baby plant does not do any drinking; for then the ground is frozen hard, and the water cannot reach it. But when the warm spring days come, the ice melts, and the ground is full of moisture. Then the seed swells with all the water it sucks in, and the baby plant drinks, drinks, drinks, all day long.

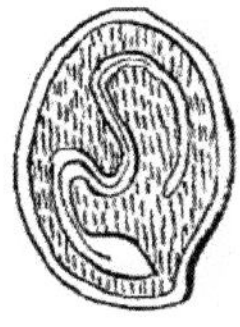

You scarcely need ask how it keeps warm, this little plant. It is packed away so snugly in the seed shell, and the seed shell is so covered by the earth, and the earth much of the time is so tucked away beneath a blanket of snow, that usually there is no trouble at all about keeping warm.

Fig. 86

But how, then, does it get air?

Well, of course, the air it gets would not keep alive a human baby. But a plant baby needs only a little air; and usually enough to keep it in good condition makes its way down through the snow and earth to the tiny openings in the seed shell. To be sure, if the earth above is kept light and loose, the plant grows more quickly, for then the air reaches it with greater ease.

So now you see how the little plant inside the peony seed gets the food and drink and air it needs for its growth.

In the picture above (Fig. 86) you get a side view

of the baby plant of the morning-glory, its unripe seed being cut in two. As you look at it here, its queer shape reminds you of an eel. But if instead of cutting through the seed, you roll it carefully between your fingers, and manage to slip off its coat, and if then you take a pin and carefully pick away the whitish, jelly-like stuff which has been stored as baby food, you will find a tiny green object which through a magnifying glass looks like the next picture (Fig. 87). The

narrow piece pointing downward is the stem from which grows the root. Above this are two leaves.

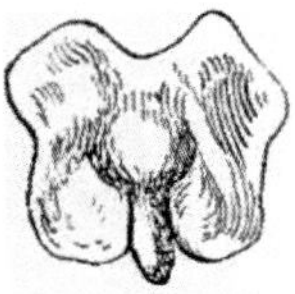

FIG. 87

This baby plant is a very fascinating thing to look at. I never seem to tire of picking apart a young seed for the sake of examining through a glass these delicate bright-green leaves. It seems so wonderful that the vine which twines far above our heads, covered with glorious flowers, should come from this green speck.

As this morning-glory is a vine which lives at many of your doorsteps, I hope you will not fail to collect its seeds, and look at their baby plants. When these are very young, still surrounded by a quantity of baby food, you will not be able to make them out unless you carry them to your teacher and borrow her glass; but when the seed is ripe, and the little plant has eaten away most of the surrounding food, it grows so big that you can see it quite plainly with your own eyes.

A SCHOOLROOM GARDEN

I WANT you children to do a little gardening in the schoolroom. You will enjoy this, I am sure.

When I was a child, I took great delight in the experiments that I am going to suggest to you; and now that I am grown up, I find they please me even more than they did years ago.

During the past week I have been doing this sort of gardening; and I have become so interested in the plant babies which I have helped into the world, that I have not been at all ready to stop playing with them, even for the sake of sitting down to tell you about them.

To start my garden, I had first to get some seeds. So I put on my hat and went down to the little shop in the village, half of which is given up to tailor work, while the other half is devoted to flower raising. The gray-bearded florist tailor who runs this queer little place was greatly interested when he heard that I wanted the seeds so that I might tell you children something of their strange ways.

"Seeds air mighty interestin' things," he said. "Be you young or be you old, there's nothin' sets you thinkin' like a seed."

Perhaps the florist tailor had been fortunate in his friends; for I have known both grown-up people and children who year after year could see the wonder of seed and baby plant, of flower and fruit, without once stopping to say, "What brings about these changes?"

PLANTS AND THEIR CHILDREN

To "set thinking" some people would take an earth-quake or an avalanche; but when this sort of thing is needed to start their brains working, the "thinking" is not likely to be good for much.

But I hope that some of you will find plenty to think about in the seeds which your teacher is going to show you; and I hope that these thoughts may be the beginning of an interest and curiosity that will last as long as you live.

The seeds which I got that morning were those of the bean, squash, pea, and corn; and your teacher has been good enough to get for you these same seeds, and she will show you how to do with them just what I have been doing this past week.

First, I filled a pot with finely sifted earth, and planted the different seeds; then I filled a glass with water, floated some cotton wool upon its surface, and in this wool laid some beans; and then my garden planting was done.

During the following days I kept the earth in the pot slightly moist. The cotton wool in the glass of water did this for itself.

And how carefully I watched my two little gardens!

For three days the pot of earth kept its secret. Nothing happened there, so far as I could see. But the beans that were laid upon the cotton wool grew fat and big by the second day, just like those that your teacher soaked over night; and by the third day their seed coats had ripped open a little way, just as your coat would rip open if it were tightly buttoned up and suddenly you grew very fat; and out of the rip in the seed coat peeped a tiny white thing, looking like the bill of a chick that is pecking its way out of the eggshell which has become too small to hold it.

Very quickly this little white tip grew longer. It curved over and bent downward, piercing its way through the cotton wool into the water.

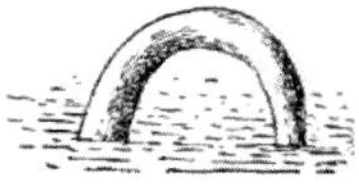

About this time the pot garden began to show signs of a disturbance. Here and there

FIG. 88

I saw what looked like the top of a thick green hoop (Fig. 88).

What had happened, do you think?

Why, first this bean had sucked in from the damp earth so much water that it had grown too fat and big for the seed coat; and it had torn this open, just like the other bean, pushing out its little white tip; and this tip had bent down into the earth and taken a good hold there, lengthening into a real root, and sending out little root hairs that fastened it down still more firmly.

But it was not satisfied to do all its growing below. Its upper part now straightened itself out, and started right up into the air. From a hoop it turned into a stem which lifted the bean clear above the earth (Fig. 89).

This bean was no longer the round object we usually call by that name; for its two halves had opened and spread outward, and from between these two halves

FIG. 89

grew a pair of young leaves.

As these leaves grew larger, the two half-beans began to shrink, growing smaller and more withered all the time (Fig. 90).

DANA'S PLANTS. — 6

76

Why was this, do you suppose?

To make clear the reason of this, to show just why the two halves of the bean grew smaller as the rest of the young bean plant grew larger, I must go back a way.

Turn to the picture of the peony seed (Fig. 84).

There you can see how the baby plant is packed away in the midst of a quantity of baby food. And in the picture of the morning-glory seed (Fig. 86) you see the same thing.

You remember that day by day the baby plant ate more and more of this food, and kept growing stronger and bigger, and that all this time the store of food kept growing smaller and smaller.

Now, if you cut open the bean, you do not see a tiny plant set in the midst of a store of food.

FIG. 90

Why is this? This is because the baby bean plant keeps its food in its own leaves.

The seed coat of the bean is filled by these leaves, for each half of the bean is really a seed leaf. In these two thick leaves is stored all the food that is necessary to the life of the baby plant; and because of all this food which they hold, the bean plant is able to get a better start in life than many other young plants.

If you soak and strip off its seed coat, and pull apart the two thick leaves, you will find a tiny pair of new leaves already started (Fig. 91); but you will see nothing of the sort in the seed of the morning-glory, for the reason that this is not so well stored with baby food as to be able to do more than get its seed leaves well under way.

The pea, like the bean, is so full of food, that it also is able to take care of a second pair of leaves.

But now to go back to the young bean plant in the schoolroom garden. We were wondering why the two halves of the bean, which are really the first pair of leaves, kept growing thinner and smaller as the second pair grew larger.

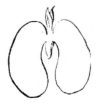

FIG. 91

Perhaps you guess now the reason for this. These first leaves, called the seed leaves, feed all the rest of the young bean plant.

Of course, as they keep on doing this, they must themselves shrink away; but they do not cease with their work till the plant is able to take care of itself.

By this time, however, the seed leaves have nothing left to live upon. They die of starvation, and soon fade and disappear.

So now you understand just what has happened to the leaves that once were so fat and large.

And I hope you will remember the difference between the seed of the morning-glory and that of the bean, — how the morning-glory packs the baby food inside the seed, of course, but *outside* the baby plant; while the bean packs it inside the two seed leaves, which are so thick that there is no room for anything else within the seed coat.

But really, to understand all that I have been telling you, you must see it for yourselves; you must hold in your hands the dried bean; you must examine it, and make sure that its seed shell is filled entirely by the baby plant; you must see it grow plump and big from the water which it has been drinking; you must watch with sharp eyes for that first little rip in the seed coat, and for the putting-out of the tiny tip, which grows later into stem and root; you must notice how the bent stem straightens out, and lifts the thick seed leaves up into the air; and you must observe how that other pair of leaves, which grows from between the seed leaves, becomes larger and larger as the seed leaves grow smaller and thinner, and how, when the little plant is able to hold its own in the world, the seed leaves die away.

And if day by day you follow this young life, with the real wish to discover its secret, you will begin to understand what the wise old florist tailor meant when he said, —

"Be you young or be you old, there's nothin' sets you thinkin' like a seed."

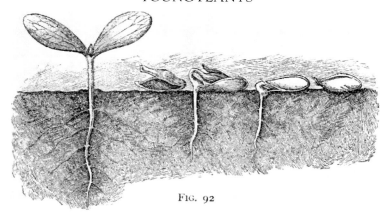

FIG. 92

A SCHOOLROOM GARDEN (*Concluded*)

THE picture at the top of this page (Fig. 92) shows you how the young squash plant comes into the world; for you remember that in my pot garden I planted some squash seeds. And I hope that in your schoolroom garden you will watch this plant as it makes its first appearance.

The baby food of the squash vine, like that of the bean, is stored away inside the seed leaves, which on this account are so large that they quite fill the seed shell. They are not so thick as those of the bean, but thick enough to hold all the nourishment that is needed to keep the young plant alive and hearty until it is big enough to shift for itself.

Very soon after this seed is laid in warm, moist earth, its little plant begins to grow too large for the seed shell, and the white stem is pushed out through the hole you notice at one end of the seed. This stem forces its way into the earth below, and puts out a root, and root fingers. And now its upper part begins to lengthen out and to straighten itself. In doing this,

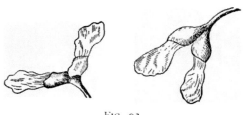

FIG. 93

it pulls the two seed leaves right out of the seed coat. If it fails at once to get rid of the seed coat, it lifts this up into the air, on top of its leaves.

Often the young maple tree comes into the world in this way, carrying its seed coat on top of its seed leaves. The maple is another plant that packs its baby food within the seed leaves instead of round about them. Perhaps your teacher has saved for you some maple keys (Fig. 93), as the fruit of the maple tree is called. If you split open a maple key, you will find hidden within one of its halves (Fig. 94) the beautiful baby tree. This is folded away so

FIG. 94

neatly that one is tempted to split open one key after another, for the pleasure of unpacking other delicate baby maples (Fig. 95).

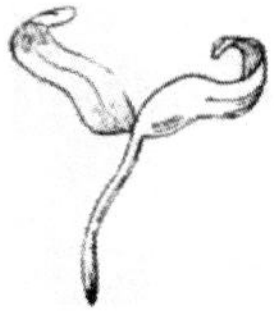

But now let us find out what has happened to the peas which I planted.

FIG. 95

Peas seem to us so much like beans, that perhaps you think the young pea baby comes into the world in the same way as the bean plant; but surely we have nothing here that looks at all like the bean plant.

We see some stems having small, thin, green leaves.

Where are the fat seed leaves, filled with the baby food that keeps the plant alive ? They are not in sight, certainly, so we must start a hunt for them.

If you will carefully remove the earth from about this little pea plant, you will soon find that the pea seed from which it is growing lies buried in the earth (Fig. 96). This pea seed, like that of the bean, is made up chiefly of what really are two seed leaves,

FIG. 96

although in the case of the pea it may seem only as a matter of politeness that we give them the name of " leaves ; " for in the pea these seed leaves lie buried in the earth, and split open just enough to allow the little pea plant to grow up into the air.

But like the seed leaves of the bean, they are fat and full of food, and care for the young plant just as devotedly as did those of the bean. When this young plant needs them no more, like those of the bean, they die of starvation.

Within the acorn, the seed leaves of the great oak tree grow together. These lie quietly in the acorn shell while sending out supplies of food to the root and stem and leaves of the young oak (Fig. 97). Walnut and chestnut leaves act much in the same manner. But these first leaves of the

FIG. 97

walnut do not grow together, as you know. Each one is packed away separately in half of the walnut shell.

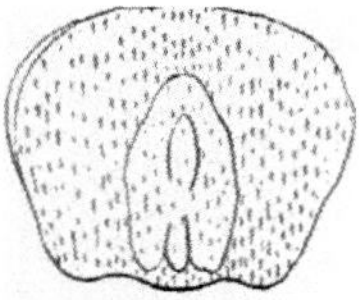

The corn has but one seed leaf, which makes it unlike all the other plants about which we have been reading; but it resembles the pea, the acorn, the walnut, and the chestnut in this, — that the one seed leaf

FIG. 98

lies buried in the earth, as do their two seed leaves.

The baby corn plant is very small. It does not fill the whole seed shell, but gets its nourishment from the food by which it is surrounded.

This picture shows you a seed or grain of corn cut in two (Fig. 98). Of course, this is much larger than life. In the center you see the tiny plant. All about is the baby food.

The next picture (Fig. 99) shows you the young corn plant.

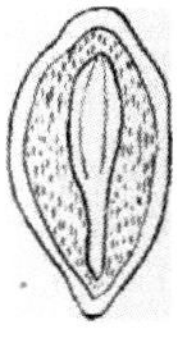

I want you to remember that this is the only plant we have seen with but one seed leaf. This one seed leaf never comes out of the seed shell. There are other plants of the same kind. All the grass plants have but one seed leaf, and the blue flag that grows in wet meadows, and all the lilies.

FIG. 99

FIG. 100

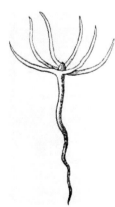

Only a few plants have more than two of these seed leaves. The pine trees are among these few. This picture (Fig. 100) shows you a baby pine tree, still cradled in its seed, surrounded by baby food; and

FIG. 101

the next one (Fig. 101) shows you the pine just starting out in the world, with its six seed leaves.

When you study the botany that is written for older people, you will find that plants are set apart in separate groups, according to the number of their seed leaves.

Strange though it may seem to you, plants with but one seed leaf have certain habits that you will not find in a plant with two seed leaves ; and a plant with two seed leaves, long after these have passed away, will show by root and stem that it had more than one seed leaf.

In your schoolroom garden I should like you to grow side by side, first a plant with but one seed leaf, next a plant with two seed leaves, and lastly a plant with more than two.

———∘∘⦂⊙⦂∘∘———

SEEDS AS FOOD

I WANT you to think for yourselves why it is fortunate for us human beings that many plants store away in their seeds so much baby food.

" Because without this the little plants would die, and we should have no new plants to make the world beautiful to live in," some child replies.

That answer is a good one ; but it is not just the answer that I wish.

Can you think of any other way in which we all benefit by the large supply of baby food that is packed away in certain seeds ?

If the right answer to this question does not occur to you, try to remember which of those seeds we have been reading about have been supplied with a specially large amount of this food.

You remember that the bean holds so much baby food in its seed leaves, that these are very fat. So do the pea, the walnut, and the chestnut. The seed of corn, also, is well filled with baby food, only in the corn seed it is packed around the outside of the seed leaves, instead of the inside.

But the squash, although it puts in its seed leaves enough food to keep its young plant well and hearty, does not lay by any great quantity of this material. Neither does the maple tree, which also stores the seed leaves with food, but does not fill them nearly so full as do the bean and the pea.

And the morning-glory, which packs its precious white jelly (this is what the little morning-glory plant likes to eat) all about its young, lays up only just enough of this to last until the baby plant breaks out of its seed shell.

Now, what difference do we find between these seeds? — between the seeds of squash, morning-glory, and maple, which have only a small supply of baby food, and those other ones, such as bean and pea and corn and walnut and chestnut, which are packed full of nourishment?

" Why, these last ones are good to eat!" you exclaim. " They are part of the food we live upon, while the squash seeds, the morning-glory seeds, and the maple seeds are not good to eat."

Yes, that is the answer which I wished. The baby food in these seeds makes " grown-up " food for us.

We get strength and nourishment from the same material which the mother plant has prepared for her young.

Now try to name the different seeds which help to make up our food. Already we have mentioned several kinds. Besides these, there is the oat seed (from which comes oatmeal), the wheat seed (from which comes flour for our bread), the coffee seed, the buckwheat seed, the peanut seed, the almond seed, and many others, some of which will come to your mind from time to time.

I wish you would make for your teacher a list of all those that you can recall; or, better still, I should like you to collect as many as you possibly can, and bring them to your next class. If you cannot find the seeds just as they grow upon the plant, you may be able to get them prepared for use. A pinch of flour, for instance, would answer for wheat seeds, of oatmeal for oat seeds.

I have in mind a number of seeds that you can easily secure, of which I have not spoken; and it will be interesting at our next meeting to see which child in this class is able to make the best exhibition of seed food.

———

AN IMPATIENT PLANT BABY

PLANT babies are not alike as to the time they take in finding their way out of the ripe seed shell into the world.

Certain seeds need only two or three days in which

to bring forth their young. Perhaps we ourselves have seen the white tip of the bean rip open its shell the second or third day after being laid upon the moist cotton wool. But if we had not given this bean plant a good chance to grow, it would have kept alive and hearty inside its shell for a long time. This is not the case with all plants. Certain seeds need to be planted soon after they are ripe. If they are not, their baby plants die.

But usually seeds take such good care of their young, that they will live for a long time, even if shut up in a dark closet or a table drawer, instead of being comfortably laid away in the warm, moist earth.

Wonderful stories are told of seeds that have sprouted after having lain buried in some Egyptian tomb for thousands of years ; but the people best fitted to judge of the truth of such stories do not believe them. There is no doubt, however, that some seeds keep their baby plants alive for many years.

Early in the summer the seeds of the red maple fall to the ground ; and soon after this the young plants find their way up into the world above. Later in the year the sugar maple sheds its seeds. These lie sleeping in the earth through the winter. When the warm spring days come, the baby plants awake, and stretch themselves, and join the hundreds of other, just-awakened baby plants that are flocking into the world above. So you see that seeds of the same family have different habits in this matter.

There is one curious tree that lives in swamps along the seashore of hot countries. It is called the mangrove.

The baby plants of this tree are so anxious to get out into the world, that they do not wait until the seeds in which they are hidden are set free from the mangrove fruit.

It is as if the little plants inside the apple seed could not wait until the apple flesh should be eaten or should decay, but insisted on struggling first out of . the seed into the apple, and then through the apple into the light and air.

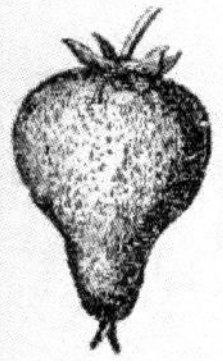

This picture (Fig. 102) shows you the mangrove fruit. It looks more like a pear than an apple In the middle of this lies hidden one seed. As time goes on, this grows bigger and bigger, trying to make room for the impatient little plant within ; but it does not grow fast enough to please this ambitious young one, which finally overcomes the difficulty by piercing the seed shell with its stem. This stem bores its way right down through the mangrove fruit, and breaks into the outer air. It keeps on growing in this way for many weeks, till at last it is a foot long (Fig. 103). Try to fancy how odd a mangrove tree must look at this time, covered with mangroves, from each one projecting this long odd-looking beak, which one could hardly guess to be the stem of the baby plant within the fruit.

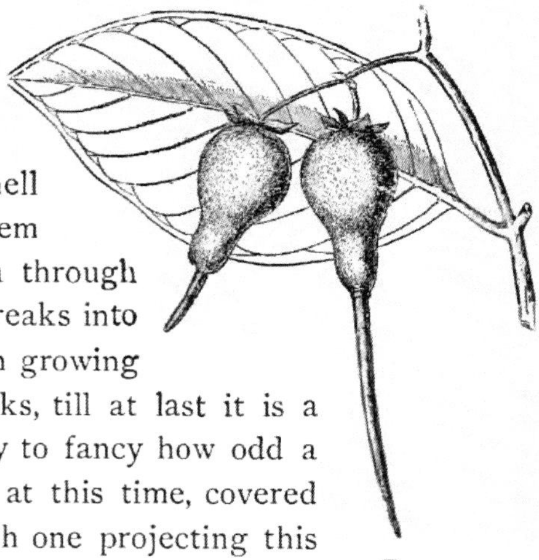

FIG. 103

We read that these long-beaked fruits bob about with every breath of wind in a fashion that gives the tree a still stranger look than on a day when the air is not stirring. Picture a pear tree from every pear of which the long stem of a baby pear tree protrudes. Would you not be eager to find one of these pears and cut it open, and see what sort of a baby plant it must be that could send out such a great stem ?

FIG. 104

But perhaps the strangest part of the story is yet to come. At last all of these great beaks fall away from the fruit; and from the broken top of each grows a little bud, such as you see in the picture (Fig. 104). When this heavy beak falls upon the muddy ground below, its pointed end strikes first, and so bores into the earth.

Even if it happens to fall into the water, it does this with so much force that it will pierce its way to the depth of eighteen or twenty inches, and yet remain standing erect when it strikes bottom, where it sends out a root. When it has secured a good hold, the little bud unfolds into four leaves. Above these grow larger, shining leaves ; and soon the ground beneath an old mangrove tree is covered with these daring little adventurers.

A HUMPBACKED PLANT BABY

NOW let us pause for a moment, and try to recall a little of what we have learned since school opened.

We learned that the fruit of a plant is the part which holds its seed, and that there are many different kinds of fruits ; that the burr of the burdock, the pod of the milkweed, the puff of the dandelion, are fruits, as well as the apple and the pear, the acorn and the walnut.

We learned that the chief importance of these fruits lies in the fact just mentioned, that they hold the seeds of the plants.

Then we learned something about the many different kinds of seeds, and of how these seeds managed to become separated from the parent plant, and to get a start in life.

Next we read of the baby plant which lies hidden within every perfect seed. We learned how this is kept safe and warm, and supplied with food, and how at last it finds its way out of the seed shell into the world.

If you have been using this book in the right way, not only have you read about these things, but you have seen them with your own eyes.

Some of the fruits you have tasted, and others you have handled.

You have examined the silky sails of the seeds which float through the air, and the hooks and claws of those little tramps that manage to steal free rides.

And some seeds you have planted. These you have watched day by day, and you have seen that the baby plants burst their seed shells much as a chick bursts its eggshell.

Now what I want you to do is this : I want you to study carefully the different parts of these little creatures that are living out their strange, beautiful lives under your very eyes. I want you to watch them from day to day ; to learn how they eat and drink and work and grow, until you feel that you know them really well.

First let us look at this bean plant which is breaking its way through the earth.

Just what do you see?

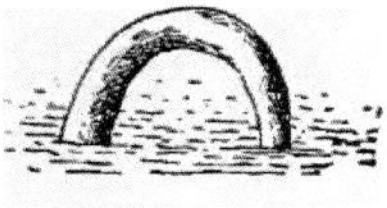

You see what looks like a thick, green hoop (Fig. 105), do you not?

What is it, this odd-looking hoop?

Perhaps some of you still think that it is the

FIG. 105

root, for I remember that I too once supposed the root was the part of the plant which first left the bean.

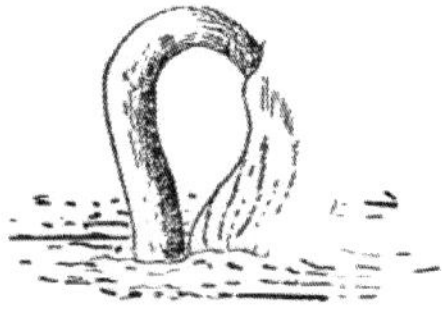

But really this made by the bent that this is the its lower end grows from its upper part flowers, and fruit.

green hoop is stem. We know stem because from the root, while grow the leaves,

FIG. 106

Certainly it is curious, the way in which this bean plant comes into the world. Why does it not grow straight up and down, do you suppose? — up with its stem and leaves, and down with its root?

But we must not forget that whenever some habit on the part of a plant has filled us with surprise, sooner or later we have discovered that the plant's reason for it was a good one.

FIG. 107

What reason can the bean plant have for coming into the world crooked?

Before reading further, try to think this out for yourselves. Try each one of you to form an idea of what the bean plant gains by pushing through the earth with this hooped stem.

I hope some of you may guess correctly. But even if you have not been successful in naming the cause of the bean plant's humped back, at least you have been working your brains; and every time you do this, you help to·keep them in good order.

If you let your brain lie idle, and allow your teacher or your book to do for you not only all the asking of questions, but also all the thinking-out of answers, it will get as dull and rusty and good for nothing as a machine that is laid by for a long time gets dull and rusty and good for nothing.

I should be sorry to think that any of you children were carrying about in your heads any such rusty, good-for-nothing brains. So if you wish to keep them bright and clean, and in good working order, you must try to do your own thinking.

And now, hoping you have tried to guess for yourselves the reason of this crooked back, I will explain it to you.

But first handle carefully the tip of one of the upper leaves on the larger bean plant. You see how delicate this is.

Then feel how firm and hard and tough is the green hoop of the plant which is just breaking through the earth.

Now suppose the bean plant had grown straight up into the air, would not its uppermost part have been the delicate leaf tips ?

Can you not see that these would have been too frail to work their way uninjured through the earth ?

DANA'S PLANTS. — 7

But by crooking its stout stem the plant opened quite easily a path for itself and for its leaves, and no harm was done anywhere (Figs. 106, 107). Was not this a clever thought? But really every step in the life of the plant is full of interest, if we watch it with sharp eyes and a brain in good order.

PART III — ROOTS AND STEMS

ROOT HAIRS

CAREFULLY pull up one of your bean plants and look at its root (Fig. 108).

You see that the root grows downward from the lower part of the stem.

This bean root looks not unlike a bunch of dirty threads, some quite thick, others very thin. If you look at these thread-like roots in a good light, perhaps you may be able to see growing from them a quantity of tiny hairs.

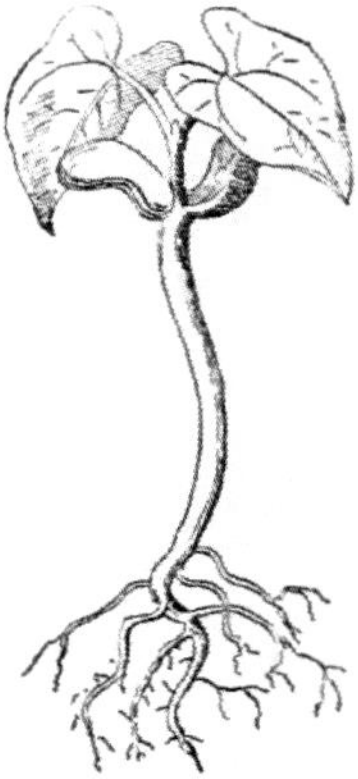

Now, what is the use of such a root as this?

Surely some of you are able to guess at the object of this root, and I will help the others to the answer.

Give a firm though gentle tug to one of the larger plants, — one of those that are growing in the pot of earth.

FIG. 108

Does it come out easily in your fingers?

Not at all. Unless you have been really rough, and used quite a good deal of strength, the little plant has kept its hold.

94

What holds it down, do you suppose?

Ah! Now you know what I am trying to get at. Its root is what holds it in place; and this holding of the plant in place is one of its uses.

Its thread-like branches are so many fingers that are laying hold of the earth. Each little thread makes it just so much the more difficult to uproot the plant.

I think you know already that another use of the root is to obtain nourishment for the plant.

These thread-like roots, you notice, creep out on every side in their search for food and drink. The water they are able to suck in easily by means of tiny mouths, which we cannot see. But the plant needs a certain amount of earth food, which in its solid state could not slip down these root throats any more easily than a young baby could swallow a lump of sugar.

Now, how is the plant to get this food, which it needs if it is to grow big and hearty?

Suppose the doctor should tell your mother that a lump of sugar was necessary to the health of your tiny baby brother, what would she do about it?

Would she put the great lump into the baby's mouth?

You laugh at the very idea. Such a performance might choke the baby to death, you know quite well.

Perhaps you think she would break the lump into small pieces, and try to make the baby swallow these; but even these small pieces might prove very dangerous to the little throat that had never held a solid morsel.

"She would melt the sugar in water, then the baby could swallow it," one of you exclaims.

That is exactly what she would do. She would melt,

or dissolve as we say, this sugar in water. Then there would be no difficulty in its slipping down the little throat; for you know when anything is thoroughly melted or dissolved, it breaks up into such tiny pieces that the eye cannot see them. When you melt a lump of sugar in a glass of water, the sugar is all there as much as it ever was, although its little grains no longer cling together in one big lump.

And so when the plant needs some food that the little root hairs are not able to swallow, it does just what the mother does. It melts or dissolves the solid food so that this is able to slip quite easily down the root throats.

But how does it manage this?

No wonder you ask. A root cannot fill a glass with water, as your mother did. Even if it could, much of this solid food which is needed by the plant would not melt in water, or in anything but certain acids; for you know that not everything will dissolve, like sugar, in water.

If I place a copper cent in a glass of water, it will remain a copper cent, will it not? But if I go into a drug shop and buy a certain acid, and place in this the copper cent, it will dissolve almost immediately; that is, it will break up into so many tiny pieces that you will no longer see anything that looks at all like a cent.

And as much of this earth food, like the copper cent, can only be dissolved in certain acids, how is the plant to obtain them? Certainly it is not able to go to the drug shop for the purpose, any more than it was able to fill a glass with water.

Fortunately it does not need to do either of these things.

If you will look closely at the root of a plant that has been raised in water, you will see that it is rough with a quantity of tiny hairs. These little hairs hold the acid which can dissolve the solid earth food. When they touch this food, they send out some of the acid, and in this it is soon dissolved. Then the little mouths suck it in, and it is carried up through the root into the rest of the plant.

Would you have guessed that plants were able to prepare their food in any such wonderful way as this? It surprised me very much, I remember, to learn that a root could give out acids, and so dissolve the earth food it needed.

ROOTS AND UNDERGROUND STEMS

IN the last chapter you learned that the root of the bean plant has two uses.

It holds the plant in place, and it provides it with food and drink. Such a root as this of the bean plant — one that is made up of what looks like a bunch of threads — is called a "fibrous" root.

The next picture shows you the root of a beet plant (Fig. 109).

Such a thick, fat root as this of the beet is called a "fleshy" root. The carrot, turnip, radish, and sweet potato, all have fleshy roots.

This beet root, like that of the bean, is useful both in holding the plant in place and in providing it with food and drink.

But the fleshy root of the beet does something else, — something that is not attempted by the fibrous root of the bean.

Here we must stop for a moment and look into the life of the beet plant.

During its first year, the beet puts out leaves; it neither flowers nor fruits, but it eats and drinks a great deal. And as it does not use up any of this food in flowering or fruiting, it is able to lay by much of it in its root, which grows large and heavy in consequence. When the next spring comes on, the beet plant is not obliged, like so many of its brothers and sisters, to set out to earn its living. This is provided already. And so it bursts into flower without delay, its food lying close at hand in its great root.

FIG. 109

So you see that a fleshy root, like that of the beet, does three things : —

1. It holds the plant in place.

2. It provides it with food and drink.

3. It acts as a storehouse.

These plants that lay by food for another year are useful as food for man. Their well-stocked roots are taken out of the ground and eaten by us before the plant has had the chance to use up its food in fulfilling

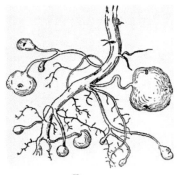

FIG. 110

its object in life, that of fruiting. Of course, when it is not allowed to live long enough to flower and fruit, it brings forth no young plants. So a habit which at first was of use to the plant becomes the cause of its destruction.

Perhaps you think that the white potato (Fig. 110) is a plant with a fleshy root.

If so, you will be surprised to learn that this potato is not a root at all, but a stem.

You think it looks quite unlike any other stem that you have ever seen. Probably you do not know that many stems grow underneath the ground, instead of straight up in the air.

FIG. 111

If you find something in the earth that you

FIG. 112

take to be a root, you can feel pretty sure that it really is a stem, if it bears anything like either buds or leaves. A true root bears only root branches and root hairs. But in this white potato we find what we call "eyes." These eyes are buds from which new potato plants will grow. Close to these are little scales which really are leaves. So we know that the potato is a stem, not a root. But this you could not

99

have found out for yourselves, even with the sharpest of eyes.

Fig. 111 shows you the thick, fat, underground stem of the cyclamen. From its lower part grow the true roots.

Next you have that of the crocus (Fig. 112), while here to the right is that of the wood lily (Fig. 113). This is covered with underground leaves.

FIG. 113

All these stems are usually called roots. In the botanies such an underground stem as that of the Jack-in-the-pulpit (Fig. 114) is named a "corm," while one like that of the crocus is called a "bulb" (Fig. 112). All have a somewhat rounded shape.

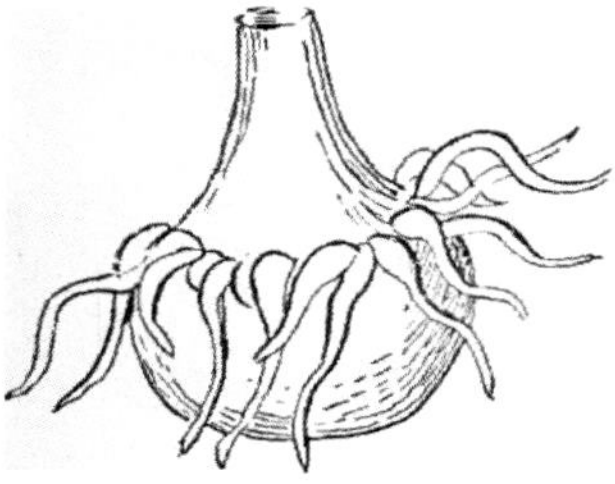

During our walks in the woods last fall, often we found the Solomon's seal, and stopped to admire its curved stem, hung with blue berries. I hope one of you boys whipped out your pocketknife and dug into the earth till you found its underground stem (Fig. 115). This was laid lengthwise, its roots growing from its lower side. From its upper side, close to one end, sprang the growing plant. But what causes those round, curious-looking scars?

FIG. 114

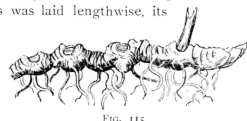

FIG. 115

100

These scars are what give the plant its name of "Solomon's seal." They are supposed to look like the mark left by a seal upon wax.

They show where the underground stem has budded in past years, sending up plants which in turn withered away. Each plant has left a scar which shows one year in the life of the underground stem.

Next spring when you find in the woods the little yellow bells of the Solomon's seal, I think you will have the curiosity to dig down and find out the age of some of these plants.

Another plant with an underground stem is the beautiful bloodroot. As its name tells you, this so-called root contains a juice that looks something like blood. Such underground stems as those of the Solomon's seal and bloodroot are called "rootstocks." Rootstocks, corms, and bulbs are all storehouses of plant food, and make possible an early flowering the following spring.

ABOVE-GROUND ROOTS

BUT before we finished talking about roots we were led away by underground stems. This does not matter much, however, for these underground stems are still called roots by many people.

Just as stems sometimes grow under ground, roots sometimes grow above ground.

Many of you know the English ivy. This is one of the few plants which city children know quite as well

as, if not better than, country children; for in our cities
it nearly covers the walls of the churches. In England
it grows so luxuriantly that some of the
old buildings are hidden beneath masses
of its dark leaves.

This ivy plant springs from a root in
the earth; but as it makes its way upward, it clings to the stone wall by means
of the many air roots which it puts forth
(Fig. 116).

Our own poison ivy is another plant
with air roots used for climbing purposes.
Often these roots make its stem look as

FIG. 116

though it were covered with a heavy growth of coarse hair.

There are some plants which take root in the
branches of trees. Many members of the Orchid family

perch themselves aloft in this
fashion. But the roots which
provide these plants with the
greater part of their nourishment are those which hang
loosely in the air. One of these orchids
you see in the picture (Fig. 117). It is
found in warm countries. The orchids
of our part of the world grow in the
ground in everyday fashion, and look
much like other plants.

These hanging roots which you see in
the picture are covered with a sponge-
like material, by means of which they suck in from the
air water and gases.

FIG. 117

In summer, while hunting berries or wild flowers by the stream that runs through the pasture, you have noticed that certain plants seemed to be caught in a tangle of golden threads. If you stopped to look at this tangle, you found little clusters of white flowers scattered along the thread-like stems (Fig. 118); then, to your surprise, you discovered that nowhere was this odd-looking stem fastened to the ground.

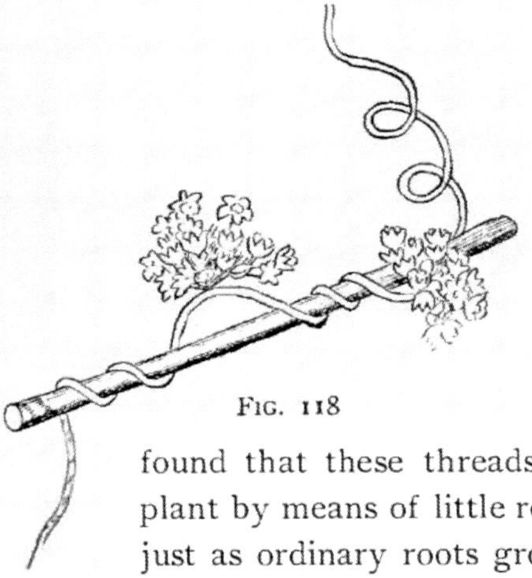

It began and ended high above the earth, among the plants which crowded along the brook's edge.

Perhaps you broke off one of these plants about which the golden threads were twining. If so, you

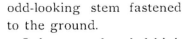

FIG. 118

found that these threads were fastened firmly to the plant by means of little roots which grew into its stem, just as ordinary roots grow into the earth.

This strange plant is called the "dodder." When it was still a baby plant, it lay within its seed upon the ground, just like other baby plants; and when it burst its seed shell, like other plants it sent its roots down into the earth.

But unlike any other plant I know of, it did not send up into the air any seed leaves. The dodder never bears a leaf.

It sent upward a slender golden stem. Soon the stem began to sweep slowly through the air in circles, as if searching for something. Its movements were like those of a blind man who is feeling with his hands for support. And this is just what the plant was doing: it was feeling for support. And it kept up its slow motion till it found the plant which was fitted to give it what it needed.

Having made this discovery, it put out a little root. This root it sent into the juicy stem of its new-found support. And thereafter, from its private store, the unfortunate plant which had been chosen as the dodder's victim was obliged to give food and drink to its greedy visitor.

And now what does this dodder do, do you suppose? Perhaps you think that at least it has the grace to do a little something for a living, and that it makes its earth root supply it with part of its food.

Nothing of the sort. Once it finds itself firmly rooted in the stem of its victim, it begins to grow vigorously. With every few inches of its growth it sends new roots deep into this stem. And when it feels quite at home, and perfectly sure of its board, it begins to wither away below, where it is joined to its earth root. Soon it breaks off entirely from this, and draws every bit of its nourishment from the plant or plants in which it is rooted.

Now stop a moment and think of the almost wicked intelligence this plant has seemed to show, — how it keeps its hold of the earth till its stem has found the plant which will be compelled to feed it, and how it gives up all pretense of self-support, once it has captured its prey.

You have heard of men and women who do this sort

of thing, — who shirk all trouble, and try to live on the work of others; and I fear you know some boys and girls who are not altogether unlike the dodder, — boys and girls who never take any pains if they can possibly help it, who try to have all of the fun and none of the work; but did you ever suppose you would come across a plant that would conduct itself in such a fashion?

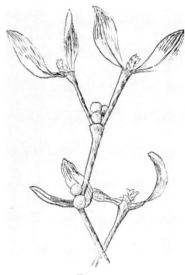

Of course, when the dodder happens to fasten itself upon some wild plant, little harm is done. But unfortunately it is very partial to plants that are useful to men, and then we must look upon it as an enemy.

Linen is made from the flax plant, and this flax plant is one of the favorite victims of the dodder. Sometimes it will attack and starve to death whole fields of flax.

But do not let us forget that we happen to be talking about the dodder because it is one of the plants which put out roots above ground.

FIG. 119

There is one plant which many of you have seen, that never, at any time of its life, is rooted in the earth, but which feeds always upon the branches of the trees in which it lives.

This plant (Fig. 119) is one of which perhaps you hear and see a good deal at Christmas time. It is an old English custom, at this season, to hang somewhere about the house a mistletoe bough (for the mistletoe is the plant I mean) with the understanding that one is free to steal a kiss from any maiden caught beneath it. And as mistletoe boughs are sold on our street corners and in our shops at Christmas, there has been no difficulty in bringing one to school to-day.

The greenish mistletoe berries are eaten by birds. Often their seeds are dropped by these birds upon the branches of trees. There they hold fast by means of the sticky material with which they are covered. Soon they send out roots which pierce the bark, and, like the roots of the dodder, suck up the juices of the tree, and supply the plant with nourishment.

Then there are water roots as well as earth roots. Some of these water roots are put forth by plants which are nowhere attached to the earth. These are plants which you would not be likely to know about. One of them, the duckweed, is very common in ponds; but it is so tiny that when you have seen a quantity of these duckweeds, perhaps you have never supposed them to be true plants, but rather a green scum floating on the top of the water.

But the duckweed is truly a plant. It has both flower and fruit, although without a distinct stem and leaves; and it sends down into the water its long, hanging roots, which yet do not reach the ground.

There are other plants which have at the same time underground roots and water roots.

Rooted in the earth on the borders of a stream sometimes you see a willow tree which has put out aboveground roots. These hang over the bank and float in the water, apparently with great enjoyment; for roots not only seem to seek the water, but to like it, and to flourish in it.

If you break off at the ground one of your bean plants, and place the slip in a glass of water, you will see for yourselves how readily it sends out new roots.

I have read of a village tree the roots of which had made their way into a water pipe. Here they grew so abundantly that soon the pipe was entirely choked. This rapid, luxuriant growth was supposed to have been caused by the water within the pipe.

So you see there are underground roots and above-ground roots and water roots. Usually, as you know, the underground roots get their food from the earth; but sometimes, as with the Indian pipe, they feed on dead plants, and sometimes, as with the yellow false foxglove, on other living roots.

WHAT FEW CHILDREN KNOW

TO–DAY we must take another look at the plants in the schoolroom garden.

By this time some of them have grown quite tall. Others are just appearing above the earth.

Here is a young morning-glory (Fig. 120). We see that its stem, like that of the bean, was the first thing to come out of the seed. This stem has turned downward into the earth. From its lower end grows the root, which buries itself deeper and deeper.

An older plant shows us that the upper part of the stem straightens itself out and grows upward, bearing with it a pair of leaves (Fig. 121).

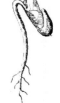

From between these starts a tiny bud, that soon unfolds into a fresh leaf, which is carried upward by a new piece of stem.

On the tip of this new piece of stem grows another bud, which also enlarges into a leaf, and in the same way as before is borne upward (Fig. 122).

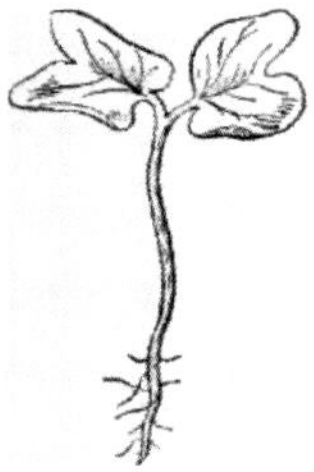

FIG. 120

In this fashion the plant keeps growing bigger and bigger. Soon branches start from the sides of the stem, and later flowers and fruits.

So we see that it is the stem which bears all the other parts of the plant.

Most people think that the plant springs from the root; but you children know better. With your own eyes, here in the schoolroom, you have seen that instead of the stem growing from the root, the root grows from the stem.

FIG. 121

That more people have not found this out, is because they do not use their eyes rightly.

Every spring hundreds and thousands of baby plants make their way out of the seed shell into the world, just as you saw the baby bean plant do, sending out first its little stem, which pointed downward into the earth and started a root. And every spring there are hundreds of thousands of men and women, and boys and girls, who go through the woods and fields, and across the parks and along the streets, as though they were blind, taking no notice of the wonders all about them.

FIG. 122

DANA'S PLANTS. — 8

108

PLANTS THAT CANNOT
STAND ALONE

ALREADY we have learned that some stems grow under ground, and that by most people these are called roots.

And among those which grow above the ground we see many different kinds.

The stem of Indian corn grows straight up in the air, and needs no help in standing erect.

Fig. 123 shows you the morning-glory plant, the stem of which is unable to hold itself upright without assistance. A great many plants seem to need this same sort of help; and it is very interesting to watch their behavior.

The stem of the young morning-glory sweeps slowly through the air in circles, in search of some support.

You remember that the curious dodder acted in this same way, and that its movements reminded us of the manner in which a blind man feels about him

109

When the morning-glory finds just the support it needs, it lays hold of it, and twists about it, and then climbs upward with great satisfaction.

I want you to watch this curious performance. It is sure to amuse you. The plant seems to know so well what it is about, and it acts so sensibly when it finds what it wants.

But if it happens to meet a glass tube, or something too smooth to give it the help it needs, it slips off it, and seems almost as discouraged as a boy would be who fails in his attempt to climb a slippery tree or telegraph pole.

Fig. 123

The bean is another plant whose stem is not strong enough to hold it erect without help.

Fig. 124

But, unlike the morning-glory, the stem of the bean does not twist about the first stick it finds. Instead it sends out many shorter stems which do this work of reaching after and twining about some support. In this same way the pea is able to hold up its head in the world.

Other plants are supported by their leafstalks. These twist about whatever sticks or branches they can find, and so prevent the plant from falling. The picture (Fig. 124) shows you how the garden nightshade climbs by its leafstalk. The beautiful clematis clambers all over the roadside thicket in the same way.

The English ivy and the poison ivy, as we have

learned already, climb by the help of roots which their stems send out into the trunks of trees and the crevices of buildings.

The stems of the Virginia creeper and of the Japanese ivy give birth to smaller stems, such as you see in the picture below. When the tips of these reach the wall, or the tree trunk up which the plant is trying to climb, they broaden out into little flat, round plates, which, like tiny claws, cling to the surface (Fig. 125).

I hope your teacher will tell you where you can find

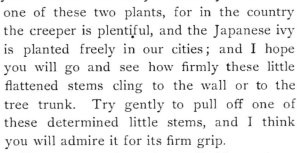

one of these two plants, for in the country the creeper is plentiful, and the Japanese ivy is planted freely in our cities; and I hope you will go and see how firmly these little flattened stems cling to the wall or to the tree trunk. Try gently to pull off one of these determined little stems, and I think you will admire it for its firm grip.

There are other than climbing plants whose stems are not strong enough to stand up straight without help.

FIG. 125

Think of the beautiful water lily. If you have ever spent a morning in a boat (as I hope you have, for it is a delightful way to spend a morning) hunting water lilies, you will remember that these flowers float on top of the water; and when you reach over to pick them, you find the tall flower stems standing quite erect in the water.

But what happened when you broke them off, and held them in your hand?

Why, these long stems proved to have no **strength at**

all. They flopped over quite as helplessly as the morning-glory vine would do if you unwound it from the wires up which it was climbing; and you saw that they had only been able to stand up straight because of the help the water had given them.

———oo°o̥°oo———

SOME HABITS OF STEMS

BESIDE the stems which stand erect without help (like that of the corn), and those which climb by means of some support (like those of the morning-glory and bean), and those which are held up by the water (like that of the water lily), there are stems which slant upward (like that of the red clover), stems which lie upon the ground (like that of the snowberry), and stems which creep (that is, which run along the ground), and which strike root, and so give rise to new plants (like those of the white clover and strawberry).

With the new plants you meet, try always to notice to which of these different classes their stems belong; for later, when you wish to use the botany and to learn the names of the plants, this habit of noticing things will help you greatly.

Then, too, with every new plant, you should find out whether its stem is round or square, and whether it is smooth or hairy, or if it is at all thorny.

The thorns and hairs which some plants scatter over their stems protect them from animals and insects, which might otherwise do them an injury.

By the thorns little snails are prevented from climbing up the stems and eating away the green leaves above; and the cows and horses are pretty sure to leave the thorny plants well alone. It is easy to understand why we find thistle plants growing thickly in the pasture, which is nearly bare of everything else. Long ago these thistles clothed themselves in an armor of prickles, and ever since they have been successful in waging war against the cattle.

Sometimes a tree will cover its lower part only with thorns. Why is this, do you suppose?

This is because only the lower branches are within reach of the cattle. Only these have any need of a suit of thorns. The wild pear, which grows in Europe, is such a tree 'as this.

A stem that is covered with hairs, and also one that is sticky in spots, serves to protect its flowers from an attack by ants, or by other insects that might do them harm; for these flowers, you remember, hold the golden dust which works such wonders when carried to another flower. And you recall, that, when bees go to plants for the sweet stuff from which honey is made, they carry this flower dust from blossom to blossom. But if the sweet stuff is given up to greedy insects, then this good work is not done; for the bees get disgusted, and stop visiting the plants which do not take more pains to please them. And so oftentimes the plant covers its stem with hairs or with sticky drops, so that the meddlesome little thieves cannot get up to the blossom at all.

So if you pick a flower which leaves your fingers sticky, you must remember that the plant is only doing its duty in trying to please the bees.

Although I have seen these plants do so many queer things that I am learning not to be surprised at their clever ways, I must own that I was a little astonished to see how anxious one of them was to save itself unnecessary trouble.

There is a plant called the "amphibious knotweed." This is a rather difficult name, I know. This word "amphibious" is applied to something that can live both in water and on land; and this plant grows sometimes in the pond or river, and sometimes on the shore.

When on land, its stem is covered with the hairs which serve to keep meddlesome insects from climbing up to its pretty balls of pink flowers. In the water there is no danger of any such attack from insects; and so when it happens to grow in the pond or river, this knowing little plant does not trouble itself to clothe with hairs its stem, but leaves this quite smooth.

Next summer I hope you will hunt up the amphibious knotweed, and will compare the smooth water stem with the hairy one that grows on land.

STEMS AND SEED LEAVES

THE smaller plants usually have green stems. The larger ones have brown, woody stems, such as you see in bushes and trees; for the trunk of the biggest tree in the world is nothing but a great stem.

The delicate green stems die down to the ground during the cold winter. Sometimes the whole plant dies, the root below as well as the stem above ground. But often the root (or what we usually call the root) lives, and sends up a fresh stem the next year.

But the woody stems live through the winter, and put out fresh leaves and branches the next spring.

Without a magnifying glass, it is difficult to see of just what the green stems of the small plants are made up; and these you can pass by for the present. But if your teacher will cut across the stem of a large rose, you can see here an outer covering, *the green skin;*

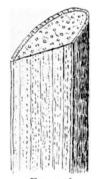

within this, a *ring of woody material;* and in the center of the stem, a *soft white stuff* called " pith."

When we were reading about seed leaves, I told you that by the stem and leaves of a plant you could tell whether it brought into the world more than one seed leaf.

Now, when a stem like that of the rose is divided into three well-defined parts, — the skin, or bark, outside ; next the woody part ; and the soft white pith in the middle, — then you can be

FIG. 126

pretty sure that the plant had more than one seed leaf.

This picture (Fig. 126) shows you a section of a cornstalk. Here you do not see the three parts that were so plain in the rose stem, for the woody part is not gathered together in a ring : it is scattered through the soft part, so that you cannot distinguish the one from the other.

Running lengthwise you see the scattered bundles of woody threads, the cut ends of which give the dotted look on top.

Now, such a stem as this of the corn shows you that the plant was born with only one seed leaf.

Try to remember the difference between these two stems.

This next picture (Fig. 127) shows a part of the trunk or stem of the fir tree.

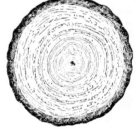

The dark outside circle is the bark.

The rings within this are the wood. Each year one of these woody rings is added to the tree, the last ring of all lying next to the bark ; so, if you count

these, you can find out how many years the tree has lived.

In the center we see the soft stuff called pith.

What do these three divisions show?

The trunk of the palm in the next picture (Fig. 128) is like the stem of the corn. The wood is not gathered in rings, but is scattered through the soft part in thread-like bundles, so that we cannot tell just the age of the tree.

And what else do you know about the palm?

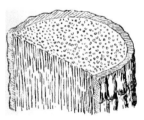

Why, you know that it came into the world with but one seed leaf. If it had had more than one, its stems would have had woody rings such as we see in the fir.

In the schoolroom you cannot see palms and firs ; but you can find a log in a wood pile which will show you

Fig. 128

just such woody rings as prove that the fir tree had more than one seed leaf.

And you can look at a stalk brought from the cornfield that will show you how the trunk of the palm tells us that this tree began life with only one seed leaf.

"WELL DONE, LITTLE STEM"

IT is wonderful how much there is to learn about everything.

We began this book with an apple, and I had no more idea than you that that apple was going to keep us busy for days.

And then the apple reminded us of its cousins, the pear and plum and peach and cherry and rose. And if we had not stopped short, we should have been introduced to so many more cousins that we should have had neither room nor time for anything else.

From fruits we went to seeds.

At first it seemed almost as though we ought to finish up the seeds in two or three readings; but this did not prove to be the case.

The mere naming of the different ways in which seeds went traveling, covered so many pages that it was all we could do to find time to tell how a few of the baby plants were cared for, and how they made their way out of the seed shell into the world.

But when we came to roots, we felt there would be no temptation to loiter by the way, for roots seemed rather dismal things to talk about. Yet it took some little time to show the different uses of a root, and to talk about air roots and water roots, as well as earth roots. It was not altogether easy to make clear just how the little root hairs keep acids on hand in which to melt the solid earth food which their throats are too delicate to swallow. And it was quite a long story when we came to the dodder, which roots in the stems of living plants, and steals all its food from them; and to those orchids whose long roots swing from tree branches and draw their nourishment from the air.

About stems, however, even I felt a little discouraged; for though it is from the stem that all other parts of a plant grow, yet it is not looked upon generally as an interesting object when studied by itself; and I dare say you children still feel that stems are less amusing than fruits, or seeds, or roots.

Still we can hardly help admiring the way in which a stem, when it lies underground, like that of the lily or the Jack-in-the-pulpit, makes its food so carefully all through the summer, and waits so patiently through the long winter in order to help its plant to burst into flower, and to ripen into fruit as soon as possible, and without more labor and food hunting when the spring comes.

When a stem, like that of the morning-glory, sweeps slowly and carefully through the air in search of something to lay hold of in its efforts to climb upward, and when, on finding this support, it makes such good use of it, we feel inclined to say, "Well done, little stem."

And when a stem on land knows how to keep off meddlers, yet has the wisdom not to take unnecessary trouble when afloat, like that of the amphibious knot-weed, then we feel that a plant gives its stem, as well as its other parts, a large supply of common sense.

PLANTS AND THEIR CHILDREN

There is a great deal more that might be said on this subject. What a plant lives on, what it eats and drinks and breathes, is very interesting to learn about. And of course the food taken in by the roots must be carried upward through the stem. But to write simply about this is difficult. As much as I think most of you can understand, I will tell you when we take up leaves.

Part IV — Buds

——◦○❀○◦——

BUDS IN WINTER

WHEN school opened in September, all the trees were covered with leaves ; and some of these trees were bent with their burden of pears and apples and peaches, while others were hung with prickly chestnut burrs or with acorns or walnuts.

But now all is changed. The woods look gray and bare ; for nearly all the leaves have fallen save those ot the oak, which are still holding fast to the branches. These oak leaves are brown and stiff and leathery. They crackle and rustle when the wind blows through them.

In the city squares you see the same change, — bare branches in place of green leaves.

At this season it is hardly worth while, perhaps you think, to go to the woods or to the park ; for there is nothing to be seen, — no leaves, no flowers, almost no fruits. Better wait till spring for any such expedition.

Here you are wrong. Provided you know what to look at, and how to look at it, there is no month of the year when the woods and parks are not full of interest.

And so at this season, when the trees are bare of leaves, better than at any other, certain things can be studied.

I have asked your teacher to bring to school to-day branches from the different trees which are looking so cold and lonely. It is nearly always possible to find the horse-chestnut, the maple, or the cherry; and we will talk especially about these branches.

On your way to school, perhaps you pass every day a horse-chestnut tree; but its branches are so far above your heads that you may never have noticed that in winter the leafless twigs bear just such buds as you see in the picture (Fig. 129), and on the branch which is before you.

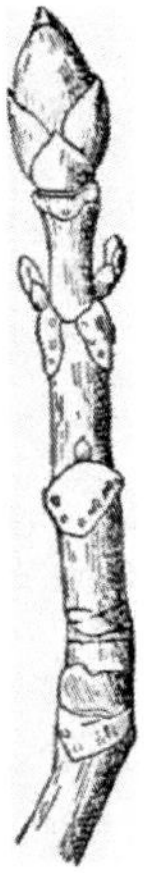

The largest bud grows on top. This is where the beautiful flower cluster that comes out in May lies hidden.

The smaller buds that grow lower down the stem hold only leaves. You see that these buds grow in pairs, one bud opposite another, and always above a sort of scar on the twig. This scar was made last fall by the breaking-off of a leaf.

Perhaps you fancy that these buds have only just made their appearance.

FIG. 129

If you have any such idea as that, you are quite wrong. Last summer, when the leaves were large and fresh, the little buds, that were not to unfold for nearly a year, began to form, growing somewhat larger as the weeks went by, and folding themselves tightly in the brown, leathery wrappings that were to keep them safe from the cold of winter.

I should like you to pull off these wrappings, and see how well the horse-chestnut tree defends from cold its baby leaves.

121

First you find about seven of these outside wrappings. The very outer ones are thick and brown, and covered with the sticky stuff that makes them proof against rain.

The next ones are brown and thick where their tips are exposed to the air, while the inner ones are green and delicate. But altogether they make a warm, snug covering for young leaves and flowers.

As for the baby leaves themselves, they are all done up in a furry stuff that keeps them from catching cold, even if a gust of wind or a few drops of rain should manage to make a way through the waterproof and almost air-tight wrappings.

So you see that the leaves and branches and young flowers of a plant or tree are looked after just as carefully as is the seed within the seed case, or the baby plant in its seed shell.

A HAPPY SURPRISE

HERE you see a branch from the red maple (Fig. 130).

On the flowering shoots three buds grow side by side. The middle, smaller one holds the leaves. These leaves do not appear until the two outer, larger buds have burst into flower clusters; for the flowers of the red maple appear before its leaves.

I want you to bring to school as many different kinds of branches as you can find, and I hope you will examine

Fig. 130

them all very carefully. Notice the position of their buds, and whether these grow close together or are scattered far apart, and whether one bud grows just opposite another; and look for the marks left by the leaves which broke off last fall.

When the buds are large enough, you will find it interesting to pull them apart (but you must do this with great care) and see how beautifully wrapped are the baby leaves and flowers.

I chose the branch of the horse-chestnut for special examination, because its large buds show their contents plainly.

When a bud grows on the tip of a stem, its work is to carry on that stem; but when it grows just above a leaf scar, you can be sure that it is a young branch. Such a branch may bear either leaves or flowers, or both.

But buds do not all grow up at the same time, or necessarily at all.

The strongest ones are the first to open. The others may keep quiet for some time, not unfolding, perhaps, unless some of the earlier ones are killed. In this case, the waiting buds try to fill the gap, and carry on the good work of clothing the tree with leaves and flowers.

Sometimes they wait over till another year, and occasionally a bud never opens at all.

You all enjoyed planting seeds, and watching them grow under your very eyes.

Now I am going to propose to you a scheme which has given me quite as much pleasure as my pot gardens.

BUDS

When the buds on the winter branches have swelled the least little bit, after a few warm days in February perhaps, go to the woods and cut several branches in places where no one will miss them, and take them home and put them in warm water, in a warm, bright corner, and see what happens.

It will be a real joy to you, watching these little buds get bigger and bigger, till the outer wrappings are forced apart, and either thrown well aside, or pushed off altogether; and you will be filled with delight when the delicate baby leaves begin to stretch themselves, or, better still, when the pure, beautiful flowers burst from the brown, dead-looking twigs.

Get branches of cherry, apple, peach, and pear; and bring in the pussy willow, the maple, the *Forsythia*, the spicebush, and, if you can find it, the mountain laurel; and if you do not pass many moments of almost breathless pleasure watching the wonders these budding branches are so eager to reveal, you are not the children I take you to be.

———⋯⋯———

SOME ASTONISHING BUDS

THERE are some plants which do not put any winter wraps on their delicate buds; and, strangely enough, these buds do not seem to suffer for lack of clothing.

In a warm country this would not surprise us. If we were going to spend the winter in the West Indies, we

DANA'S PLANTS. — 9

should not carry our furs with us, for we should not meet any weather cold enough to make them necessary; and so perhaps in the West Indies the buds have no more need of winter clothing than we ourselves.

But if we were to spend the Christmas holidays somewhere in our Northern mountains, if we were going for skating and coasting to the Catskills or the Adirondacks, we should not fail to take with us our warmest clothes.

And yet, if we walked in the Adirondack woods, we should meet over and over again a shrub bearing naked buds, their folded, delicate leaves quite exposed to the bitter cold.

This shrub is the hobblebush, the pretty flowers of which you see on p. 246.

I do not understand any better than you why this hobblebush does not tuck away its baby leaves beneath a warm covering. Neither do I understand how these naked leaves can live through the long, cold winter. I should like very much to satisfy myself as to the reason for this, for they do live and flourish; and I wish that such of you children as know the home of the hobblebush (and it is common in many places) would watch this shrub through the winter, and see if you can discover how it can afford to take less care of its buds than other plants.

There is one tree which seems to shield its buds more carefully in summer than in winter. This tree is the buttonwood. It grows not only in the country, but in many of our city streets and squares. You know it by the way in which its bark peels in long strips from its trunk and branches, and by the button-like balls which hang from the leafless twigs all winter.

If you examine one of these twigs, now that they are bare of leaves, you see the buds quite plainly; but if it is summer time, when the leaves are clinging to the branch, you see no buds, and suppose that they are not yet formed.

But here you are wrong.

"How can that be?" you ask. You looked carefully, and nowhere was there any sign of a bud.

But you did *not* look everywhere, after all.

If very carefully you had pulled off one of the leaves, you would have found the young bud tucked safely away beneath the hollow end of the leafstalk. This leafstalk fitted over it more neatly than a candle snuffer over a candle (Fig. 131).

Try this for yourselves next summer. I think you will be pleased with this pretty arrangement.

We learned that the potato, even though it is buried in the earth and does not look like it, is really one of the thickened stems of the potato plant.

FIG. 131

The "eyes" of the potato look as little like buds as the potato itself looks like a stem. Yet these "eyes" are true buds; for, if we leave our potatoes in the dark cellar till spring, the "eyes" will send out slender shoots in the same way that the buds on the branches of trees send out young shoots.

As I told you before, the usual place for a bud is just between the stem and the leafstalk, or the scar left by the leafstalk; but if a stem is cut or wounded, oftentimes it sends out buds in other than the usual places.

This habit accounts for the growth of young shoots from stumps of trees, and from parts of the plant which ordinarily do not give birth to buds.

Some buds never open while fastened to the stem of the parent plant; but after a time they fall to the ground, strike root, and send up a fresh young plant.

FIG. 132

The tiger lily, the plant that grows so often in old gardens, bears such buds as these. We call them "bulblets" when they act in this strange fashion.

Perhaps even more surprising than this is the fact that leaves sometimes produce buds.

In certain warmer countries grows a plant called the *Bryophyllum.* If you look carefully at the thick, fleshy leaves of this plant, along its notched edges you will see certain little dark spots; and if you cut off one of these leaves and pin it on your window curtain, what do you suppose will happen?

Well, right under your eyes will happen one of the strangest things I have ever seen.

From the row of dark spots along the leaf's edge, springs a row of tiny, perfect plants (Fig. 132).

And when these tiny plants are fairly started, if you

127

lay the leaf on moist earth, they will send their roots into the ground, break away from the fading leaf, and form a whole colony of new plants.

Now, those dark spots along the leaf's edge were tiny buds; and the thick leaf was so full of rich food, that when it was broken off from the parent plant, and all of this food was forced into the buds, these were strong enough to send out roots and leaves, and to set up in life for themselves.

It will not be difficult for your teacher to secure some of these leaves of the *Bryophyllum*, and to show you in the schoolroom this strange performance.

All children enjoy wonderful tricks, and I know of nothing much prettier or more astonishing than this trick of the *Bryophyllum*.

Part V — Leaves

HOW TO LOOK AT A LEAF

TO-DAY we begin to learn what we can about the leaves of plants. I hope that enough fresh green leaves have been brought to school to allow every child here to have one on the desk before him, so that he may see, as far as is possible, just what is being talked about.

This picture (Fig. 133) shows you the leaf of the quince. Now, suppose you held in your hand a leaf fresh from the quince tree, and were asked to describe it to a blind person, how would you tell about it?

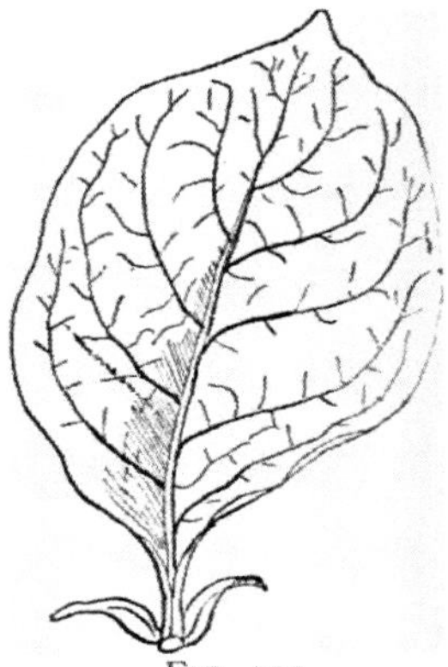

You would begin, I fancy, by saying, "This leaf is green," for the color of an object is one of the things we notice first.

Next perhaps you would describe its shape. "This quince leaf is rounded, yet it is too long to be called a round leaf." So you would use the word "oblong."

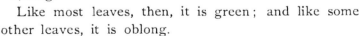

Fig. 133

Like most leaves, then, it is green; and like some other leaves, it is oblong.

129

Now look at this picture (Fig. 134) of the maple leaf. This, you see, is not oblong, but three-pointed.

What other differences do you notice between these two leaves?

You do not seem quite sure as to whether there are any other differences. But do you not notice that the edge of the maple leaf is cut into little teeth, like the edge of a saw, while the edge of the quince leaf is smooth?

And let me tell you here, that when I speak of a leaf, I speak not only of the enlarged flat surface we call the "leaf blade," but also of the "leafstalk." A leaf usually consists of a leafstalk and a leaf blade, though some leaves are set so close to the stem that they have no room for any stalks of their own.

"Oh! then," you answer, "the leafstalk of the maple is much longer than that of the quince, and there are little bits of leaves at the foot of the quince leafstalk which the maple is without."

FIG. 134

You have done very well, and have noticed just those things which you should.

The shape of the leaf blade, whether the edge of this is toothed, the length of the leafstalk, and whether this has any little leaves at its foot where it joins the stem, are things always worth noticing.

Now take your leaves and hold them up against the

light, or else look at the picture of the quince leaf, and study carefully the make-up of the blade.

You see that this is divided lengthwise by a heavy rib which juts out on the lower side. From this "midrib," as it is called, run a great many smaller lines. These are called "veins." And from these branch off still smaller veins that bear the name of "veinlets." And somewhat as the paper is stretched over the sticks of a kite, so from the leaf's midrib to its edge, and from vein to vein, is drawn the delicate green material which makes up the greater part of the leaf.

What I wish you to learn this morning is, *how to look at a leaf.*

Before using our brains rightly, we must know how to use our eyes. If we see a thing as it really is, the chances are that our thoughts about it will be fairly correct.

But it is surprising how often our eyes *see wrong.*

If you doubt this, ask four or five of your playmates to describe the same thing, — some street accident, or a quarrel in the playground, which all have seen, or something of the sort, — and then I think you will understand what I mean by saying that few people see correctly.

THE MOST WONDERFUL THING IN THE WORLD

IT would be quite a simple matter to interest you children in plants and their lives, if always it were possible to talk only about the things which you can see with your own unaided eyes.

I think a bright child sees better than many a grown person, and I think that it is easier to interest him in what he sees.

And then plants in themselves are so interesting and surprising, that one must be stupid indeed if he or she finds it impossible to take pleasure in watching their ways.

But about these plants there are many things which you cannot see without the help of a microscope, and these things it is difficult to describe in simple words. Yet it is necessary to learn about them if you wish really to feel at home in this beautiful world of plants.

After all, whatever is worth having is worth taking some trouble for; and nothing worth having can be had without trouble. So I hope when you children come to parts of this book that seem at first a little dull, you will say to yourselves, " Well, if we wish really to know plants, to be able to tell their names, to understand their habits, we must try to be a little patient when we come to the things that are difficult."

For even in your games you boys have to use some patience; and you are quite willing to run the risk of being hurt for the sake of a little fun.

And you girls will take no end of trouble if you happen to be sewing for your dolls, or playing at cooking over the kitchen stove, or doing something to which you give the name "play" instead of "work."

I only ask for just as much patience in your study of plants; and I think I can safely promise you that plants will prove delightful playthings long after you have put aside the games which please you now.

So we must begin to talk about some of the things which you are not likely to see now with your own eyes, but which, when possible, I will show you by means of pictures, and which, when you are older, some of you may see with the help of a microscope.

Every living thing is made up of one or more little objects called "cells."

Usually a cell may be likened to a tiny bag which holds a bit of that material which is the most wonderful thing in the whole world, for this is the material which has *life*.

Occasionally a cell is nothing but a naked bit of this wonderful substance, for it is not always held in a tiny bag.

This picture (Fig. 135) shows you a naked plant cell, much magnified, that swims about in the water by means of the two long hairs which grow from one end of the speck of life-giving material.

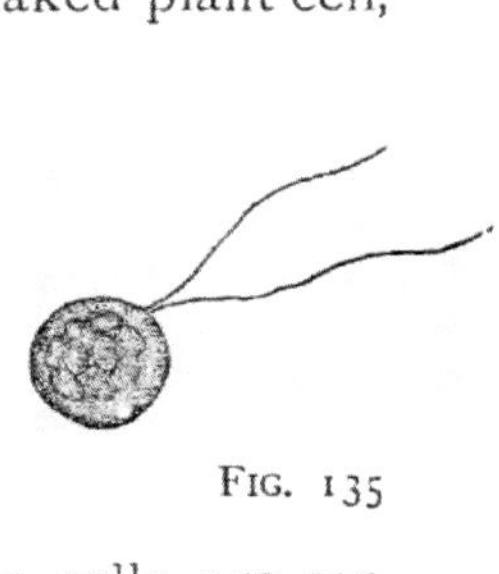

FIG. 135

The next picture (Fig. 136) shows you a seed cut across, and so magnified that you can see plainly its many cells.

In the middle portion of the seed the cells are six-sided, and laid against one another in an orderly and beautiful fashion, while the outer ones are mostly round.

All animals, we ourselves, all plants, began life as a single cell.

Sometimes a cell will spend its life alone. When the time comes for it to add to the life of the world, it divides into two or more "daughter cells," as they are

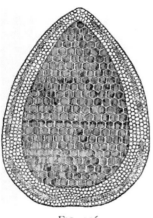

called. These break away from one another, and in like manner divide again.

But usually the single cell which marks the beginning of a new life adds to itself other cells; that is, the different cells do not break away from one another, but all cling together, and so build up the perfect plant or animal.

By just such additions the greatest tree in the forest grew from a single tiny cell.

FIG. 136

By just such additions you children have grown to be what you are, and in the same way you will continue to grow.

Every living thing must eat and breathe, and so all living cells must have food and air. These they take in through their delicate cell walls. The power to do this comes from the bit of living substance which lies within these walls.

This strange, wonderful material within the little cell is what is alive in every man and woman, in every boy and girl, in every living thing, whether plant or animal.

PLANTS AND THEIR CHILDREN

We know this much about it, and not the wisest man that ever lived knows much more.

For though the wise men know just what things go to make up this material, and though they themselves can put together these same things, they can no more make life, or understand the making of it, than can you or I.

But when we get a good hold of the idea that this material is contained in all living things, then we begin to feel this; we begin to feel that men and women, boys and girls, big animals and little insects, trees and flowers, wayside weeds and grasses, the ferns and rushes of the forest, the gray lichens of the cliffs and fences, the seaweeds that sway in the green rock pools, and living things so tiny that our eyes must fail to see them, — that all these are bound into one by the tie of that strange and wonderful thing called life; that they are all different expressions of one mysterious, magnificent idea.

While writing that last sentence, I almost forgot that I was writing for boys and girls, or indeed for any one but myself; and I am afraid that perhaps you have very little idea of what I am talking about.

But I will not cross it out. Why not, do you suppose?

Because I feel almost sure that here and there among you is a girl or boy who will get just a little glimmering idea of what I mean ; and perhaps as the years go by, that glimmer will change into a light so bright and clear as to become a help in dark places.

But the thought that I hope each one of you will carry home is this, — that because this strange something found in your body is also found in every other living thing, you may learn to feel that you are in a way a sister or brother, not only to all other boys and girls, but to all the animals and to every plant about you.

————o◦◦◦◦oo————

HOW A PLANT IS BUILT

NOW we know that the plant, like yourself, began life as a single cell; and we know that the perfect plant was built up by the power which this cell had of giving birth to other cells with like power.

Suppose that a brick were laid upon the earth as the foundation of a wall; and suppose that this brick were able to change into two bricks. Suppose that the new brick were able to form another brick in the same manner, and that this power should pass from brick to brick; and suppose that all these bricks were able to arrange themselves one upon another in an orderly fashion, so that they could not easily be moved from their places.

Now, if you can see this brick wall growing up, you can see something of how the cells of a plant grow up and arrange themselves.

But though it is fairly easy to see how the plant cells form one from another, that does not explain how they come to make a plant, with its many different parts, with its root and stem, its branches, leaves, and flowers.

One thing can divide and make two things of the

same sort; but it is not easy to see how it can make things that are quite different from itself.

Now, if this difficulty as to the building-up of plants and animals has come into your minds, you are only puzzled by what has puzzled hundreds of people before you; and all these hundreds of people have found the puzzle quite as impossible to solve as the king's horses and the king's men found it impossible to put Humpty Dumpty together again.

A good many questions that we cannot answer come into our minds; but if we look honestly for the answers and do not find them, then we can be pretty sure that for the present it is safe to leave them unanswered.

As cell is added to cell in the building-up of plant life, some wonderful power forces each new cell to do the special work which is most needed by the growing plant.

Sometimes this new cell is needed to help do the work of a root, and so it begins to do this work, and becomes part of the root; or else it is needed to do stem work, and goes to make up the stem, or leaf work, and is turned over into the leaf.

A healthy cell is born with the power to do whatever is most needed.

HOW A PLANT'S FOOD IS COOKED

SOME time ago we learned that the little root hairs, by means of their acid, are able to make a sort of broth from the earthy materials which they could not swallow in a solid state.

137

But before this broth is really quite fit for plant food, it needs even more preparation.

Why do we eat and drink, do you suppose?

"Because we are hungry." That is the direct reason, of course. But we are made hungry so that we shall be forced to eat; for when we eat, we take into our bodies the material that is needed to build them up, — to feed the cells which make the flesh and bone and muscle.

And this is just why the plant eats and drinks. It needs constantly fresh nourishment for its little cells, so that these can live, and grow strong enough to make the new cells which go to form, not bone and flesh and muscle, as with you children, but fresh roots and stem and leaves and flowers and fruits.

If these little cells were not fed, they would die, and the plant would cease to live also.

And now what do you think happens to the broth that has been taken in from the earth by the root hairs?

As we have said, this broth needs a little more preparation before it is quite fit for plant food. What it really wants is some *cooking*.

Perhaps you can guess that the great fire before which all plant food is cooked is the sun.

But how are the hot rays of the sun to pierce the earth, and reach the broth which is buried in the plant's root?

Of course, if it remains in the root, the earth broth will not get the needed cooking. It must be carried to some more get-at-able position.

Now, what part of a plant is usually best fitted to receive the sun's rays?

Its leaves, to be sure. The thin, flat leaf blades are spread out on all sides, so that they fairly bathe themselves in sunshine.

So if the broth is to be cooked in the sun, up to the leaves it must be carried.

And how is this managed? Water does not run uphill, as you know. Yet this watery broth must mount the stem before it can enter the leaves.

Water does not run uphill ordinarily, it is true; yet, if you dip a towel in a basin of water, the water rises along the threads, and the towel is wet far above the level of the basin.

And if you dip the lower end of a lump of sugar in a cup of coffee, the coffee rises in the lump, and stains it brown.

And the oil in the lamp mounts high into the wick.

Perhaps when you are older you will be able somewhat to understand the reason of this rise of liquid in the towel, in the lump of sugar, in the lamp wick. The same reason accounts partly for the rise of the broth in the stem. But it is thought that the force which sends the oil up the wick would not send the water far up the stem. And you know that some stems are very tall indeed. The distance, for example, to be traveled by water or broth which is sucked in by the roots of an oak tree, and which must reach the topmost leaves of the oak, is very great.

Yet the earth broth seems to have no difficulty in making this long, steep climb.

DANA'S PLANTS. — 10

139

Now, even wise men have to do some guessing about this matter, and I fear you will find it a little hard to understand.

But it is believed that the roots drink in the earth broth so eagerly and so quickly, that before they know it they are full to overflowing. It is easier, however, to enter a root than it is to leave it by the same door; and the result is, that the broth is forced upward into the stem by the pressure of more water or broth behind.

Of course, if the stem and branches and leaves above are already full of liquid, unless they have some way of disposing of the supply on hand, they cannot take in any more; and the roots below would then be forced to stop drinking, for when a thing is already quite full to overflowing, it cannot be made to hold more.

But leaves have a habit of getting rid of what they do not need. When the watery broth is cooked in the sun,

FIG. 137

the heat of the sun's rays causes the water to pass off through the little leaf mouths. Thus the broth is made fit for plant food, and at the same time room is provided for fresh supplies from the root.

If you should examine the lower side of a leaf through a microscope, you would find hundreds and thousands of tiny mouths, looking like the little mouths in this picture (Fig. 137).

Some of the water from the earth broth is constantly passing through these mouths out of the plant, into the air.

140

A STEEP CLIMB

IT is all very well, you may think, to say that the pressure from the root sends the water up through the stem; but when we cut across such a stem as a tree trunk, one finds it full of wood, with a little tightly packed soft stuff in the center, and not hollow like a water pipe, as one would suppose from all that has been said about the way the water rises in the stem.

No, a stem is not a hollow pipe, or even a bunch of hollow pipes, it is true; and it does seem something of a question, how the water can force its way through all this wood; and even if one hears how it is done, it is not an easy thing to make clear either to grown people or to children. But I will see what I can do; and I know that you really love these plants and trees, and will try to be a little patient with them and with me.

The water, or liquid, when it mounts a stem or tree trunk, takes a path that leads through the new-made cells. Each young cell wall is made of such delicate material that it allows the water, or broth, to filter through it, just as it would pass through a piece of thin cloth. And so it makes its way from cell to cell, along the stem, more slowly than if it were passing through a hollow tube, but almost as surely. It is true, the earth broth does not reach the leaves above without having given up something to the little cells along the road. These seem to lay hold of what they specially need for their support, while the rest is allowed to pass on.

I want your teacher to prove to you by a little experiment that water makes its way up a stem.

LEAVES

If she will place in colored water the stem of a large white tulip, cutting off its lower end under the liquid, those parts whose little cells are in closest connection with the stem will soon begin to change color, taking the red or blue of the water; for a freshly cut stem has the same power as the root to suck in water eagerly and quickly.

———oo⁃o⁃oo———

HOW A PLANT PERSPIRES

WE cannot see the water as it passes from the tiny leaf mouths into the air. Neither can we see the water that is being constantly carried from the surface of our bodies into the air. But if we breathe against a window pane, the scattered water in our breath is collected by the cold of the glass in a little cloud; and if we place the warm palms of our hands against this window pane, in the same way the cold collects the water that is passing from the little mouths in our skin, and shows it to us as a cloud on the glass.

Heat scatters water so that we cannot see it, any more than we can see the lump of sugar when its little grains are scattered in hot water; but cold gathers together the water drops so that we are able to see them.

This is why you can "see your breath," as you say, on a cold day. The cold outside air gathers together the water which was scattered by the heat of your body.

If you place against the window pane the under side of the leaves of a growing plant, the water passing from the tiny leaf mouths collects on the glass in just such a damp cloud as is made by the moist palms of your warm hands.

When water passes from your hands, you say that you are perspiring; and when water passes away from the plant, we can say that the plant perspires. Some plants perspire more freely than others. A sunflower plant has been known to give off more than three tumblers of water a day by this act of perspiration.

There is a tree, called the *Eucalyptus*, whose leaves perspire so freely that it is planted in swampy places in order to drain away the water.

Of course, the more quickly the leaves throw off water, the faster the fresh supply pushes up the stem.

If the leaves do their work more quickly than the roots make good the loss, then the plant wilts.

When a leaf is broken from a plant, it soon fades. Its water supply being cut off, it has no way of making good the loss through the leaf mouths.

Just as the air in a balloon keeps its walls firm, so the water in the leaf cells keeps the cell walls firm.

As a balloon collapses if you prick it with a pin, and let out the air, so the cell walls collapse when the cells lose their water; and when the cell walls of a leaf collapse, the leaf itself collapses.

HOW A PLANT STORES ITS FOOD

WE see that the water is drawn away from the earth broth into the air by the heat of the sun, just as water is drawn from the broth we place on the stove by the heat of the fire; and that when this has happened, the plant's food is cooked, and is in condition to be eaten.

But this broth does not lose all its water. There is still enough left to carry it back through the leaf into the branches and stem, and even down into .the root once more.

In fact, the prepared food is now sent to just those parts of the plant which most need it.

Perhaps it is laid up beneath the bark, to help make new buds which will burst into leaf and flower another year.

Or perhaps it goes down to help the roots put out new branches and fresh root hairs.

Or possibly it is stowed away in such an underground stem as that of the lily, or the crocus bulb, and is saved for next year's food. Once in a while some of this prepared food is stored in the leaf itself.

When a leaf is thick and juicy ("fleshy," the books call it), we can guess that it is full of plant food.

Do you recall the *Bryophyllum*, — the plant we talked about a few days ago? Its wonderful leaves, you remember, gave birth to a whole colony of new plants.

You may be sure that these leaves had refused to give up all the food sent to them for cooking in the sun. You can guess this from their thick, fleshy look, and you can be sure of this when you see the baby plants spring from their edges; for without plenty of nourishment stored away, these leaves could never manage to support such a quantity of young ones.

144

LEAF GREEN AND SUNBEAM

BUT the earth broth which the roots supply is not the only article of importance in the plant's bill of fare.

The air about us holds one thing that every plant needs as food.

This air is a mixture of several things. Just as the tea we drink is a mixture of tea and water, and milk and sugar, so the air is a mixture of oxygen and nitrogen, and water and carbonic-acid gas.

Oxygen, nitrogen, and carbonic-acid gas, — each one of these three things that help to make the air is what we call a gas, and one of these gases is made of two things. Carbonic-acid gas is made of oxygen and carbon.

Now, carbon is the food which is needed by every plant. But the carbon in the air is held tightly in the grasp of the oxygen, with which it makes the gas called carbonic-acid gas.

To get possession of this carbon, the plant must contrive to break up the gas, and then to seize and keep by force the carbon.

This seems like a rather difficult performance, does it not? For when a gas is made of two different things, you can be pretty sure that these keep a firm hold on each other, and that it is not altogether easy to tear them apart.

Now, how does the plant meet this difficulty?

You cannot guess by yourselves how this is done, so I must tell you the whole story.

145

LEAVES

Certain cells in the plant are trained from birth for this special work, — the work of getting possession of the carbon needed for plant food. These little cells take in the carbonic-acid gas from the air; then they break it up, tearing the carbon from the close embrace of the oxygen, pushing the oxygen back into the air it came from, and turning the carbon over to the plant to be stored away till needed as food.

Only certain cells can do this special piece of work. Only the cells which hold the green substance that colors the leaf can tear apart carbonic-acid gas. Every little cell which holds a bit of this leaf green devotes itself to separating the carbon from the oxygen.

Why this special power lies in a tiny speck of leaf green we do not know. We only know that a cell without such an occupant is quite unable to break up carbonic-acid gas.

But even the bit of leaf green in a tiny cell needs some help in its task. What aid does it call in, do you suppose, when it works to wrench apart the gas?

In this work the partner of the bit of leaf green is nothing more or less than a sunbeam. Without the aid of a sunbeam, the imprisoned leaf green is as helpless to steal the carbon as you or I would be.

It sounds a good deal like a fairy story, does it not, — this story of Leaf Green and Sunbeam?

Charcoal is made of carbon. About one half of every plant is carbon.

The coal we burn in our fireplaces is the carbon left upon the earth by plants that lived and died thousands of years ago. It is the carbon that Leaf Green and

Sunbeam together stole from the air, and turned over into the plant.

If one looks at a piece of coal with the eyes which one keeps for the little picture gallery all children carry in their heads, one sees more than just a shining, black lump. One sees a plant that grew upon the earth thousands of years ago, with its bright green leaves dancing in the sunlight; for without those green leaves and that sunlight, there could be no coal for burning to-day. And when we light our coal fire, what we really do is to set free the sunbeams that worked their way so long ago into the plant cells.

It is more like a fairy story than ever. Sunbeam is the noble knight who fought his way into the cell where Leaf Green lay imprisoned, doomed to perform a task which was beyond her power. But with the aid of the noble Sunbeam, she did this piece of work, and then both fell asleep, and slept for a thousand years. Awakening at last, together they made their joyful escape in the flame that leaps from out the black coal.

In truth, a sunbeam and a flame are not so unlike as to make this story as improbable as many others that we read.

And because I have told it to you in the shape of a fairy story, you must not think it is not true. It is indeed true. Everywhere in the sunshiny woods and fields of summer, the story of Leaf Green and Sunbeam is being lived. But when the day is cloudy or the sun sets, then there is no Sunbeam to help the Princess, and then no carbon is stolen from the air.

PLANT OR ANIMAL?

D ID you ever stop to ask yourself, "What is the difference between a plant and an animal?" because this is the place where that question should be answered.

"Why, an animal is *altogether* different from a plant," you answer, perhaps a little scornfully. "I have no trouble in telling which is which."

It is very natural that you should feel this way. A cow or a horse, for example, is not at all like a tree; and when you think of animals, you think of the ones you know best, and likewise of plants.

But wise men have discovered plants that look and act so much like animals, and animals that look and act so much like plants, that at one time they say, "Now, these are animals, surely," and a little later exclaim, "No, after all, these are plants;" and they take a long time to make up their minds as to whether certain objects are plants or animals.

And already even you children have discovered that the plants you know best belong to families, and have children, and care for them in a very motherly fashion; that they drink earth food with their roots, and eat carbon food with their leaves; and soon you will find that they do many other things which once upon a time you would have thought it a great joke to be told a plant could do.

You remember my telling you of one little plant cell that could swim; and there are some animals,

148

you know, that are rooted to one spot as we usually think only a plant is rooted.

What, then, *is* the difference between a plant and an animal?

Leaf Green and Sunbeam between them put life into what had no life before; and the living plant matter, which they help to make, is that which animals cannot make themselves, yet which they cannot live without, for this living matter is absolutely necessary to them as food.

And the one real difference between a plant and an animal is this, — a plant can make out of certain dead substances the living matter that all animals must have for food; an animal cannot do this.

HOW WE ARE HELPED BY LEAF GREEN AND SUNBEAM

THE cell in which Leaf Green lives has no little mouths such as we saw in the picture some time ago.

Its walls are so delicate that the carbonic-acid gas passes through them quite easily, — as easily as the gas escaping from an unlighted jet in the schoolroom could pass to your nose even if you wore a veil, or as easily as water would pass through a piece of muslin.

But between Leaf Green's cell and the outer air are other cells, — those which make up the outer covering or skin of the leaf. These are arranged so as to form the openings or mouths about which we have read. By means of these mouths the gas makes its way through the leaf's thick skin.

The plant needs as food the carbon in this gas, and so keeps fast hold of it; but the oxygen is not needed for this purpose, and so it is pushed back into the air.

Now, we learned in the last chapter of one very great service rendered to animals by plants. We learned that plants took carbon from the air, and turned this into food for animals.

But there is still another way in which plants serve animals. And once more it is the work of Leaf Green and Sunbeam that is of such importance to us; for when they take hold of the carbon, making it into living food for man and beast, they take from the air the gas that is poisonous, and send back into the air the gas which gives life and health.

This poisonous gas which they lay hold of, you remember, is carbonic-acid gas ; and carbonic-acid gas is what we animals send out of our bodies with every breath, for it is the part of the air which poisons us. When the schoolroom is so close that our heads ache, it is because so many children have been breathing out this gas, and we are forced to take it back into our bodies again.

But when this gas is stolen by the plant, and robbed of its carbon, it is no longer carbonic-acid gas. Nothing of it is left but the oxygen which is pushed out through the cell walls ; and this oxygen is as good to breathe as the other gas (carbon and oxygen mixed) is bad.

So the plant finds good what we find poisonous. It takes in and keeps that which hurts us (the carbon), and sends out that which helps us (the oxygen).

So you see that our lives depend on the lives of plants in two ways : —

1. The plants give us the food we need for life.

2. The plants take from the air the gas that poisons us, and give to the air the gas which we need for life and health.

And in both cases it is Leaf Green and Sunbeam who are making life possible for us.

Remember the great services of these two fairies when next you pass a green tree which is bathing itself in sunshine.

HOW A PLANT BREATHES

PERHAPS you have heard people say that it is not good to sleep in a room with plants.

They say this, because they have heard that at night the plant does not give out oxygen, but that it does give out the poisonous carbonic-acid gas.

Now, you children know that part of this statement is true.

You know that the plant cannot give out oxygen at night, because at that time there is no Sunbeam about to help Leaf Green tear apart carbonic-acid gas and send the oxygen back into the air.

But how about the other part of the statement?

Is it true that at night plants give out the poisonous carbonic-acid gas?

Both day and night, plants give out carbonic-acid gas; for though plants, save in the sunlight, cannot eat by means of their little green cells, they can breathe through the tiny mouths (Fig. 137) on the under side of the leaf by night as well as by day.

And when either a plant or an animal breathes, it takes the life-giving oxygen from out the air mixture, and keeps it for its own use. But poisonous carbonic-acid gas is sent back into the air. Now, the question is, whether a plant does most good or most harm to the air by taking in and sending out the different gases.

Of course, it does good when it lets the oxygen out through its cell walls, and stores away the carbon within itself; and it may seem to do harm when through its leaf mouths it breathes in oxygen and breathes out carbonic-acid gas.

There is only one key to unlock the matter, and that is this, — to find out whether the plant does most towards poisoning or towards purifying the air.

And that has been found out already.

Wise men say that Leaf Green and Sunbeam do much more good to the air than the little breathing mouths do harm. The two good fairies take away a great deal of poison, and send back a great deal of the helpful oxygen ; while the tiny mouths neither rob the air of much oxygen nor give it much poison. Indeed, the harm they do is so small compared with the great good accomplished by Leaf Green and Sunbeam, that even at night you need not worry at the thought that you have plants in your room.

Perhaps you wonder that a plant does these two things that are so exactly opposite to each other.

But a plant must breathe as well as eat; for when it breathes, it takes in the precious oxygen which is just as necessary to its life as to ours.

In summer, by the dusty roadside, you see plants almost white with dust, looking quite ill and lifeless.

And they are both ill and lifeless ; for their little leaf throats are so choked that they cannot breathe in the oxygen they need, and in consequence they are being slowly suffocated.

THE DILIGENT TREE

NOW we have learned three things about plants, and especially about leaves. We have learned —

1. That they perspire.
2. That they eat and drink.
3. That they breathe.

They perspire when the water passes through the leaf mouths into the air.

They eat when Leaf Green and Sunbeam together manage to take the carbon out of the carbonic-acid gas which has made its entrance through the leaf mouth and the cell wall. They drink when the roots suck in water and earth broth.

They breathe when the leaf mouths take from the air the oxygen, and give back to it carbonic-acid gas.

The veins and veinlets, of which you see so many running through a leaf, act in something the same way as the water pipes of a city; for through these veins the watery food, the earth broth, is carried to the different cells.

When one knows all that we know even now about a plant, one looks at a tree covered with leaves with a good deal of admiration.

Just think of what is being done inside that quiet-looking tree! Think of the millions of cells that go to make it up, each cell having its own work to do! Think of the immense amount of business being carried on within the trunk, inside the branches, and especially in each green leaf! And when you have the chance, notice how hard each leaf tries to get just as much sun and air as it possibly can.

In the first place, the thin, flat leaf blades are so spread out that every part is exposed to the light and air.

Then notice how the leaves are placed in reference to one another.

Almost every single one is fastened to the tree so as to get its fair share of sunshine.

When you think of the many thousands of leaves borne by one tree, it astonishes you to see how seldom one leaf gets in another's light.

And the shapes of leaves are always suited to their arrangement on the tree.

If you should take the leaves of a chestnut tree and replace them by the leaves of a maple, you would find the maple leaves all getting in each other's way, or else you would see that they were taking up a great deal more room than necessary.

But when a leaf is studied on its own tree, one sees that its shape is the very best that could be imagined for its position.

And in the smaller plants we notice this same thing.

And when you remember that Leaf Green cannot feed the plant unless Sunbeam comes to her assistance, you realize how necessary it is that each leaf be within the reach of Sunbeam's visits.

DANA'S PLANTS. — 11

155

LEAVES AND ROOTS

YOU will be surprised to learn that the way in which a plant's leaves grow tells us something of the way in which its roots grow.

Many of you have been overtaken far from home in a rainstorm, and have sought shelter under a spreading tree. The ground directly beneath the tree has kept almost dry even after some hours of rain, but the earth just under the tips of the spreading branches got very wet: for the great tree acted like a large umbrella; and when the raindrops fell upon the smooth leaves, which sloped outward and downward, they rolled from leaf to leaf till they reached the very lowest, outermost leaves of all. From these they fell to the ground, just as the drops that gather upon your umbrella run outward and downward to the umbrella's edge, and then off upon the ground.

So you can see that the circle of earth which marks the spread of the branches above must be specially wet, as it received a great part of the rain which fell upon the whole tree.

And whenever you see a tree which sheds the rain water in such a circle, you can be pretty sure that, if you should dig into the earth a ditch which followed this circle, you would soon reach the tips of the new root branches of the tree.

You know that the root does the drinking for the plant; and only the newest parts of the root, the fresh root tips, are really good for work of this sort. You remember that the earth food is carried up the stem to the leaves in a watery broth ; and that if the water supply should give out, the new plant cells would not get the broth which helps them to grow, and to put out other cells, and so to build up the plant.

Now, as only the new root branches, near their tips, are able to drink, if the water should leak through the earth in equal quantities everywhere, much of it would be wasted; but when this water is collected in certain spots within reach of the new root branches, there is good reason to believe that these will be able to satisfy their thirst.

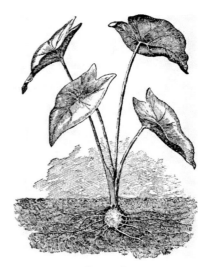

FIG. 138

By the shedding of the rain from the tips of the spreading branches above, the water is collected in a ring, and so sinks into the earth ; and the root branches below spread out in just the same direction as the tree branches above, till they find what they need, and drink their fill.

So by the way in which a tree sheds the rain, you can tell just where its root branches reach out underground.

In smaller plants you see much the same thing. Fig. 138 shows a plant called the *Caladium*. You can see that the raindrops must roll outward down these

157

leaves, and fall upon the earth just above the tips of the root branches.

Fig. 139 shows you the rhubarb plant. This has quite a different sort of root. Now, if the rhubarb leaves were like those of the *Caladium*, unless the rhubarb root-branches changed their direction, these root-branches would grow very thirsty indeed.

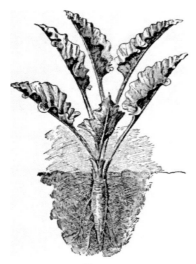

But as it is, the water pours down these leaves toward the center of the plant, and reaches the ground almost directly over the straight, fleshy root, with its downward-growing branches; and we see that these root-branches are watered by the leaves above just as carefully as are those of the *Caladium*.

By knowing one thing about a plant, often you can guess that another thing is so.

You understand now that when the leaves of a plant shed rain water after the fashion of the *Caladium*, the chances are that its root-branches spread out as far as the drip of the water; and that the root of the rhubarb points almost straight downward, is told you by the drip of water from the rhubarb leaves.

LEAF VEINS

SOME time ago you learned that from the stem of a plant you could guess the number of seed leaves which it brought into the world, and that in the same way from the seed leaves you could guess what kind of a stem it would build up.

From the way in which a leaf is veined you can guess both of these things. You can guess what sort of a stem belongs to the plant, and with how many seed leaves it began life.

When the little veins run in and out, forming a sort of network, we say that the leaf is "net-veined."

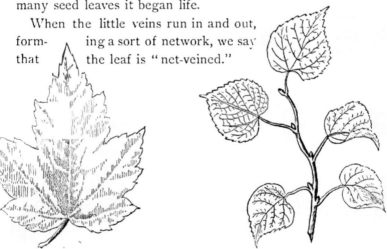

FIG. 140

FIG. 141

FIG. 142

These leaves of the quince (Fig. 140), the maple (Fig. 141), and the basswood (Fig. 142) are all net-veined.

159

Net-veined leaves are borne by plants which brought into the world more than one seed leaf; and with the net-veined leaf we can expect to find that stem which comes with more than one seed leaf, — a stem where the skin or bark, the woody rings, and the soft central pith, are clearly separated one from another.

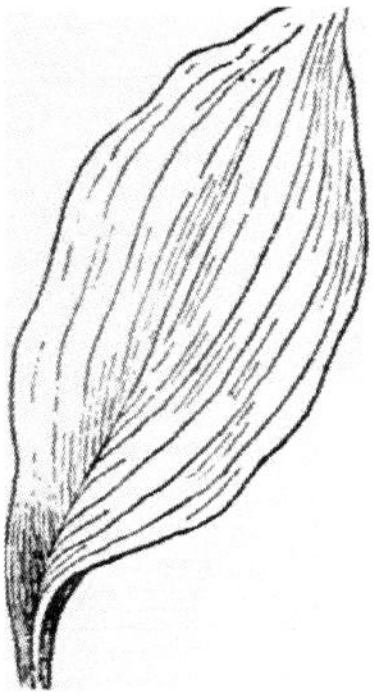

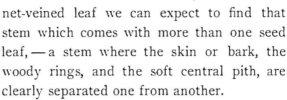

FIG. 143

But a leaf such as that in Fig. 143 or that in Fig. 144, where the veins do not branch off in a network, but run in unbroken lines side by side, — such leaves as these tell you that they are borne by plants which started life with only one seed leaf, and which have such a stem as the cornstalk, where you see no woody rings or central pith.

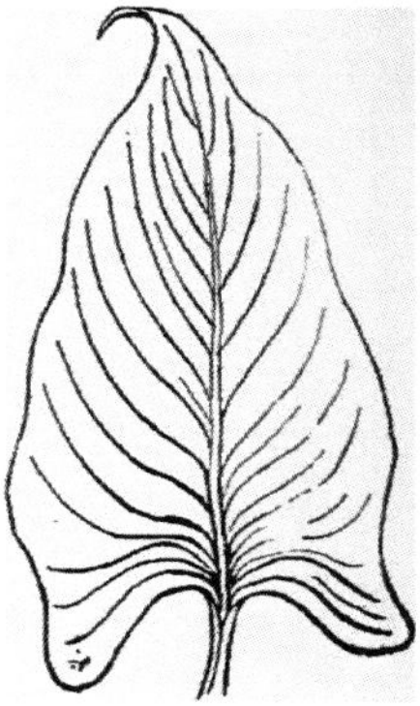

These leaves are called " parallel-veined."

FIG. 144

I fear that you find all this a little difficult to understand and to remember; but if you read it patiently, when you study the botany for older children, I think it will come back to you and make your lessons easier.

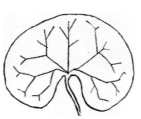

LEAF SHAPES

A S I told you before, we should notice always the shape of a leaf.

It is much easier to describe some new plant we have met on our walks if we remember the shape of its leaves.

Next summer I hope you will make a collection of leaves, pressing and keeping them. I think you will be amazed at their great variety in shape.

Fig. 145

Some you find long and narrow, others almost round. Some are arrow - shaped, others star - shaped, others needle-shaped (Fig. 145). Some are three-pointed like the maple leaf (Fig. 146); others deeply - parted, like the oak leaf (Fig. 147).

Fig. 146

161

FIG. 147

Sometimes a large leaf is cut up into several little leaves. These little leaves are called "leaflets."

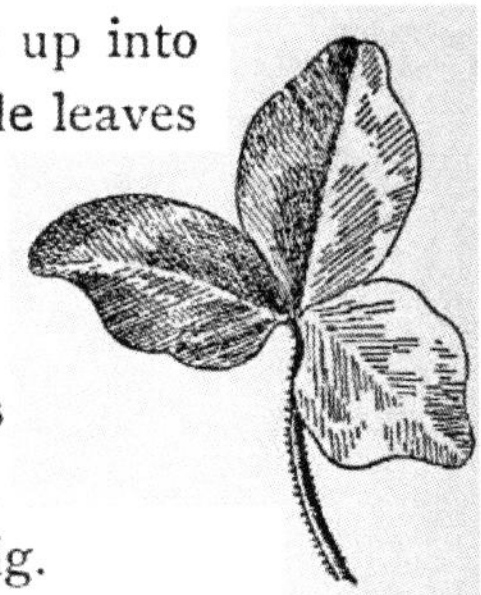

The clover leaf (Fig. 148) has three leaflets.

The locust leaf (Fig. 149) is cut into a great many leaflets.

The edge of one leaf (Fig. smooth, while that of another is cut into little teeth (Fig. 151) like the teeth of a saw.

FIG. 148

I should like to know how many of you children, without looking even at a picture save such as you carry in that little gallery in your head, could describe correctly the shapes of some of our common leaves. I should like to ask you to draw on the blackboard the rough outlines of any leaves

FIG. 149

FIG. 150

FIG. 151

that you remember. If you think you could not do this, will you not try, when next you see a leaf, to carry off in your mind such a picture of it as to enable you to outline

162

it on the blackboard when you go back to the school-room?

Really it does not take any more time to see a thing correctly than to see it incorrectly. It takes a little more sense, that is all.

It takes some sense to give even one minute of honest thought to the thing you are looking at.

You know some children who never seem to have all their thoughts in one place at a time, and who in consequence never see anything really well.

It is better to stop doing a thing altogether than to do it in a foolish sort of way; and it is foolish to start to do even the smallest thing, and yet not do it.

The child who looks at even a leaf in a way to make it possible for him to draw the outline of that leaf five minutes later, is likely to be the child who goes in for both work and play with all his heart, and who comes out as far ahead on the playground as he does in the schoolroom.

Now, after that lecture, which some of you need badly enough (and which I will tell you, as a great secret, I need not a little myself), I want to point out a few more of the things that are worth noticing in a leaf.

But perhaps it is better to save them for another chapter.

HAIRY LEAVES

NOTICE always whether a leaf is smooth or hairy. Do you remember the mullein that sends up its tall spires over the hill pasture? The grayish leaves of this mullein are so hairy that they feel almost like wool. What is the use of all this hair? It is not likely that a plant would wrap itself in this hairy coat except for some good reason.

It is believed that this coating of the mullein prevents animals from eating the leaves, and so destroying the plant. In the mouth, these hairs slip from the leaf blade, and cause a most unpleasant sensation.

But usually the hairs on a leaf are helpful because they prevent too much perspiration or giving-off of water. The more freely the hot sun beats upon a leaf, the more quickly the water is drawn away from it. You can see just how this is by hanging a wet towel in front of the fire. In a very short time the heat from the burning coals draws the water from the towel. But put a screen between the fire and the towel, and the water passes off more slowly.

Now, the hairs on that side of the leaf which faces the sun act as a screen from its fierce heat. We have learned how important it is that the leaf should not part with its water more quickly than the roots can make up the loss. We know that when a leaf does this, it wilts just as a leaf wilts when it is picked and cut off from its water supply, on account of the collapse of the walls of the many little cells which are emptied of water.

So you can understand that plants which grow in dry, sunny places, where there is little drinking water for the roots, and where the sun beats constantly on the leaves, must take every care that there is no waste of water.

And if you keep your eyes open, you will discover that many of the plants which grow in such places screen themselves from the full heat of the sun by a coat of hairs.

The plant called "life everlasting" is one which grows in dry, open, sunny places. It clothes its leaves with silky hairs, and so prevents them from throwing off too quickly the small amount of water its roots are able to provide. Without this silky coat, the sun would suck its leaves quite dry of water.

Sometimes a leaf has only a few of the little leaf mouths through which most of the water passes. As these mouths are wide open only in the sunlight, and as often the rest of the leaf is covered with a thick skin which prevents the water from slipping away (as a little of it nearly always does) through the cell walls, such a leaf will hold its water supply and keep fresh for a long time. Such leaves as these we find on what we call "evergreen" plants. The pines and hemlocks which light up the woods all winter have these thick-skinned, few-mouthed leaves, which throw off so little water that even when the ground is frozen hard, and gives no drinking water to the roots, they are able to keep fresh by the careful way in which each one hoards its own little supply.

165

WOOLLY AND "DUSTY" LEAVES

CURIOUSLY enough, some plants put on a hairy coat for just the opposite reason from the one which makes life everlasting clothe itself in that fashion. Life everlasting fears lest its leaves throw off their water, or perspire too quickly.

Down by the stream that runs through the meadow grow great clusters of the pink-flowered steeple bush. If you look at the lower sides of the leaves of the steeple bush, you see that they are very woolly. As this wool is not between the sun and the leaf blade, it cannot be meant to protect the leaves from the heat of the sun; and indeed in this wet meadow, close to the river, never mind how quickly the leaves throw off their water, the roots can have no difficulty in finding close by more than enough to make good the loss. No, the fact is that these leaves need to throw off water very freely indeed to make room for the ever-fresh supply that is pushing up the stem, and their woolly covering is intended to help them do this very thing. Its object is to aid perspiration. In swampy places the moisture rises every night from the wet ground, and settles on the plants about. The little mouths on the under surfaces of the leaves of the steeple bush would soon be clogged with the moisture rising from below, if they were not protected in some way; and if they became so clogged, they could not throw off the water with which the whole plant is charged. Thus, by having this thick coat of hair, the water that otherwise would cling to the outer surface of the leaf blade is kept at a distance from the little mouths, and these are not interrupted in the performance of a duty so necessary to the health of the plant.

This same habit of coating its lower leaf surfaces with hair, you notice in the speckled or swamp alder, a shrub which grows also in wet places, and therefore runs the same risk of having its leaf mouths clogged with water.

So when you see only the upper surface of a leaf covered with hair, you can guess that the object of the plant is to prevent too much perspiration; but when you see only its lower side clothed in this same way, you can guess that the plant fears too little perspiration.

Sometimes you find a plant with leaves which have a coating of what looks almost like dust on one or both of their surfaces. This dust we call "bloom." We see it in apples and grapes, as well as on leaves. It is made up of a waxy material which is put forth by the plant just as it puts forth hair. This bloom the plant uses also as a help to free perspiration. By thus clothing its leaves it shields the little mouths from water clogging; and so you can be sure that the little mouths have not been filled with water, and thus prevented from doing their work.

The cabbage leaf has mouths on both of its surfaces, and so both sides are covered with this protecting bloom. If you dip a cabbage leaf in water and then shake it, the drops roll off and leave it quite dry.

PRICKLES AND POISON

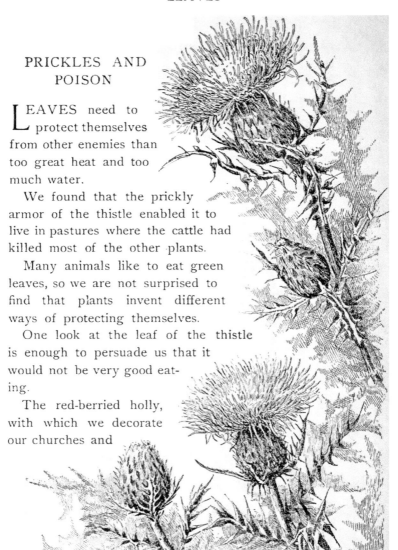

LEAVES need to protect themselves from other enemies than too great heat and too much water.

We found that the prickly armor of the thistle enabled it to live in pastures where the cattle had killed most of the other plants.

Many animals like to eat green leaves, so we are not surprised to find that plants invent different ways of protecting themselves.

One look at the leaf of the thistle is enough to persuade us that it would not be very good eating.

The red-berried holly, with which we decorate our churches and houses at Christmas time, is another plant with prickly leaves.

Some plants cover their leaves with bristles, which the cattle dread almost as much as the stout prickles.

As we read before, the mullein defends its leaves by a fuzzy coat of hair. Such an armor as this is less warlike than that of the thistle, but quite as effective.

Other plants fill their leaves with juices which are either poisonous or unpleasant.

It seems as if animals guessed the presence of these unfriendly juices by the plant's smell, for they will munch the different growing things all about such a plant as this, and leave the harmful leaves severely alone.

The nettles cover their leaves with stinging hairs. These stiff hairs break off when handled, burying themselves in the flesh, and sending out a burning acid that punishes severely the meddler, man or beast, as it may happen to be.

By this time I think you realize that leaves are well worth noticing. And when you have looked at a leaf so fully as to be able to carry in your mind its outline, I hope you will then discover whether it wears a coat of hair, or a dusty bloom, or a prickly armor, or a thick, evergreen skin, and that you will decide what enemies it is trying to escape.

SOME CRUEL TRAPS

HAVE you ever seen a leaf like the one in this picture (Fig. 152)?

It is shaped something like a pitcher; and the plant on which it grows has been named the "pitcher plant."

The pitcher plant lives in low, wet places, such as the shaded swamp, or the marsh down by the lake.

On account of curious leaves it is brought the cities, and is sold on the street corners or at the flo- rists'.

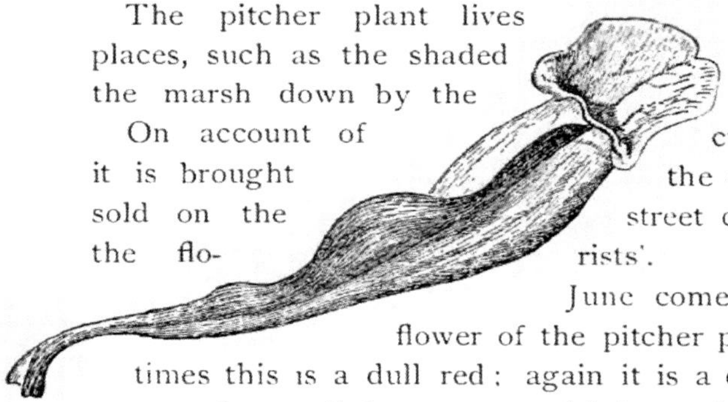

June comes the great flower of the pitcher plant. Some- times this is a dull red; again it is a delicate pink or perhaps a light green; and it has a faint, pleasant fragrance.

FIG. 152

Next June I hope that some of you children will find these beautiful flowers and these curious leaves.

Why should a leaf be shaped like a pitcher, do you suppose?

These leaves are not only pitcher-like in shape, but also in their way of holding water; for if you succeed in discovering a settlement of pitcher plants, you will find that nearly every pitcher is partly filled with rain water. Usually this water is far from clear. It ap- pears to hold the remains of drowned insects; and sometimes the odor arising from a collection of these pitcher plants is not exactly pleasant.

PLANTS AND THEIR CHILDREN

Perhaps you wonder how it happens that dead insects are found in every one of these pitchers; and possibly you will be surprised to learn that apparently these curious leaves are built for the express purpose of capturing insects.

It is easy to understand that these odd leaves are not so well fitted as more simple ones to cook the plant's food in the sun, or to take carbon from the air; but if they are unfitted to provide and prepare ordinary food, possibly they are designed to secure food that is extraordinary.

It seems likely that the pitcher plant is not content to live, like other plants, upon the simple food that is taken in from the earth and from the air. We are led to believe that it wishes something more substantial; that it needs a *meat* diet; and that to secure this, it teaches its leaves to capture flies and insects in order that it may suck in their juices.

These leaves are veined in a curious and striking fashion. The bright-colored veins may convince the insects of the presence of the sweet nectar in which they delight. At all events, in some way they are tempted to enter the hollow leaf; and, once they have crawled or tumbled down its slippery inner surface, they find it impossible to crawl back again, owing to the stiff hairs, pointing downward, which line the upper part of the pitcher.

Even if they have wings, it is difficult for them to fly upward in so straight a line as would be necessary to effect their escape.

When tired out in their efforts to get out of this cruel

trap, they fall into the water at the bottom of the pitcher, and are drowned. Their bodies decay and dissolve; and it is thought that this solution is taken in by the leaf, and turned over to the plant as food.

It is just the old, sad story of the spider and the fly, you see, only now it is the pitcher and the fly.

But be sure to examine one of these pitchers if you possibly can, and then you will understand better how the whole thing is managed.

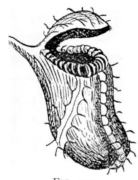

FIG. 153

The leaf in this picture (Fig. 153) for it is a leaf, you cannot find in our North American swamps. It grows on a plant called *Nepenthes*, a plant which lives in hot countries far from the United States.

The leaf in the picture is full grown, and all ready for its work of trapping animals. Before it was old enough to do this, the lid which is now lifted was laid nicely across the opening to the pocket, and so prevented any unseasonable visits.

Sometimes these pockets are so large as to be able to hold and to hide from sight a pigeon. They are gayly colored, and the rim around their border is covered with a sugary, tempting juice. So you can guess that the animals in search of nectar are not slow in accepting the invitation offered by color and sweets, and that some of these are imprudent enough to venture across the sticky edge. In this event they are pretty sure to lose their footing on the slippery inner surface of the pocket, and to fall into the watery liquid with which it is filled. Even if they do not slip immediately, their efforts to crawl back over the rim are defeated by a row of teeth such as you see in the picture.

The liquid at the bottom of the leaf is not rain water, as in the pitcher plant. It is given out by the leaf

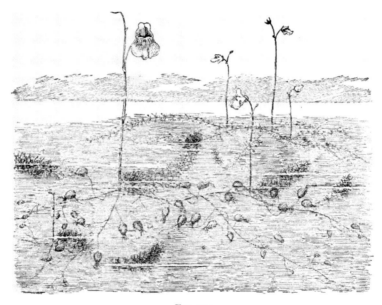

FIG. 154

itself; and it contains an acid which dissolves the animals' bodies, so that their more nourishing parts can easily be taken in by certain little cells which line the lower part of the pocket, and which have been brought up to this work.

The next picture (Fig. 154) shows you a water plant. It is called the "bladderwort," because of the little bags

or bladders which you see growing from the branches
under water. The little bladders are traps set for water
animals, which swim into them in their wish, perhaps,
to escape some enemy. But they are quite unable to
swim out again; for the door into the bladder is transparent, and looks like an open entrance with a nice
hiding place beyond. It opens easily from the outside,
but is so arranged that it will not open from within.
So when the poor little animal hurriedly swims into
what seems to it a cozy resting spot, and draws a long
breath of relief at getting safe inside, it is hopelessly
caught, and must slowly starve to death, for there is no
chance of escape. It may live for nearly a week in this
prison; but at last it dies. Its body decays, and is
taken in as food by the cells set apart for that purpose.

Strangely enough, though we ourselves do not hesi-
tate to kill animals for food, and sometimes, I am sorry
to say, for nothing but amusement, we give a little
shiver of disgust when we find these plants doing the
same thing. Some lines that came out in one of the
magazines a few years ago express this feeling : —

> " What's this I hear
> About the new Carnivora?
> Can little plants
> Eat bugs and ants
> And gnats and flies?
> A sort of retrograding!
> Surely the fare
> Of flowers is air,
> Or sunshine sweet.
> They shouldn't eat
> Or do aught so degrading."

MORE CRUEL TRAPS

THE plants about which we read in the last chapter do not take any active part in capturing insects. They set their traps, and then keep quiet. But there are plants which lay hold of their poor victims, and crush the life out of them in a way that seems almost uncanny.

This leaf (Fig. 155) belongs to a plant which lives in North Carolina. It is called Venus's flytrap.

You see that the upper, rounded part of the leaf is divided by a rib into two halves. From the edges of these rounded halves run out a number of long, sharp teeth; and three stout bristles stand out from the central part of each half. When an insect alights upon this horrible leaf, the two halves come suddenly together, and the teeth which fringe their edges are locked into one another like the fingers of clasped hands.

FIG. 155

The poor body that is caught in this cruel trap is crushed to pieces. Certain cells in the leaf then send out an acid in which it is dissolved, and other cells swallow the solution.

After this performance the leaf remains closed for from one to three weeks. When finally it reopens, the insect's body has disappeared, and the trap is set and ready for another victim.

The next picture (Fig. 156) shows you a little plant which is very common in our swamps, — so common that some of you ought to find it without difficulty next summer, and try upon it some experiments of your own.

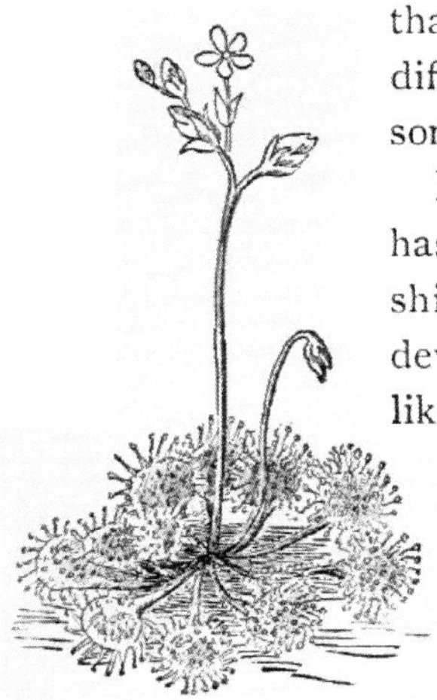

It is called the "sundew." This name has been given to it because in the sunshine its leaves look as though wet with dew. But the pretty drops which sparkle like dew do not seem so innocent when you know their object. You feel that they are no more pleasing than is the bit of cheese in the mouse trap.

When you see this plant growing in the swamp among the cranberry vines and the pink orchids, you admire its little white flowers, and its round red-haired leaves, and think it a pretty, harmless thing. But bend down and pluck it up, root and all, out of the wet, black earth. Carry it home with you, and, if you have a magnifying glass, examine one of its leaves.

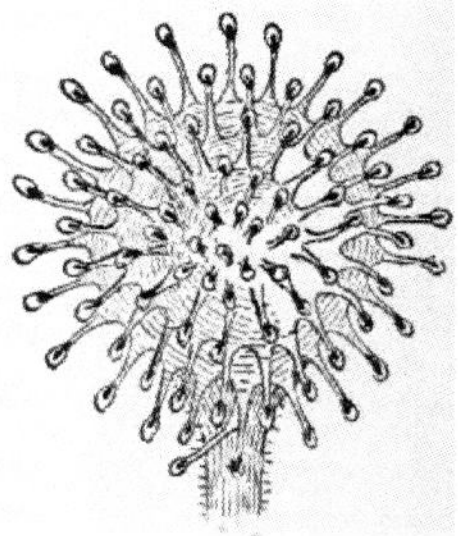

FIG. 156

The picture (Fig. 157) shows you a leaf much larger than it is in life. The red hairs look like pins stuck in a cushion, and the head of each pin glistens with the drop that looks like dew.

But the ants and flies do not take these drops for dew. They believe

FIG. 157

them to be the sweet nectar for which they long, and they climb or light upon the leaves in this belief.

176

And then what happens?

The next two pictures will show you (Figs. 158, 159).

The red hairs close slowly but surely over the insect, whose legs are already caught and held fast by the sticky drops it mistook for nectar, and they hold it imprisoned till it dies and its juices are sucked in by the leaf.

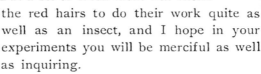

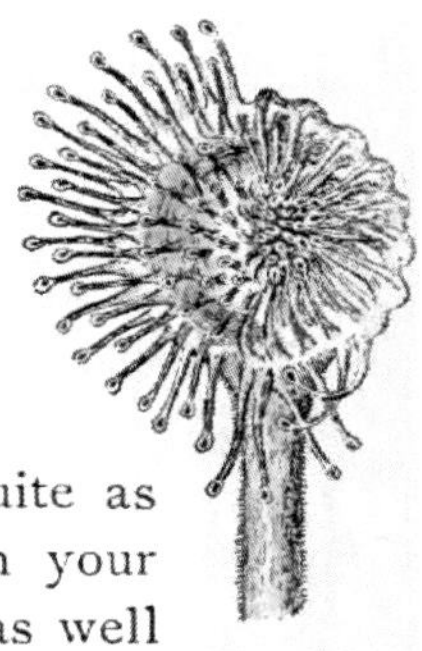

I should like you to satisfy yourselves that these leaves act in the way I have described. But a bit of fresh meat will excite the red hairs to do their work quite as well as an insect, and I hope in your experiments you will be merciful as well as inquiring.

FIG. 158

FIG. 159

So you see that the little sundew is quite as cruel in its way as the other insect-eating plants. But its gentle looks seem to have deceived the poet Swinburne, who wonders how and what these little plants feel, whether like ourselves they love life and air and sunshine.

> "A little marsh-plant, yellow-green
>   And tipped at lip with tender red,
>   Tread close, and either way you tread,
> Some faint, black water jets between
>   Lest you should bruise its curious head.
>
> "You call it sundew: how it grows,
>   If with its color it have breath,
>   If life taste sweet to it, if death
> Pain its soft petal, no man knows.
>   Man has no sight or sense that saith."

LEAVES

THE FALL OF THE LEAF

YOU know that in autumn nearly all the leaves fall from the trees. To be sure, a few trees (such as the pines and hemlocks) and some plants (such as the laurel and wintergreen and partridge vine) do hold fast their leaves all winter; but these are so few as compared with the many plants which lose their leaves, that they hardly count.

Perhaps you never stopped to wonder why most plants get rid of their leaves before winter comes on; but you feel pretty sure now that there is some good reason for a habit that is adopted by nearly all the plants that live in this part of the country.

When we were talking about the way in which leaves defend themselves from different dangers, we found that evergreen leaves, the leaves which hold fast to the tree and keep fresh all winter, manage to keep their water safe inside their cells by wearing a very thick skin, and by not having too many little leaf mouths. For when a leaf has a thin skin and a great many mouths, its water leaks away very quickly. And if many such leaves should remain upon a plant into the winter, might it not happen that they would let off all its water at a time when its roots could not find any more in the frozen ground? And thus might not the leaves kill the plant by draining it quite dry?

So you can see why it is well for most plants to shed their leaves before winter comes on and the root's drinking water is turned into ice.

178

But when a plant is about to shed its leaves, it takes care not to waste the precious food which they hold. This food it draws back into its stem and roots, laying it away in safe places beneath the buds which are to burst another year.

It is this action on the part of the plant which changes the color of the leaves every fall. That material which makes them green is broken up, and part of it is taken away. That which is left is usually yellow or brown or reddish, and gives the leaves the beautiful colors we see in our October woods.

So whenever you see the woods changing color, losing their fresh green and turning red and yellow, you can be sure that the trees have begun to prepare for winter. You know that they are stowing away their food in warmer, safer places than can be supplied by the delicate leaves. And when all the food has been drawn out of the leaves, and packed away in the right spots, then the plant finishes a piece of work it began some time before. This piece of work is the building-up of a row of little cells just where the leaf-stalk joins the stem or branch. When this row is complete, it acts almost like a knife, loosening the stalk from the stem.

Then the leaf's life work is over; and with the first breeze, the empty shell, which is all that is left, breaks away from the parent plant, and drifts earthward.

Part VI — Flowers

THE BUILDING PLAN OF THE CHERRY BLOSSOM

ONE day your teacher brought to school a branch broken from the cherry tree. This she placed in water, standing the tumbler on the sunny window sill; and now its buds have burst into a glory of white blossoms.

To-day I want you to study the flower of the cherry; for if you know all about this flower, which is put together in a rather simple way, one that is easy to study, it will not be so difficult for you to understand other, less simple flowers.

You may wonder why I do not wait till the cherry tree outside is in blossom; but if we waited till May, other flowers, which are not built on quite so simple a plan, would have come and gone, and you would not have been able to understand them so well as if you had first studied the simple make-up of the cherry blossom.

Last fall we learned a little about this flower, but we had only its picture to help us in our work: so I think it well to begin all over again.

In looking at the cherry blossom (Fig. 160), we should first notice the green cup which holds the rest of the flower.

This cup is divided into five green leaves.

During the babyhood of the flower, when it was quite too young to face the cold, windy world, these green leaves were folded together so as to shut away from all harm its more delicate parts.

Above this green cup we see a circle made up of five white leaves. These pretty leaves are spread outward as if they were quite proud of themselves, and eager to attract attention.

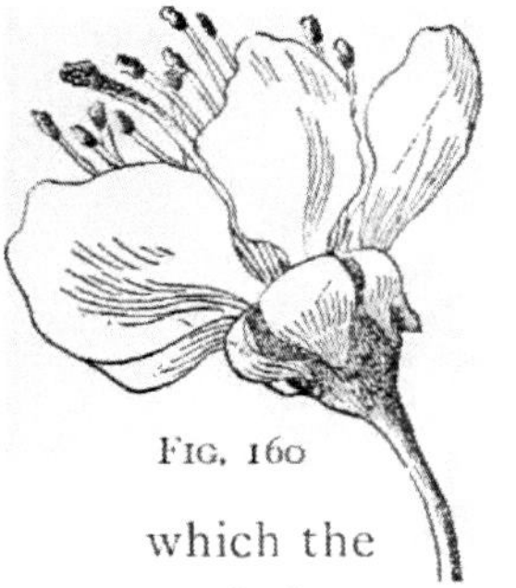

FIG. 160

And that is just what they are trying to do; for the cherry blossom is not wise enough to know that here in the schoolroom there are no bee visitors to bring it yellow dust, and to help it grow into a cherry. These leaves are the little handkerchiefs which the cherry tree, just like the apple tree we read about long ago, uses in signaling the bees.

Within the circle of white leaves you see a quantity of what we named "pins with dust boxes." You remember that these dust boxes hold the powdery material which is as wonderful as Cinderella's fairy godmother in its power to do strange and surprising things.

And in the very center of the flower you find a single "pin," as we called it, with a flat top which is not a dust box.

But you remember that at the foot of this pin is another sort of box, a seedbox (Fig. 161).

181

FLOWERS

And you have not forgotten that it is on the flat top of this pin that the bee brushes the yellow dust which gives new life to the seed below, and turns the little case of the seedbox into the juicy cherry.

So now what do we find in the cherry blossom? We find

1. A green cup cut above into separate leaves.
2. A circle of white leaves.
3. Some pins with dust boxes.
4. One pin with a seedbox.

Here you have the plan on which the cherry blossom is built (for flowers, like houses, are built on different plans), and the building plan of the cherry blossom is one of the simplest of all. So it is well, before studying more difficult flowers, to feel quite at home with this one. And you must try

FIG. 161

to remember first what work each part of the flower is expected to perform; for you see that the leaves of the green cup, the pretty white leaves, the pins with dust boxes, and the pin with a seedbox, have each and all their special task, — a task which they alone are able to accomplish.

Now, in talking about a flower it is troublesome to use a great many words where one would answer every purpose, so I will tell you what these different parts of the flower have been named; and by taking a little trouble to remember these names, we can save a good deal of time.

The green cup is called the "calyx."

"Calyx" is a Greek word meaning "cup."

The circle of leaves which grow above the green cup or calyx is called the "corolla."

"Corolla" comes from a word which means "crown."

The pins with dust boxes are called "stamens."

"Stamen" comes from a word meaning "to stand."

The pin with a seedbox is called the "pistil."

"Pistil" is another form of the word "pestle." A pestle is an instrument used in the drug shops for pounding and mixing medicines. You might ask to look at one the next time you are sent to the drug shop, and then you can see for yourselves if it really looks like its namesake, the pin with a seedbox.

Perhaps at first you may find it a little difficult to bear in mind these four words with their meanings; but soon they will become quite easy, and will save you much trouble.

Green cup, — calyx.

Circle of flower leaves, — corolla.

Pins with dust boxes, — stamens.

Pin with seedbox, — pistil.

If you remember the names of these four parts of the flower, how the different parts look, and what they do, you will have made a good start in the study of flowers.

LILIES

I THINK most of you know by sight at least one of the three following flowers.

I have asked for pictures of three different kinds of lilies, so that the city and country children alike may recognize an old friend; for every spring the white Easter lily (Fig. 162) stands outside the flower shops, and decorates the churches, and travels through the streets in the peddler's cart; while in summer time the country is bright with the wood and meadow lilies (Figs. 163, 164).

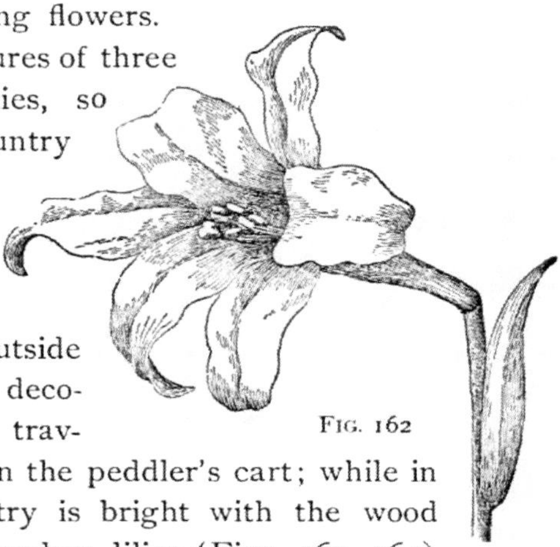

FIG. 162

FIG. 163

And I hope that even now one of the living blossoms is before you, for I want you to see for yourselves what plan these lilies use in flower building.

The building plan of the cherry, you remember, began with a green cup or calyx.

Do you find in the lily any green cup?

No, there is nothing of the sort in the lilies. You see only a circle of flower leaves. In the last chapter you learned to call such a circle the corolla. But the wise men say that without a calyx there cannot be a real corolla. So in the lily we will speak of the "flower leaves" instead of the corolla.

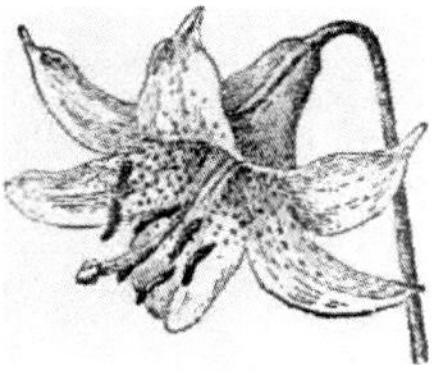

Next we find six of the pins with dust boxes, or the stamens.

And then we come to the pin with a seedbox below, or the pistil.

So the building plan of the lily has only three divisions : —

FIG. 164

1. Flower leaves.
2. Stamens.
3. Pistil.

If you look at the lower side of the outer row of flower leaves, you will see that they are streaked with green; and that when the flower is still in bud, only the green, thick parts of these leaves are exposed to the wind and cold, while the more delicate parts of the blossom are hidden almost as snugly as though they were covered by the leaves of a green cup or calyx.

These lilies are pleasant flowers to study. Their different parts are so large and simple that you have no doubt as to what they are meant for. The bees could hardly overlook their great, showy handkerchiefs; and the heaping dust boxes must powder the visiting bees so freely with golden or brownish dust, that plenty of this is sure to be carried

FIG. 165

185

to the pistil of a neighboring blossom; and the flat tip of this pistil is so large and so sticky, that, once the dust is brushed upon it, it is sure to stay there until its wonderful work is accomplished.

The gay tulip (Fig. 165) is a cousin to the lily. It is built on almost the same plan. There is no green cup in the tulip; but every tulip has

1. Flower leaves.
2. Stamens.
3. Pistil.

The tip of the tulip's pistil is divided into three parts.

ABOUT STAMENS

LET us take a good look at the stamens of the Easter lily. There are six of these. Each dust box is fastened to the tip of a tall stalk. Fig. 166 shows you a single stamen from the Easter lily. It is drawn somewhat larger than life. Its box has opened, and is letting out some grains of dust.

There are many different kinds of stamens. I will show you some pictures that will give you an idea of their great variety. Here is one taken from the flower of the shin leaf (Fig. 167). The dust makes its escape through two little openings at the very top of the box.

That shown in Fig. 168 is from the barberry. The sides of the box open like a door which is hinged on top. This arrangement lets out a quantity of dust.

FIG. 166

FIG. 167

DANA'S PLANTS. — 13

Here is a collection of stamens of different sorts.

Fig. 169 has two boxes at the top of its stalk. and so has Fig. 171. Fig. 172 has a cross-piece, with a good-sized box at one end, and only the little beginnings of a box at the other. Fig. 170 has a similar crosspiece, with a box at one end only.

You see that flower faces show quite as much variety as do the faces of the people you know. You must not expect to find stamens all alike, any more than you would expect all the boys and girls you know to have noses of the same shape, or hair of the same color.

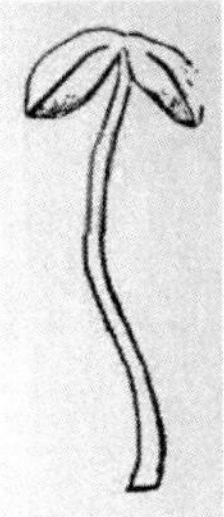

FIG. 168

FIG. 169

FIG. 170

FIG. 171

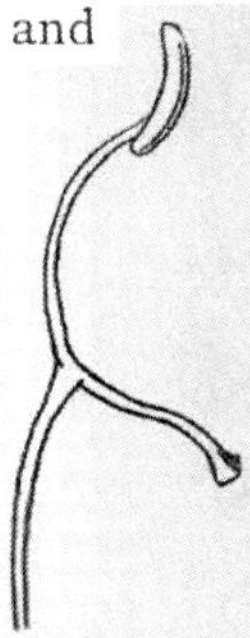

FIG. 172

This picture (Fig. 173) shows you all the stamens of the pea blossom. Do you notice that quite a number

of these (nine, in fact) grow together close about the pistil, while the tenth one stands alone? That is a strange custom always observed by the stamens of the pea.

Next we see all the stamens from one of the tiny flowers of the golden-rod (Fig. 174). These are very much larger than life. There are five of them, fastened together in a sort of tube. Split open this tube and flatten

FIG. 173

FIG. 174

it out. Now they look like five little sisters, arm in arm (Fig. 175).

And here, again joined in a tube, we see the stamens of the mallow (Fig. 176). From the hollow of this tube stand out the tops of the mallow's pistils.

Some flowers have so many stamens that you would find it almost impossible to count them. This little

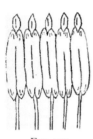

FIG. 175   FIG. 176   FIG. 177

blossom (Fig. 177), the enchanter's nightshade (drawn much larger than life), has only two.

I hope that you children, from now on, will be un- willing to pass by a flower without looking to see whether its stamens are few or many; and I hope you will try to carry away in your minds a clear idea of the size and shape of their dust boxes.

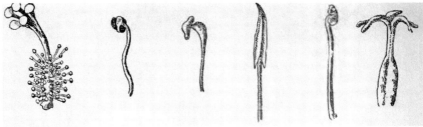

FLOWER DUST, OR POLLEN

WHEN a child smells a flower, he is apt to put his nose right into the middle of the blossom, and to take it out with a dab of yellow dust upon its tip.

When he brushes off this dust, of course he does not stop to think that each tiny grain holds a speck of the wonderful material we read about some time ago, the material without which there can be no life.

And probably he does not know that the dust grains from the lily are quite unlike those which he rubs upon his nose when he smells a daisy; that different kinds of flowers yield different kinds of flower dust.

If you should look through a microscope at a grain of flower dust from the lily, you would see an object resembling Fig. 178.

Fig. 179 shows a grain from the

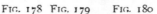

FIG. 178   FIG. 179   FIG. 180   FIG. 181   FIG 182

189

pretty blue flower of the chicory. Fig. 180 is a dust grain from the flower of the pine tree. Fig. 181 is from the laurel, and the odd-looking Fig. 182 is from a dust box of the evening primrose.

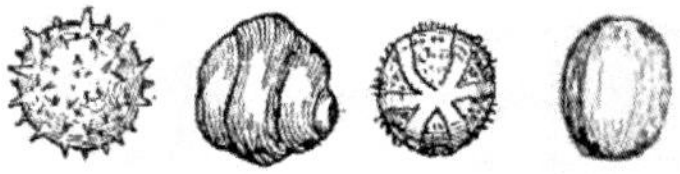

FIG. 183

The next picture (Fig. 183) shows you a group of dust grains from flowers of different kinds, one looking like a porcupine, another like a sea shell, another like some strange water animal, and all, I fancy, quite unlike any idea you may have had as to the appearance of a grain of flower dust.

When you are older, I hope it may be your good luck to see through a microscope some of the odd shapes and curious markings of different kinds of flower dust, or "pollen," as this flower dust is called in the books.

And now that you know something of the appearance of flower dust, perhaps you wish to learn a little more of the way in which it ,helps the flower to turn into the fruit.

ABOUT PISTILS

BUT first you must know a little something about the pistil, if I am really to make clear to you how the flower dust helps the flower to change into fruit.

This picture (Fig. 184) shows you the pistil of the lily. At the foot of this pistil, you remember, is the

FIG. 184 box which holds the lily's seeds.

The top of the lily's pistil is quite large and somewhat flat. It is almost as sticky as if it had received a dab of glue.

This flat top dwindles below into a stalk, which grows larger again at its lower end.

Now take a sharp knife and cut open lengthwise this pistil.

The lower, thicker part, seen through a magnifying glass, looks like Fig. 185. You see a great many baby seeds fastened to a central wall. Each one of these seeds holds a speck of the wonderful material without which there is no life. But this speck of life has not the power to make the seed grow into a plant. To do this, the seed must have some outside help; and this help can come only from a grain of flower dust.

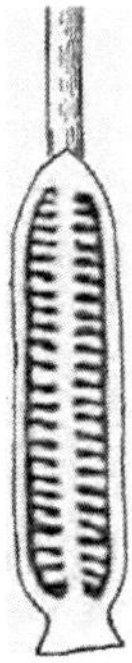

Perhaps you wonder how a dust grain brushed on the pistil's flat top can ever reach the baby seeds hidden away in the seedbox.

I could not tell you to-day how this is done were it not for those wise and patient men and women who have spent days and weeks and months, and even years, in watching and studying the ways of plants.

FIG. 185

But first let me ask you a question.

What happens when a healthy seed falls on moist ground?

Why, it seems to take in the moisture, and to thrive upon it. It swells up, and at last it bursts open, and it sends a root down into the earth.

Now, something not altogether unlike this happens when a lily dust grain falls upon the moist tip of a lily pistil. The dust grain sucks in the moisture. It grows bigger and bigger. The outer skin becomes too small for the swelling contents. At last it bursts open, letting out a little tube.

This little tube works its way down through the stalk of the pistil, almost as a root pushes down into the earth, and at last it reaches one of the seeds in the seedbox below.

And into this tiny seed the little tube pushes its way.

The tube has carried with it that speck of wonderful living material which every dust grain holds. And when this living speck has been added to that which the seed already holds, a great change begins to come about.

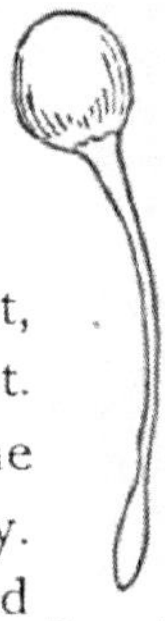

This new touch of life, added to that already present, gives the lily seed the power to grow into a lily plant.

The other dust grains that were brushed upon the flat top of the lily's pistil act in just the same way. Apparently without difficulty the different tubes find their way to the different seeds, till at last each one

FIG. 186

has received the fresh touch of life without which it cannot grow into a lily plant.

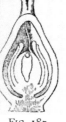

I cannot show a lily dust grain in the act of sending out its life-bearing tube; but above is a dust grain (Fig. 186) from the thorn apple. You see that it has burst open, and that a tube is pushing its way out.

This picture (Fig. 187) is that of a pistil seedbox cut open, showing you a tube that is working its way from the dust grain above to a tiny seed in the seedbox below.

FIG. 187

As I told you in the last chapter, the name "pollen"

has been given to this wonder-working flower dust.   A grain of flower dust is a grain of pollen.

In many flowers you will find a pistil much like the one that you see in the lily.

But there are as many different kinds of pistils as there are different kinds of stamens.

This pistil (Fig. 188) is from the grass of Parnassus, that pretty white flower which you find in the wet meadows in August and September.   It has no real stalk, you see, like that of the lily ; but it is quite thick

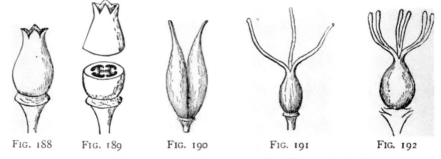

FIG. 188   FIG. 189   FIG. 190   FIG. 191   FIG. 192

all the way from top to bottom.   In Fig. 189 it is cut across, showing the seeds inside.

Many pistils that are joined in one piece below, where the seeds are held, separate above into two or more parts.   Fig. 190 shows the seed holder of a saxifrage, divided into two pieces above ; Fig. 191 gives that of the Saint John's-wort, separating into three parts ; that of the sundew (Fig. 192) separates into six parts. Fig. 193 is a section of the pea flower.   This is cut lengthwise so as to show you the seeds which line the inner surface of the pistil.   Here you have the baby pea pod.

193

All these flowers have only one real pistil, — one pistil which may persuade you, by the way in which it separates above, into thinking that there are more than one. So you must be on your guard in this respect, and remember that flowers have a way of playing tricks with all but the most wide-awake of boys and girls. Look long and carefully before you declare that a flower has only one pistil.

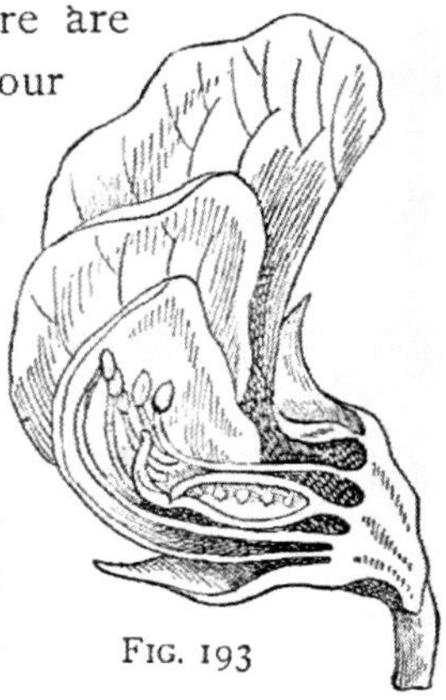

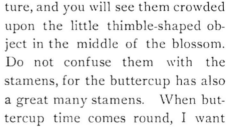

FIG. 193

Here we see half of a buttercup (Fig. 194). The buttercup has a great many entirely separate pistils. Look

FIG. 194

sharply at the picture, and you will see them crowded upon the little thimble-shaped object in the middle of the blossom. Do not confuse them with the stamens, for the buttercup has also a great many stamens. When buttercup time comes round, I want every one of you to look at these many pistils and stamens.

The next picture (Fig. 195) shows you a strawberry. In the strawberry blossom the pistils are so small, and so crowded, and so hidden by the many stamens, that it is not easy to see them ; and so I show you the full-grown berry, with little pistils scattered all over its surface. Each of those tiny objects which stand out on the strawberry is a separate pistil.

FIG. 195

194

Whenever you look at a flower, I want you to remember that its bright flower leaves will soon fade and fall, and that its stamens will lose their pollen and wither away, but that the pistil or pistils will remain, turning at last into the ripened fruit, — the fruit which is the end, the aim, the object, of the plant's life.

THE FIRST ARRIVAL

I SHOULD like to ask each of you children to tell me what flower you believe to be first to come in the spring.

Some of you have never stopped to think about this. But there are sure to be a few among you who will name one special flower as the earliest of the year.

195

FLOWERS

Perhaps even in March you may have ventured into the woods to look for the lovely, fragrant, waxlike blossoms of the trailing arbutus. You know the sheltered hollow where the snow first melts ; and there the delicate pink flowers make you glad with their beauty, and with the thought of the good time coming. To some of us this first hunt for the arbutus is one of the great events of the year. It means the beginning of long, delicious hours in the fresh air, with birds and trees and butterflies and wild flowers as our chosen companions.

But not all of you will agree that this trailing arbutus is the first spring flower. Many think the violet can lay claim to this honor. The yellow violet especially may be found in the woods before the trees have put forth their leaves.

And some say that the little blue liverwort (sometimes this is pink or white) is the earliest of all ; and others vote for the spring beauty, or for the yellow adder's tongue, or for the Dutchman's breeches, or for the anemone.

And still others say that the marsh marigold, the shining flower that in April gilds the wet meadows, leads the procession.

But you are wrong, every one of you. The earliest blossom of the year makes its appearance long before any of these flowers you have mentioned.

The first plant to blossom knows better than to proclaim the change of season by anything so fragile as a violet, an anemone, a spring beauty. It sends out its rather coarse little flowers under the protection of a tough waterproof hood, which shields them from the rude winds and nipping cold.

This plant bears the ugly name of skunk cabbage (Fig. 196). Its broken stem and leaves give out an odor which at once persuades you that its title is deserved.

In the swamps the skunk cabbages send up by the dozen the curious purple hoods which curl about the thick clusters of little flowers. When you come across a colony of these queer-looking objects, no wonder it never occurs to you that the first flower of spring is at hand. The great shiny hoods look more like snails than like flowers ; and indeed usually the flowers are not in sight at all, so well are they shielded by these hood-like leaves.

FIG. 196

But each little hidden flower has four flower leaves, four stamens, and one pistil. When they have been dusted with pollen by fly visitors, and are preparing to turn into fruit, the purple hoods wither away. Then the plant sends up clusters of large bright green leaves. In June you see these great leaves everywhere in the wet woods.

So if you wish to be on hand to welcome the very first flower of the year, you must begin to keep your eyes open by the end of February. You must visit the swamps each day, and look for the purple hoods inside which are snugly hidden the little blossoms of the skunk cabbage.

And I advise you now to take a sheet of paper and

make a list of the plants as you find them in flower. Put down the date of each blossom as it appears, and the place where you find it. If you begin to do this as children, and keep it up when you are older, you will take real delight in the habit. Each year it will interest you more and more to turn back to the old lists and discover whether the flowers are on time, or whether they are late or early in making their first appearance.

I hope your teacher will start you at once with such a list; for the sooner you begin, the more complete will be your pleasure in this delightful season.

PUSSY WILLOWS

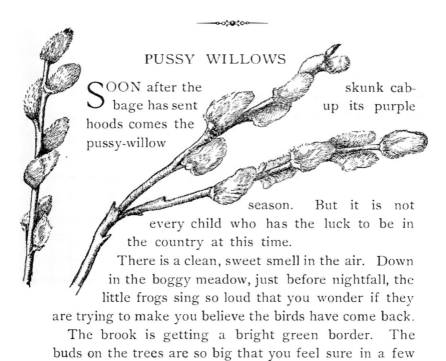

SOON after the skunk cabbage has sent up its purple hoods comes the pussy-willow season. But it is not every child who has the luck to be in the country at this time.

There is a clean, sweet smell in the air. Down in the boggy meadow, just before nightfall, the little frogs sing so loud that you wonder if they are trying to make you believe the birds have come back.

The brook is getting a bright green border. The buds on the trees are so big that you feel sure in a few hours they must burst open. And you know that each new day may bring with it some happy surprise, — a bird, a leaf, or a flower that you have not seen for many a long month.

So when you find the willow branches set thick with silken pussies, you know that a happy time has begun, at least for you country children.

And even the city children learn to love these soft pussies when they are placed in tall vases on the teacher's desk.

If you look carefully at the different branches, you see that they bear different kinds of pussies ; and your teacher will tell you, or perhaps you will discover yourselves, that these different branches were broken from different trees.

Do you know what each " pussy," or tassel, is made up of?

Each tassel is made up of many tiny flowers.

FIG. 197

But willow flowers are built on quite a different plan from cherry flowers. If you pick apart one of these tassels, and examine a single blossom, you will find it hard to believe that it is a flower at all.

On one branch the tassels are all golden yellow. The flowers that make up these yellow tassels have neither flower leaves nor pistils. Each blossom has two stamens which are fastened to a little fringed leaf, and nothing more. Such a flower, much magnified, is given in the picture (Fig. 197). The golden color comes from the yellow pollen which has been shaken from the dust boxes.

The other branch is covered with silvery green

tassels. Each flower in these tassels is made up of a single pistil, which is also fastened to a little fringed leaf (Fig. 198).

So you see the building plan used by one kind of pussy-willow flowers is nothing but two stamens; while the plan used by the other kind is still simpler, it is nothing but one pistil.

The golden dust is carried by the bees from the willows which bear dust boxes to those other willows whose flowers have only seedboxes.

When they have given to the bees their pollen, the yellow tassels fade away; but the silvery green tassels, on account of their seedboxes, grow large and ripe, turning into the fruit shown in Fig. 62, p. 61; and this fruit is one of the kind which scatters its seeds abroad by fastening them to silky sails.

FIG. 198

ALDERS AND BIRCHES

THERE is another shrub or low tree growing along the brook's edge which flowers almost as early as the willows.

This is the alder.

Perhaps you noticed last fall that these alders were hung with a quantity of little green tassels. These tassels did not fall off with the leaves in November. Through the long winter they clung to the shrub Sometimes they wore little coats of ice which made them look like the glass ornaments on a Christmas tree.

When the warm weather came, they put off their ice coats, and grew larger and longer, and at last let out a quantity of stamens.

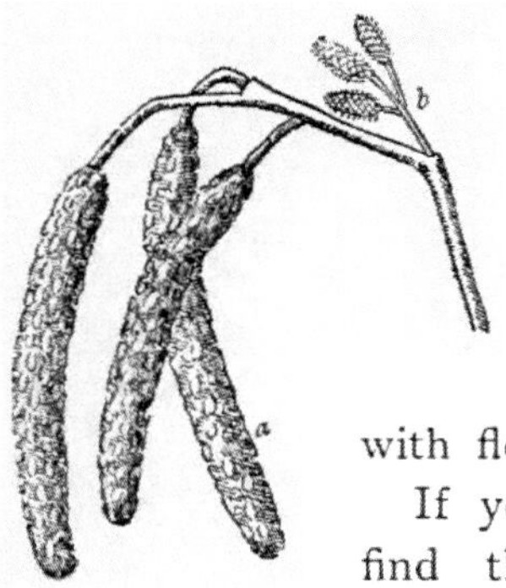

But on the same alder tree that bears these tassels with flowers made up of stamens or dust boxes (Fig. 199, *a*), you find also the tassels with flowers made up of pistils (Fig. 199, *b*).

If you make a search, you will find the little upright clusters composed of these flowers with pistils.

Late in the year, when these clusters have turned into fruit, they look like this picture (Fig. 200).

The pretty birches are cousins

FIG. 200

to the alders, and keep house in much the same way, bearing the tassels with stamens (Fig. 201, *a*) and the little clusters made up of flowers with pistils (Fig. 201, *b*) on the same tree.

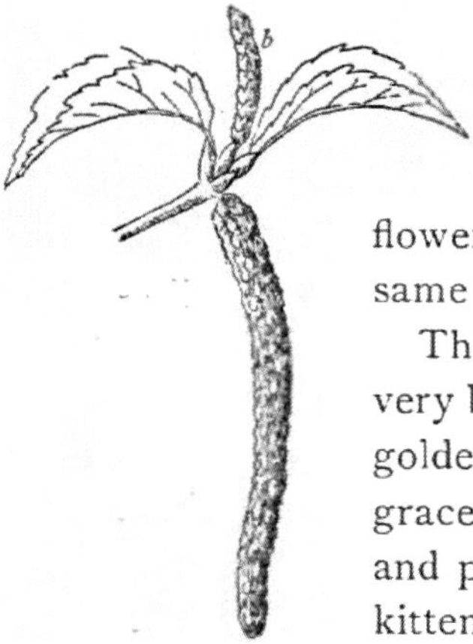

The tassels on some of the birches are very beautiful. When full grown, they are golden yellow, and so long and soft and graceful that one feels like stroking them and playing with them as he would with a kitten.

FIG. 201

I hope every country child who reads

201

this book and does not already know the willows, the
alders, and the birches, will make their acquaintance
this spring, and will examine their two
kinds of flowers. And I hope that
branches from the different trees will
be brought into the city schoolroom, so
that all can see these flowers, which are
among the very earli- est of the year.

THE GREAT TREES

M OST people seem surprised to learn that all kinds
of trees have flowers. In March and April they
go to the woods in search of the trailing arbutus, the
violet, the anemone; and when they have picked a
quantity of these, they come home and say, "These are
the only flowers we saw to-day."

But if they had looked overhead, up into the trees,
they would have seen many more; for each tree has its
own flower, and most of the trees blossom very early in

DANA'S PLANTS. — 14

the year, before they put out their leaves. There is a good reason for this, which I will tell you by and by.

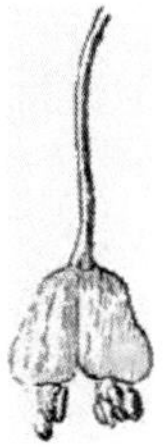

One of the early trees to flower is the swamp maple. In March or April its bright red blossoms tinge the wet woods with warm color. Sometimes the snow lies thick on the ground at this season, and the little red flower clusters fall, and look wonderfully pretty against the smooth white sheet which is drawn beneath the trees.

FIG. 202

At the same season, in our city parks and streets, sharp eyes will discover the yellowish blossoms of the silver maple. Both of these trees flower before they leaf.

The building plan used by maple flowers is rather confusing. In one flower you will find both calyx and corolla, but not in another. One

FIG. 203

blossom will have both stamens and pistils, another will have no pistils. Fig. 202 shows you a blossom from the sugar maple. It has stamens, but no pistils. Next you see what was once a flower containing both stamens and pistils (Fig. 203).

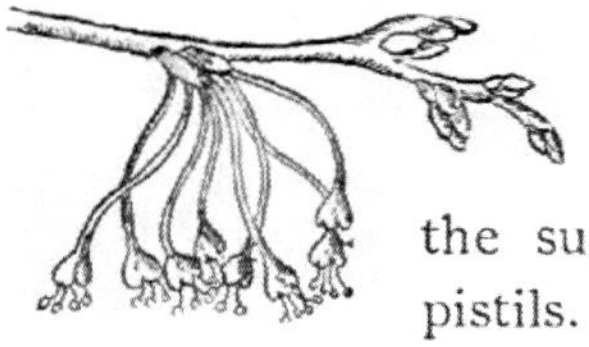

FIG. 204

The withered stamens can still be seen; and the pistil is turning into the well-known maple key.

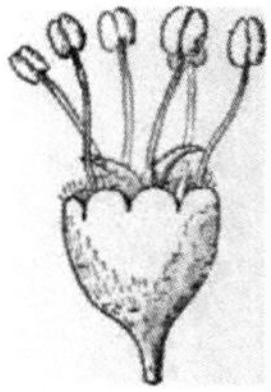

The great elms also put out their flowers before their leaves. Here you see a flower cluster from the white elm (Fig. 204). Fig. 205 shows you one of these little flowers enlarged; and in Fig. 206 you have the blossom cut open so as to display its pistil, which grows into the winged fruit you saw on p. 62.

FIG. 205

In some of our city streets grows the poplar. Its flowers are crowded into long green tassels. Many of these fall to the pavement below, and lie there, looking like great caterpillars. These tassels are those which bear the flowers with stamens. Now, if we were in the woods, we should be pretty sure to find near by another poplar whose tassels do not fall so quickly. This is because these are made up of flowers with pistils. They cling to the tree not only till they have been powdered with pollen from the neighboring poplar, but till their tiny seeds have had time to ripen and are ready to start out on their life journey.

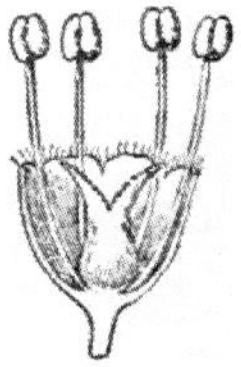

FIG. 206

THE UNSEEN VISITOR

I PROMISED to tell you why so many of the trees flower before they leaf.

Many of these tree blossoms are neither bright enough to attract the attention of the bees and butterflies, nor so fragrant as to tempt the passing insects to visit them; for when the flower handkerchiefs are not large and bright enough to signal the bees, the blossom often gives notice of its presence by a strong perfume. How, then, is the pollen from one flower to reach the pistil of another? And especially how can this be arranged when the flowers with pollen may live quite a way off — on another tree, in fact — from the flowers with pistils?

"Perhaps the birds carry it," suggests some child.

But if these little flowers are not beautiful enough, or sweet-smelling enough, to please the bees and butter-flies, it is hardly probable that the birds will pay them any attention.

So let us go out into the woods with our eyes and our ears wide open, and see if we can discover some flower visitor that does not ask for fine clothes and sweet smells.

Through the bushes comes the lisp of the song spar-row. From overhead falls the note of the bluebird. The bees are buzzing about the golden willow tassels. On the top of an old tree trunk a butterfly is drowsing in the sun's rays. But already we know that neither bird, nor bee, nor butterfly will go out of its way to help our pale, scentless little tree blossoms.

A squirrel darts from under cover, and runs along the stone wall. Among the dead leaves at our feet a little striped snake lies in a sluggish coil. But squirrel and snake would be alike useless as flower visitors.

We are almost tempted to give up trying to guess the answer to the riddle. Somewhat discouraged, we stop to rest on an old log overgrown with delicate mosses.

A soft, sighing sound creeps through the pines at the foot of yonder hill. Over the little hollow sweeps a gust of wind. A faint cloud, as of dust, fills the air. One of the children begins to sneeze. Where can the dust come from? The roads are still deep with mud. And, besides, ordinary dust does not make us sneeze as though it were pepper.

Ah, my friend, you are getting warm, very warm indeed; for this dust is no dried earth from the high-

road.   No, it is made up instead of golden grains from
the dust boxes that are swaying in the wind on yonder
trees.   And as the trees just now are bare of leaves,
the journey of the pollen through the air is an easy
matter.   It is carried along by the wind, settling here,
there, and everywhere, sometimes in our throats and
noses in such a fashion as to make us sneeze, but also
on the tops of many little pistils whose seeds cannot
ripen without its gift of new life.

And so, although we have not seen the visitor who
befriends these little flowers that are neither beautiful
nor fragrant, we have heard his voice as it came whispering through the pines; and we know that this
whisper is the gentle voice of the wind.

Now you understand that it is well for those trees
whose flowers depend upon the wind for their pollen,
to blossom before their leaves are out, and thus likely to
interfere with the pollen in reaching its destination.

PLANT PACKAGES

O N your walks through the woods these spring days I want you to notice the neat and beautiful way in which plants do their packing; for the woods now are full of plant packages, — little bundles of leaves and flowers, done up with the greatest care.

Some of these have just appeared above the ground. Others have burst from the branches of the trees and shrubs.

Of course, a plant does not like to send its young, delicate leaves and flowers

FIG. 207

into the cold world without wrapping them up, any more than your mother would like to send your baby brother out for the first time without a great deal of just such bundling-up.

And so well wrapped are many of these plant babies, that it is not an easy matter to guess just what they are, what kinds of leaves and flowers will appear when the wrappings have been thrown aside.

Sometimes the package looks like the sharp-pointed object in the picture at the head of this chapter (Fig. 207). Soon the leaves push their way out of their papery envelope, and before long our friend Jack-in-the-pulpit himself appears.

Sometimes it is such a woolly roll as you see in the next picture (Fig. 208). This roll soon un-curls into a pretty fern (Fig. 209).

The beech tree folds its leaves like fans (Fig. 210). The preceding picture (Fig. 211) shows you how carefully and cleverly the hobblebush packs its young leaves.

During their babyhood many leaves wear a hairy coat as a protection from both cold and heat; but when their green skin becomes thicker, they throw this off.

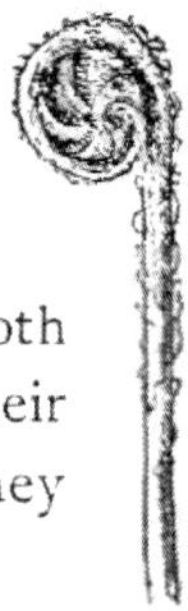

Most of these plant packages are very interesting and beautiful,

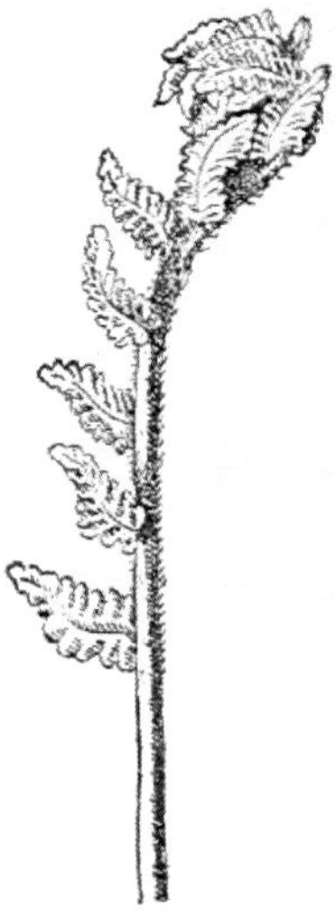

FIG. 208   FIG. 209

and well worth your attention. I wish that during these weeks of early spring the country schools would hold exhibitions of these babes in the woods, asking each child to bring what he considers a good specimen of a plant package.

FIG. 211

FIG. 210

208

UNDERGROUND STOREHOUSES

L ONG ago we learned that certain plants stow away the food which they are not fitted to use at the time in those thick underground stems which most people call roots.

This food they hold over till the next year.

It is often a surprise, these spring days, to see how suddenly a little plant will burst into blossom. One does not understand how it has had time to get up such a display. Had it been obliged to depend for food upon new supplies taken in by its roots and leaves, the flower would have put off its first appearance for many a day.

So when a plant surprises you with any such sudden and early blossoms, you can be pretty sure that its food supply has been on hand all winter.

Both in the garden and in the woods you can see for yourselves that this is so. In the garden perhaps the earliest flower to appear is the lovely little snowdrop. The snowdrop's food is stored away in the "bulb," as we call its thick, underground stem, which lies buried in the earth.

The other early garden flowers, such as the hyacinth, crocus, daffodil, and tulip, are able to burst into beautiful blossoms only because of the care and labor with which they laid by underground provisions last year.

And in the woods at this season you find the yellow adder's tongue, spring beauty, anemone, wake-robin, Jack-in-the-pulpit, wild ginger, and Solomon's seal. Each of these plants has stores of food hidden in its underground stem. This may take the shape of a bulb, or a tuber, or a rootstock ; but in any case it shows you at once that it is a little storehouse of food.

A collection of the different kinds of underground stems which serve as storehouses for the early-flowering plants would be quite as interesting to work over as a collection of plant packages.

DIFFERENT BUILDING PLANS

THIS morning let us take a stroll in the woods with the idea of noticing the different building plans used by the early flowers.

First we will go to the spot where we know the trailing arbutus is still in blossom. Pick a spray, and tell me the plan of its flower.

"There is a small green cup, or calyx, cut into five little points," you say ; "and there is a corolla made up of five flower leaves."

But stop here one moment. Is this corolla really made up of five separate flower leaves ? Are not the flower leaves joined in a tube below ? If this be so, you must say that this corolla is five-lobed, or five-pointed, not that it has five flower leaves.

"And there are ten pins with dust boxes, or stamens."

Yes, that is quite right.

"And there is one of those pins with a seedbox below, one pistil, that is, but the top of this pistil is divided into five parts."

Well, then, the building plan of the trailing arbutus runs as follows : —

1. Calyx.
2. Corolla.
3. Stamens.
4. Pistil.

So far, it seems the same plan as that used by the cherry tree, yet in certain ways this plan really differs from that of the cherry blossom. The calyx of the cherry is not cut into separate leaves, as is that of the arbutus; and its corolla leaves are quite separate, while those of the arbutus are joined in a tube.

The cherry blossom has more stamens than the arbutus. Each flower has but one pistil. But the pistil of the arbutus, unlike that of the cherry, is five-lobed.

So, although the general plan used by these two flowers is the same, it differs in important details.

Above you see the flower of the marsh marigold (Fig. 212). Its building plan is as follows : —

1. Flower leaves.
2. Stamens.
3. Pistils.

This, you remember, is something like the building plan of the easter lily. The lily has a circle of flower leaves in place of calyx and corolla. So has the marsh marigold. But the lily has six flower leaves, one more than the marsh marigold, and only six stamens, while the marsh marigold has so many stamens that it would tire one to count them.

211

And the lily has but one pistil (this is tall and slender), while the marsh marigold has many short, thick ones, which you do not see in the picture.

So these two flowers use the same building plan in a general way only.   They are quite unlike in important details.

The pretty little liverwort and the delicate anemone use the same building plan as the marsh marigold.   This is not strange, as all three flowers belong to the same family.

FIG. 213

The yellow adder's tongue is another lily.   It is built on the usual lily plan : —

1. Six flower leaves.
2. Six stamens.
3. One pistil.

The wild ginger (Fig. 213) uses the lily plan, inasmuch as it has no separate calyx and corolla ; but otherwise it is quite different.   It has no separate flower leaves, but one three-pointed flower cup.   It has stamens, and one pistil which branches at its tip.

The next picture (Fig. 214) shows you the seedbox, cut open, of the wild ginger.

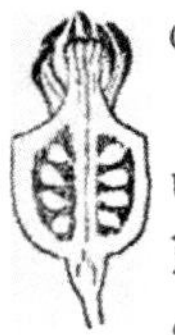

FIG. 214

To find this flower, your eyes must be brighter than usual.   It grows close to the ground, and is usually hidden from sight by the pair of round, woolly leaves shooting up from the underground stem, which tastes like ginger.   This thick underground stem is the storehouse whose stock of food makes it possible for the plant to flower and leaf so early in the year.

Fig. 215 shows you the pretty wake-robin.   This is a lily.   But it is unlike the lilies we already know, in

FIG. 216

that its calyx and corolla are quite distinct, each having three separate leaves. It has six stamens, and one pistil with three branches.

The general building plan of the violet (Fig. 216) is the old one of calyx, corolla, stamens, pistil. But the leaves of this calyx (Fig. 217) are put together in a curious, irregular fashion; and the different leaves of the corolla are not of the same shape and size as in the cherry blossom. Then the five stamens of the violet are usually joined about the stalk of the

FIG. 215

FIG. 217   FIG. 219   FIG. 220   FIG. 218

pistil in a way that is quite confusing, unless you know enough to pick them apart with a pin, when they look like this picture you see above, to the right (Fig. 218).

The garden pansy (Figs. 219, 220) is cousin to the violet. You notice at once that it uses just the same building plan.

The wild geranium (Figs. 221, 222) is put together almost as simply as the cherry blossom.

FIG. 221

FIG. 222

213

FLOWERS

A more beautiful flower than the columbine it would be difficult to find (Fig. 223). Its graceful hanging head and brilliant coloring make it a delight to the passer-by.

FIG. 223

It has not the fragrance of some other flowers, but for this there is a good reason.

The columbine is so brightly colored that the nectar-hunting bee can see it from a great distance.

It is only when a blossom is so small and faintly colored as to be unlikely to attract the eye, that it needs to make its presence known in some other way than by wearing gay clothes. By giving out fragrance it notifies the bee that material for honey making is on hand.

So you see that a pale little flower with a strong fragrance is just as able to attract the bee's attention as is a big flower with its bright flower handkerchiefs. A big flower with bright flower handkerchiefs does not need to attract the bee by its perfume.

Perhaps you will be somewhat surprised to learn that this columbine uses the old plan, calyx, corolla, stamens, pistil.

In the columbine the calyx as well as the corolla is brightly and beautifully colored, and only the botanist can tell which is which. In this way many flowers confuse one who is only beginning their study. So you must try to be patient when you come across a flower whose coloring and shape make it impossible for you to say what is calyx and what is corolla. You should

214

turn both over into the one division of flower leaves, and when older you may be able to master the difficulty.

The pretty fringed polygala (Fig. 224) is one of these confusing flowers. You find it in the May woods. Its discovery is such a delight, that one is not apt to make himself unhappy because he cannot make out all its parts.

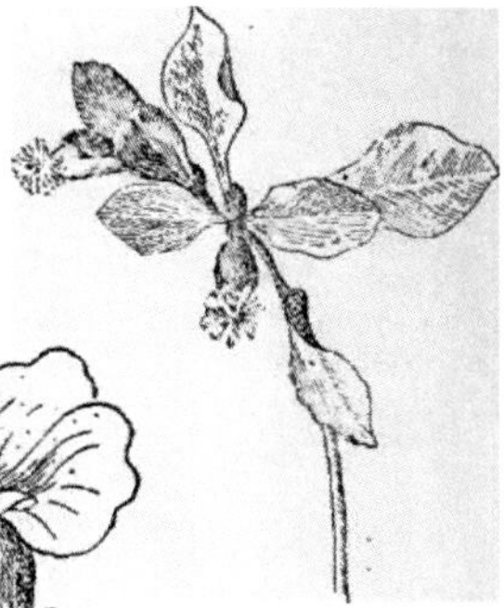

The jewelweed (Fig. 225), the plant which blossoms down by the brook in August, is another of these puzzling blossoms.

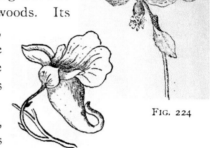

FIG. 224

FIG. 225

A CELEBRATED FAMILY

DO you know this pretty flower (Fig. 226)?

It is the yellow lady's slipper. It lives deep in the woods of May, perhaps part way up the mountain side. It has several sisters. One of these is the pink lady's slipper, which blossoms just a little later. Another is the white lady's slipper. This comes late in June, and is one of the loveliest of our wild flowers.

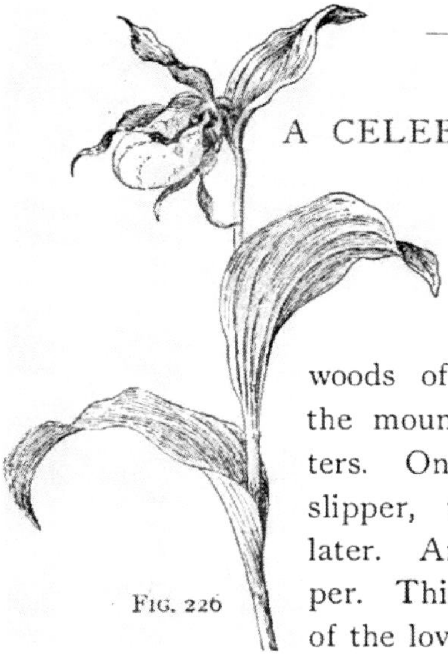

FIG. 226

215

These three sisters belong to a celebrated family, that of the Orchids.

The Orchid family is noted for the beauty of its flowers, and for the pains which these take to attract the attention of the bees.

The building plan used by the orchids is too difficult for you to learn yet awhile. Perhaps the orchids take more trouble than any other flowers to have their pistils well dusted with pollen. A good landing place for the bee is provided; signs are hung out to point the way to the hidden nectar; and if directions are followed, the pistil is sure to receive the wished-for pollen.

FIG. 227

This picture (Fig. 227) shows you an orchid which you see in the windows of flower shops during the winter. It comes to us from far South, not growing out of doors in our climate.

Its building plan would almost serve for a wayside tavern. You can see that the pocket would answer as a front doorstep, making a convenient landing place for bee or butterfly.

The dark spots on the upper flower leaf point downward to the refreshment room.

Even more curious than this one are other orchids which grow in far-away places.

In their efforts to please, they wear the most striking colors, and take on a variety of fantastic shapes.

216

One of them dresses itself much like a bee. In this way perhaps it secures a visit from the real bee.

Another is called the baby orchid, because in the center of each flower is an object which really looks like a fairy baby.

There are some ten or twelve orchids which are common in our Northern woods. I hope you children will keep on the lookout for them all summer.

Just now you could not tell whether or not a flower was an orchid. But if you come across a plant whose flowers look as though they were built to serve as wayside taverns for the bees, why, carry them to your teacher, and ask her to find out for you whether they belong to the Orchid family.

But it is only fair to tell you that some of our orchids bear flowers so small and insignificant that you would hardly guess them to be members of so distinguished a family.

CLEVER CUSTOMS

ON this page you see a picture of the garden foxglove.

The garden foxglove is an English wild flower. It is so striking and beautiful that it was brought across the sea to decorate our gardens.

We can guess that the spots within each bell are the signposts leading to the refreshment room.

The yellow false foxglove (Fig.

228), which grows wild in our woods in midsummer, is a less brilliant flower than its English cousin, and is without the spots that serve as signposts.

Our wood and meadow lilies (Figs. 229, 230) are well fitted to secure bee visitors. Their colors are brilliant enough to catch the eye of the most unobserving of bees in its voyage across the meadow, and their spots vivid enough to lead it at once to the refreshment room.

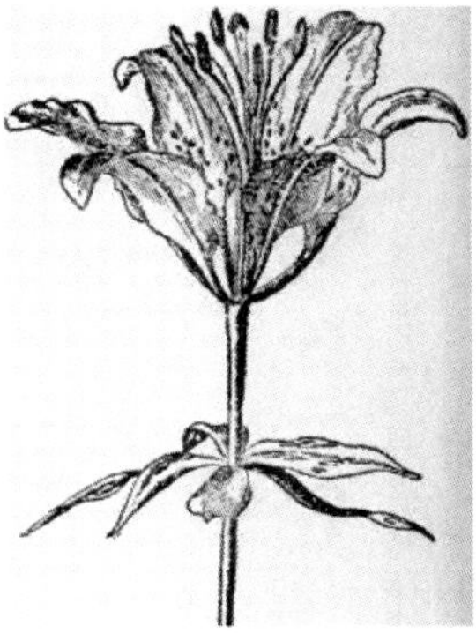

Try for yourselves to follow these markings with your tongue, and you will win the bee's reward, a sweet drop of nectar.

FIG. 228

Whenever you see a flower with such vivid markings as these, it will be worth your while to play the bee, and start a honey hunt.

Sometimes the sweet drop lies at the base of the flower leaves, as in the lilies; sometimes in a pocket, as in many of the orchids; sometimes it is in the bottom of a long spur such as you see in the columbine, violet, and nasturtium (Fig. 231).

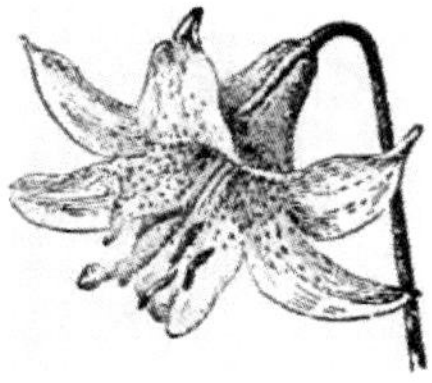

FIG. 229

Fig. 232 shows you the beautiful flowers of the mountain laurel.

FIG. 230

These flowers play a clever trick on their bee visitors. They wish to make perfectly sure that their pollen will be carried from one blossom to another, and so they set a little trap.

219

In a freshly opened blossom each stamen is bent over, as you see they are bent over in the picture (Fig. 233).

Their dust boxes are caught in little pockets of the flower cup. When a bee lights on a flower (Fig. 234), the jar causes the dust boxes to spring from the pockets with so much violence that the pollen is shaken over the body of the visiting bee, which is sure to leave some of

FIG. 231

it on the pistil of the next flower.

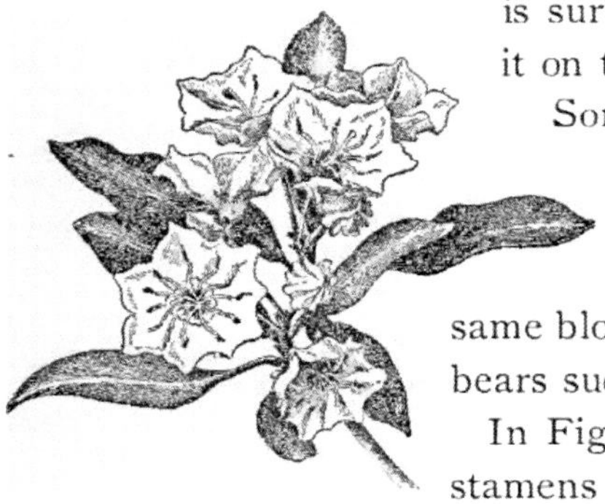

Some flowers take special care to prevent their pistils from being dusted with pollen from the dust boxes of the same blossom. The fireweed bears such blossoms as these. In Fig. 235 you see that the stamens of the fireweed are

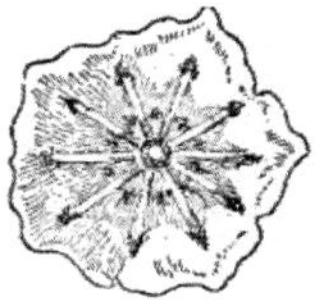

FIG. 232 large and ripe, and ready to

FIG. 233

shed their pollen ; but the pistil is bent sideways, pushing its closed tip quite out of the corolla, and out of reach of any pollen from a neighboring stamen.

Fig. 236 shows you another blossom from

FIG. 234

FIG. 235

FIG. 236

this same plant. The stamens have shed their pollen, and are quite dry and withered; but its pistil has straightened itself, and spreads out its four tips so as to receive the pollen from another flower.

It is believed that those seeds which are touched with life by pollen from another flower are more likely to change into healthy, hardy plants than those which are quickened by the pollen of their own flower.

Such of you as live near the sea know the lovely sea pinks (Fig. 237), which make a rosy carpet across the salt meadows early in August. The stamens and pistils of this sea pink act in the same way.

FIG. 237

FLOWERS THAT TURN NIGHT INTO DAY

ALREADY we have read that certain flowers attract insects rather by their fragrance than by their brilliancy of coloring.

It is interesting to learn that some blossoms open

usually only during the night. Of course, if these flowers hope to receive visitors, and get their share of pollen, they must devise some means of making known their presence to those insects which are awake and at work in the darkness.

You can understand that at night the brightest colors would be useless. A red flower is less easily seen in the darkness than a white or a yellow one; so night-opening flowers nearly always wear a white or yellow dress.

And not only this: to make sure that they will not be overlooked, and so miss the chance of ripening their seeds, they send out a strong fragrance as soon as the night falls. Through the deepest gloom this message of invitation reaches the wandering moth.

Do you know the evening primrose (Fig. 238)? There ought to be no need of asking you this, for it is one of our commonest wayside plants. But perhaps you have hardly noticed it, because ordinarily only at night is its flower wide awake.

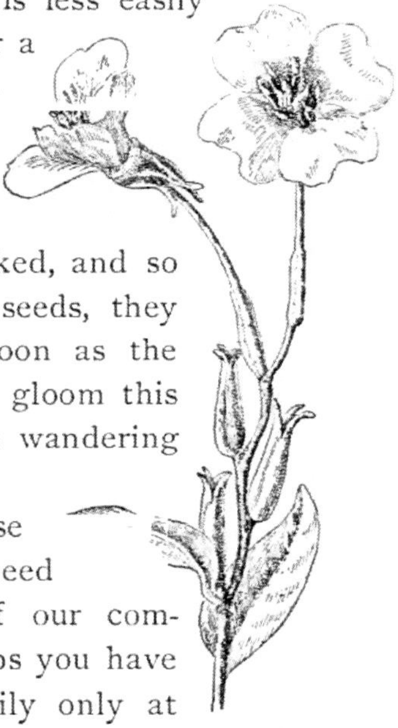

FIG. 238

When the sun has set, this pale yellow blossom unfolds, and gives out a strong, sweet fragrance, which means that it is "at home" to visitors.

After one short summer night it dies.

But during its little life the chances are that its invitation has been accepted by the pretty pink moth which oftentimes you find asleep in the faded flower cup.

222

The moth visitor has brought its hostess the pollen from another blossom, and has powdered the pistil's four spreading tips, so that the little primrose seeds below get the needed touch of life, and the short life of the flower has not been in vain.

If you keep on the lookout, you are likely to come across one of these yellow flowers with the sleepy pink moth inside its cup. I have caught this little fellow napping so often, that I have wondered if the nectar of the evening primrose might not have the effect of a sleeping potion. But after all, I suppose that pretty pink moths, like boys and girls, are likely to be dull and sleepy in the daytime if they have been up too late the night before.

HORRID HABITS

DID you ever know that some plants manage to attract insects in ways that are quite disgusting to us human beings?

While spending a morning in the woods, some of you may have noticed an odor so unpleasant that you were driven to find another resting place.

Perhaps you thought that this unpleasant smell was caused by the decaying body of some dead animal; but had you known the truth, you would have laid the blame where it rightly belonged.

And where was that, do you think?

Why, to that beautiful climbing plant close by, with large, thick leaves, and clusters of pale, greenish flowers, that were twisting all about the bushes. This plant it was that caused all the disturbance. It is called the "carrion vine" on account of the carrionlike odor of its flowers. Its pollen is carried from one little blossom to another by tiny flies, drawn to the spot by a smell like that of decaying flesh. These flies would pass carelessly over the sweet-smelling carpet of the partridge vine, they would scorn the invitation of the evening primrose; but the odor which drives us hurriedly from our cozy corner induces them to gather together in hundreds. Whether they come, actually expecting to find decaying flesh, I cannot say.

In some countries grows a plant which not only smells like decaying flesh, but which adds to the deception by its red, beefy look, thus doubly attracting the flies which like this sort of food.

THE STORY OF THE STRAWBERRY

IN the wood which edges the meadow is a hollow where it is almost sure to be cool and shady. Let us find our way there this morning, and see how we can amuse ourselves.

At first we want only to enjoy the wind which is coming through the trees, or to lie back on the grass and spy out the bird which is singing overhead, or else to laugh at the red squirrel which is scolding away at a great rate just above us.

Suddenly our eyes fall on a cluster of ripe, shining wild strawberries. Bird and squirrel are forgotten, for no fruit of all the year is prettier to look at than the wild strawberry; and, what is more important, no other fruit has such a delicious flavor of the woods and fields.

Soon we have eaten all the berries within reach. The creeping vines lead us out into the meadow, where we push aside the long grasses and pick one ripe mouthful after another. At last we are satisfied to go back to our shady nook.

225

The little white blossoms that a few weeks ago were so plentiful have nearly all disappeared. Who among you can tell me

FIG. 239

FIG. 240

FIG. 241

how these juicy berries have managed to take the place of the blossoms?

Why, ever so many of you can tell me much of the story, at any rate. It is very nearly that of the apple and cherry

FIG. 242

and plum and pear. The nectar-hunting bee carried the pollen of its many stamens from one strawberry blossom to another, leaving some of it on the flat tips of its numerous pistils. Down the pistils' stalks went the tiny life bearing tubes which pushed their way into the little seeds below.

So far, the story of the strawberry is not new to us; but just here it begins to differ from the stories of the apple and pear, of the plum and peach and cherry. The flowers of all these trees had but one seedbox. But each of the many little strawberry pistils has a separate seedbox; and when the little seeds within get their touch of new life, the flat, cushionlike object (Fig. 241) which bears these many pistils begins to act in a most surprising manner.

FIG. 243

FIG. 244

This flat flower cushion swells upward and outward

(Fig. 242), growing big and juicy and sweet, bearing its pistils (Fig. 243) with it.

And so in the strawberry blossom it is the flat cushion hidden out of sight which grows into the delicious fruit.

A COUSIN OF THE STRAWBERRY

THE strawberry is a member of the great Rose family. Among its many cousins we find the blackberry and the raspberry.

The blackberry blossom (Fig. 245) also has five white leaves, and a center made up of pistils and stamens.

When its white flower leaves fall, and its empty dust boxes wither, we see the blackberry begin to take the place of the blossom, just as we saw the strawberry take the place of the strawberry blossom (Fig. 246).

But now we are about to discover the way in which the blackberry differs from the strawberry.

Cannot some boy or girl tell me in what way they are different?

" One is black, and the other is red."

But that is not the answer I want. Perhaps it is hardly likely that any child could guess what I have in mind. Still a little exercise in guessing is as good for your brains as gymnastics are good for your bodies.

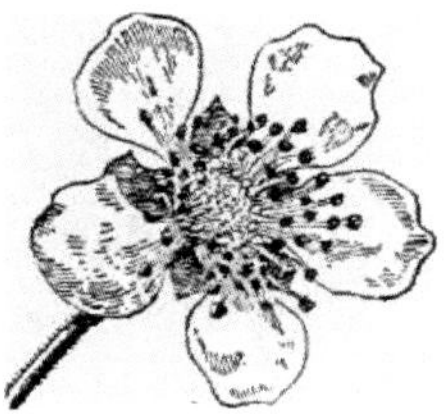

Now I will tell you what this difference is; and I want you to try and understand it clearly, so that you will be able to explain it to others, for I doubt if the grown-up people could give any better answers than you. I think your fathers and mothers will be both surprised and pleased when you show them some summer day how truly different are these two berries.

FIG. 245

You remember that in the strawberry we saw plainly that it was the flat flower cushion which swelled into the ripe strawberry, — the cushion which was quite hidden by the many pistils; and though these pistils were scattered thickly all over the ripe, red fruit, these little pistils with their seedboxes were too small and dry to add flavor or richness to the berry.

But if we watch the growth of this blackberry, we see that things are different.

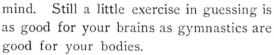

FIG. 246

We see that the pistils of this fruit do not remain small and dry, as with the strawberry. No, indeed! their little seedboxes grow bigger and juicier every day, and they turn from green to red and from red to black. They do not remain hard to the touch, but become so soft that a slight pressure will bruise them and stain your fingers purple. And we enjoy eating the full-grown blackberry (Fig. 249) because a quantity of these juicy seedboxes are so packed upon the juicy flower cushion that together they make a delicious mouthful (Figs. 247, 248).

The flower cushion of the blackberry

FIG. 247   FIG. 248   FIG. 249

is long and narrow, not broad and flat like that of the strawberry.

So do not forget that in the strawberry we enjoy eating the ripened flower cushion, while in the blackberry the juicy seedboxes give to the fruit more of its size and flavor than does the flower cushion.

ANOTHER COUSIN

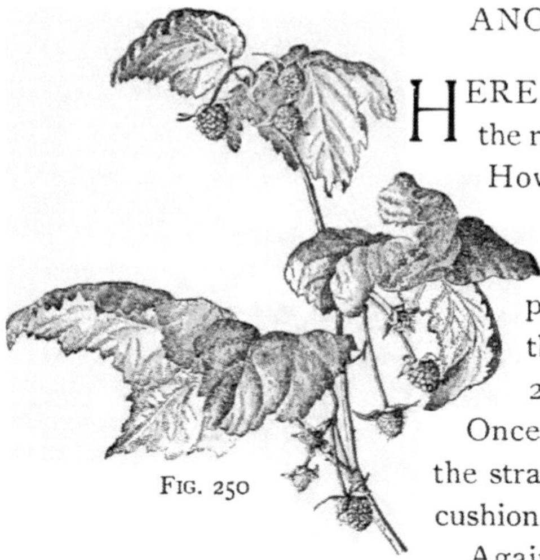

HERE we see a branch from the raspberry bush (Fig. 250). How is the raspberry unlike both strawberry and blackberry? Let us place side by side these three berries (Figs. 251, 252, 253).

Once more we observe that the strawberry is the flat flower cushion grown big and juicy.

Again we see that the seed-boxes of the blackberry packed upon the swollen flower cushion make up much of the fruit.

FIG. 250

But in the raspberry we find that the red, ripe seed-boxes alone make the berry which is so good to eat.

FIG. 251

FIG. 252

FIG. 253

When we pick this raspberry, we find that the flower cushion remains upon the plant, instead of coming off in our fingers and helping to make a luscious morsel, as with the other two fruits (Figs. 254, 255).

I hope you will remember how these three berries differ one from another.

Why the blossoms of these three plants grow into berries in three different ways, we do not know; but our time has been well spent if we remember that they do change in these three ways.

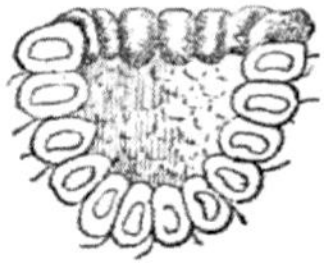

FIG. 254

FIG. 255

The more we see and question and learn, the more pleasure we shall find in our own lives, and the better able we shall be to make life pleasant for others.

232

PEA BLOSSOMS
AND PEAS

THE Pea family is a large one, and it is worth our while to find out what plan it uses in flower building.

Let us look at a pea blossom and see of what parts it is made up.

"There is the green cup, or calyx," you say.

Yes, that is plain enough. It is cut up into five little leaves.

"And there is a circle of flower leaves, which makes the corolla."

Let us pull apart both calyx and corolla, and place the separate leaves as in the picture (Fig. 256).

The five smaller leaves, the ones marked *ca*, are the green leaves of the calyx.

233

The five larger ones, marked *co*, belong to the corolla. These, you notice, are not all alike. The upper one is much the largest.

The two side ones are alike.

In the real flower the two lower ones are joined so as to form a little pocket.

And what else do you find?

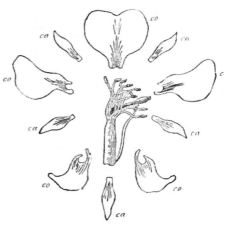

Now, if you do not pull apart the pea blossom, you find nothing else. But you know that the seed-holding fruit is the object of the flower's life, and that so this flower is pretty sure to have somewhere either a pistil with its seedbox, or stamens with their dust boxes, or both; for without the seeds of the seedbox, and the pollen of the dust boxes, no fruit can result.

So, knowing that the pea blossom cannot give birth to a pea pod without stamens and pistil, let us have a search for these.

As I told you, the two lower leaves of the corolla are joined so as to form a sort of pocket (Fig. 257). Now, surely, a pocket is meant to hold something. So take a pin and slit open this pocket. As the two sides spring apart, out flies some golden pollen, and we see that the little pocket is far from empty. It holds ten stamens and one pistil.

FIG. 257

DANA'S PLANTS. — 16

If you look at these carefully (Fig. 256), you see that one stamen stands alone, while the other nine have grown together, forming a tube which is slit down one side. This tube clings to the lower part of the pistil.

Now, if you pull this tube away, what do you see?

You see a little, green, oblong object, do you not (Fig. 258)?

And what is it? Do you not recognize it?

Why, it is a baby pea pod. Within it lie the tiny green seeds (Fig. 259) which are only waiting for the

FIG. 258 fresh touch of life from a pollen grain to grow bigger and bigger till they become the full-grown seeds of the pea plant, — the peas that we find so good to eat when they are cooked for dinner.

So, after all, the building plan of the pea blossom is nothing but the old-fashioned one which reads

1. Calyx.
2. Corolla.
3. Stamens.
4. Pistil.

Had I not told you to do so, I wonder if you would have been bright enough to pull apart the little pocket and discover the stamens and pistil.

What do you think about this?

THE CLOVER'S TRICK

HERE you see the bees buzzing about the pretty pink clover heads, — the sweet-smelling clover that grows so thickly in the fields of early summer.

Can you tell me what plan the clover uses in flower building?

You will not find this easy to do. Indeed, it is hardly possible, for the clover plays you a trick which you will not be able to discover without help.

You believe, do you not, that you are looking at a single flower when you look at a clover head?

Well, you are doing nothing of the sort. You are looking at a great many little clover flowers which are so closely packed that they make the pink, sweet-scented ball which we have been taught to call the clover blossom.

It is incorrect to speak of so many flowers as one ; and whenever we say, " This is a clover blossom," really we ought to say, " These are clover blossoms." We might just as well take a lock of hair—a lock made up of ever so many hairs — and say, " This is a hair." Now, you all know it would not be correct to do this, and no more is it correct to call a bunch of clover blossoms "a blossom." But as most people do not understand this, undoubtedly the mistake will continue to be made.

Fig. 260 shows you one little flower taken out of the ball-like clover head.

Can you think of any good reason why so many of these little flowers should be crowded together in a head?

What would happen if each little blossom grew quite alone?

Why, it would look so small that the bee could hardly see it. And sweetly though the whole clover head smells, the fragrance of a single flower would be so slight that it would hardly serve as an invitation to step in for refreshments.

FIG. 260

So it would seem that the clover plant does wisely in making one good-sized bunch out of many tiny flowers, for in this way the bees are persuaded to carry their pollen from one blossom to another.

The moral of the clover story is this: Be very careful before you insist that you hold in your hand or see in the picture only one flower.

MORE TRICKS

CAN you think of any other flowers that deceive us as the clover does?

Early in May we see in the woods a tree that is very beautiful. It is covered with what seem to be white blossoms. This tree is the flowering dogwood, and it tricks us somewhat in the same way as does the clover; for in this picture (Fig. 261) you see what nearly every one believes to be a single flower of the dogwood. And if some time ago you had been asked to give the building plan of the dogwood flower, you would have been pretty sure to say that the four large white leaves formed its corolla.

Here you would have been quite mistaken; for instead of one large flower, the picture shows you a number of tiny blossoms, so closely packed, and so surrounded by the four white leaves, that they look like only one blossom.

Fig. 261

Try to get a branch from the dogwood tree (only be sure to break it off where it will not be missed), and pull apart what looks so much like one large flower.

First pull off the four white leaves. Then you will have left a bunch of tiny greenish blossoms. Look at one of these through a magnifying glass. If eyes and glass are both good, you will see a very small calyx, a corolla made up of four little flower leaves, four mites of stamens, and a tiny pistil, — a perfect little flower where you never would have guessed it.

But all by themselves they would never be noticed: so a number of them club together, surrounding themselves with the showy leaves which light up our spring woods.

In Fig. 262 you see the flower cluster of the hobble-bush.

238

The hobblebush has still another way of attracting attention to its blossoms. It surrounds a cluster of those flowers which have stamens and pistils, and so are ready to do their proper work in the world, with a few large blossoms which have neither stamens nor pistils, but which are made up chiefly of a showy white corolla. These striking blossoms serve to call attention to their smaller but more useful sisters.

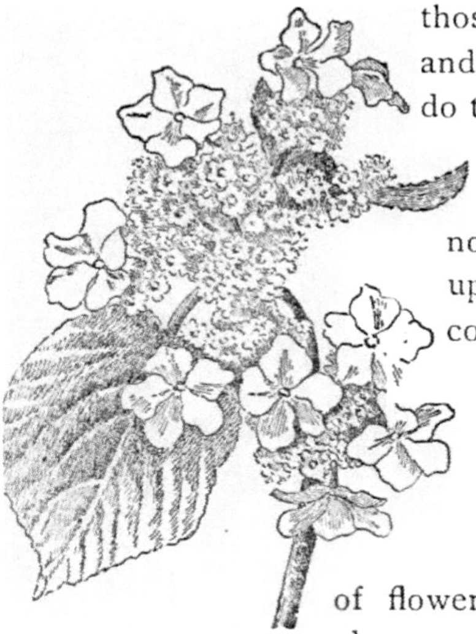

Sometimes a whole plant family will play this trick of putting a quantity of flowers in one bunch or cluster.

FIG. 262

The wild carrot (Fig. 263) is one of our commonest wayside weeds, a torment to the farmer, but a beautiful plant nevertheless. Each one of its lace-like flower clusters is made up of many flowers, — flowers which are too small to live alone, and so have decided to keep house together.

You will notice that here, as with the hobblebush, the outer flowers are larger and more showy than the inner ones. They seem to feel that with them rests the reputation of the family; that they must make the most of themselves, and do all in their power to attract the bees and butterflies.

FIG. 263

239

The wild carrot belongs to the Parsley family. All the members of this family collect a great many little flowers into one fairly large cluster.

———o◦⦂◦o———

AN OLD FRIEND

THERE is one plant (Fig. 264) which you city children ought to know almost as well as the country children. In the back yards and in the little squares of grass which front the street, it sends up its shining stars; and as for the parks, they look as if some generous fairy had scattered gold coins all over their green lawns.

FIG. 264

Now, what is this flower which is not too shy to bring its brightness and beauty into the very heart of the crowded city?

It is the dandelion, of course. You all know, or ought to know, this plucky little plant, which holds up its smiling face wherever it gets a chance.

And now, I am sure, you will be surprised to learn that this dandelion, which you have known and played with all your lives, is among those mischievous flowers which are laughing at you in their sleeves, and that regularly it has played you its "April fool;" for, like the dogwood and the clover, this so-called dandelion is not a single flower.

No, what you call a dandelion is a bunch made up of a great many tiny blossoms.

If you pull to pieces a dandelion head, you will find a quantity of little yellow straps. Each little strap is a perfect flower.

Now, if you had been asked for the building plan of the dandelion, you would have looked for the calyx, and you would have thought you had found it in the green cup which holds the yellow straps.

And when you were looking for the corolla, perhaps you would have said, "Well, all these yellow things must be the flower leaves of the corolla."

But when you began your hunt for stamens and pistils, you would have been badly puzzled; and no wonder, for these are hidden away inside the yellow straps, the tiny flowers of the dandelion.

So remember that when you cannot find the stamens and pistils within what you take to be the single flower, you will do well to stop and ask yourself, "Can this be one of the plants which plays tricks, and puts a lot of little flowers together in such a way as to make us think that they are one big flower?"

THE LARGEST PLANT FAMILY IN THE WORLD

THE dandelion belongs to the largest plant family in the world. All the members of this family have the dandelion trick of bunching together a quantity of little flowers. From this habit the family takes its name. It is called the "Composite" family, because with it, that which looks like one flower is composed of many flowers.

To this great family belong some of the flowers which you know best ; and if you are not to be fooled again and again, you must learn to tell by its blossoms whether a plant is a member of the Composite family. This will not be difficult if you will be patient, and pull to pieces a few of the flower heads which I am going to describe, and examine carefully the building plan used by the separate flowers.

Fig. 265 shows you the field daisy. This pretty flower is an old friend ; and many of you know that its beauty is no comfort to the farmer, who finds it a sign of poor soil, and a nuisance, and does his best to get rid of it.

FIG. 265

As you know, the central part of the daisy is bright yellow, and the narrow leaves which stand out in a circle around its yellow center are pure white.

Now, if I had asked you some time ago for the building plan of the daisy, I think you would have told me that the arrangement of little green leaves underneath the flower head made up the calyx, and naturally you would have believed the white leaves above to have formed the corolla ; and the chances are that the yellow center would have seemed to be a quantity of stamens. As for the seed holders, you might have said, "Oh, well! I suppose they are hidden away somewhere among all these stamens."

It would not have been at all strange or stupid if you had answered my question in this way.

I know of no plant which dresses up its flowers more cleverly, and cheats the public more successfully, than this innocent-looking daisy ; for not only does it deceive boys and girls, but many of the grown-up people who love flowers, and who think they know something about them, never guess how they have been fooled by the daisy. Indeed, some of them will hardly believe you when you tell them that when they pick what they call a daisy, they pick not one, but a great many flowers; and they are still more surprised when they learn that not only the yellow center of the daisy is composed of a quantity of little tube-shaped blossoms, but that what they take to be a circle of narrow white flower leaves is really a circle of flowers, each white strap being a separate blossom.

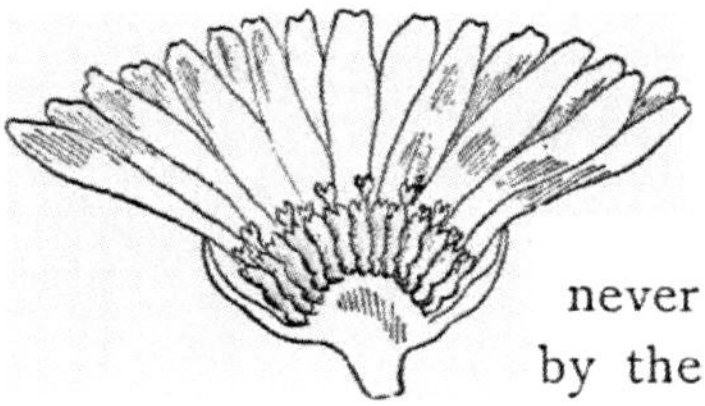

FIG. 266

I dare not try to tell you how many separate blossoms you would find if you picked to pieces a daisy and counted all its flowers, — all the yellow ones in the center, and all the white outside ones, — but you would find a surprisingly large number.

FIG. 267

The picture above (Fig. 266) shows you a daisy cut in two, and next you have one of the white outer flowers (Fig. 267). This flower, as we must call it, has a pistil, but no stamens. The pollen is brought by flies from the yellow central flowers to this pistil.

Here (Fig. 268) you see a picture of one of those yellow flowers which have both stamens and pistil inside its tube.

FIG. 268

243

If you children once make yourselves well acquainted with the make-up of the daisy, seeing with your own bright eyes (not believing it just because I tell you it is so) that there are many little flowers where most people think they see only one big one, you will never forget it as long as you live; and you will know something that many of the big people about you do not know. Some day while walking across the fields I think you will enjoy surprising them by pulling to pieces a daisy, and explaining to them this favorite flower trick.

ROBIN'S PLANTAIN, GOLDEN-ROD, AND ASTER

ALONG the roadsides, in the month of May, grows a flower which you children call a blue daisy. This has the yellow center of the field daisy; but the narrow outer flowers which surround the yellow center are not white, they are blue.

The real name of this flower is "robin's plantain." It is not a daisy, though it belongs to the same big family. Here, too, the yellow center is made up of many little tube-shaped flowers.

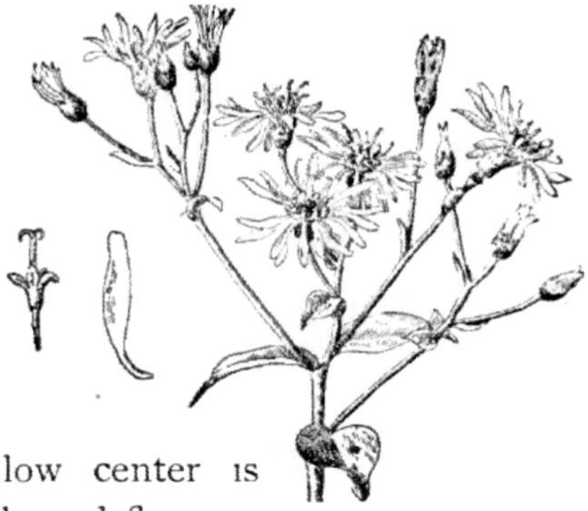

Later in the year the fields are white and purple with beautiful asters (Fig. 269). It is easy to

FIG. 269

see that these asters are own cousins to robin's plantain. Their flower heads are put together in the same way, and many of the asters wear the same blue or purple dress (Fig. 269).

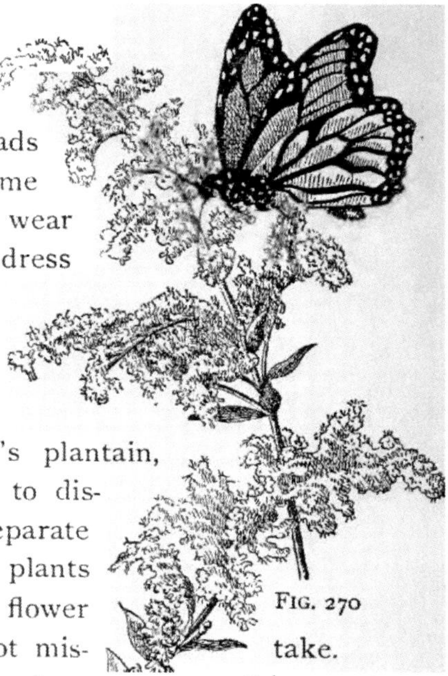

When once you have become acquainted with the secret of dandelion and daisy and aster and robin's plantain, you will find it quite easy to discover their little separate flowers. All these plants have large, plain flower heads that you cannot mis-

FIG. 270

take.

But with some members this great Composite family you are going to have more

FIG. 271 trouble, unless you take your time and keep your wits about you.

Just when the asters begin to border the roadsides in the month of August, the golden-rod (Fig. 270) hangs out its bright yellow flowers. This golden-rod is one of the plants which you may find a little troublesome; for its little flowers are so tiny, that even when a number of them are fastened together in a bunch, the whole bunch looks like a very small blossom (Fig. 271).

FIG. 272 In each of these little bunches or heads (for when a number of flowers are packed together in this way, we call the whole bunch a "head") there are a few of the strap flowers (Fig. 272) on the outside, and a few tube

245

flowers (Fig. 273) in the center; but the outer strap flowers are so small that you can hardly believe they are really flowers, and the tube flowers look hardly larger than ordinary stamens. To see them at all clearly, you must use a good magnifying glass.

And you must search very patiently for the tiny bunch (Fig. 271) which is the head of the golden-rod. Next you must pick to pieces this little head, separating the outer from the inner flowers.

In hunting for a single head in this great yellow flower cluster, you must look for the little cup-like arrangement, the tiny greenish or yellowish leaves; for each head is held in one of these small cups.

FIG. 273

Although the golden-rod is one of the most difficult of all the flowers to understand, once you have seen for yourselves how each little head is held in its tiny cup, you will find it easy enough to pick out its single flowers, and then you will have mastered the secret of the golden-rod.

246

THE LAST OF THE FLOWERS

WE found, you remember, that the dandelion head was made up entirely of strap flowers; and we saw that the daisy and aster and golden-rod were made up partly of strap flowers, and partly of tube flowers.

And here you have a great thistle head (Fig. 274). If you should pull it to pieces, you would find only tube flowers.

The Composite family always makes up its head in one of these three ways, using either nothing but strap flowers, or nothing but tube flowers, or else using tube flowers for the center of the head, and strap flowers for the outside.

FIG. 274

Now, I hope you will remember these three ways in which this important family puts together its little flowers.

FLOWERS

When you go into the garden where a big sunflower (Fig. 275) is trying to peep into your neigh-
bor's yard, I hope your eyes will be
sharp enough to see that this sunflower is a cousin to the field daisy,
and that, although its brown center is much larger than the daisy's
golden eyes, it is made up of tube
flowers (Fig. 276) shaped much
like the tube flowers of the daisy.

And you will notice, I am sure,
that the yellow circle about this brown center is
made up of strap flowers (Fig. 277) just like the
white circle about the daisy center.

Fig. 275

And what is that which falls like a golden shower
from the great brown center of the sunflower? Ah,
you know well that that is the precious pollen which
powders thickly the visiting bees and butterflies, and
goes to make new sunflower plants.

Fig. 276 The picture at the head of this chapter shows the
wild sister of the garden sunflower.

When you come across the bright blue flower of
the chicory, you will be reminded, I hope, of your
dear old friend the dandelion; for the chicory head,
like that of the dandelion, is made up entirely of
strap flowers.

But when you pick a spray of everlasting, whose
white and yellow clusters you find on the rocky hill-
sides, you will have to use your eyes with great care
if you are to discover that here, as in the great purple
thistle head, are nothing but tube flowers.

Fig. 277

248

Part VII — Learning to See

A BAD HABIT

IN fact, if you are to see any of the things that are really worth seeing, you must study the art of using your eyes. You must *learn to see*.

This world is full of things that are beautiful and interesting, things that do not cost money, that can be had for the seeing.

School is nearly over now, and during the weeks that lie before you there will be many hours which you children can call your own.

I wonder what you will do with these holiday hours?

Of course, you will play a great deal; at least, I hope you will, for we need play almost as much as we need work. But one does not play every minute, even in the holidays. I hope that all of you will spend a part of your holidays in trying to be a little useful to your mothers.

But even then there will be some time left for other things, — things that are not work, and that are not exactly play, yet that are a little of each, and so perhaps better than either play or work alone.

Among these "other things" I hope "learning to see" will find its place. I wish that every child who reads this book would make a resolution that during these coming holiday weeks he will "learn to see."

There are many different ways of doing this. The children in the city can learn this great lesson as well as those who live in the country. There is much to be seen in the city besides people and houses, and horses and wagons. There are the clouds of the sky by day, and its stars by night. There are the trees in the squares, the birds and flowers in the parks, and much besides.

The children who live by the sea do not have the great forest trees that grow among the mountains; but for this loss they can comfort themselves by the beautiful rose mallows (see the picture at the head of this chapter) that grow in the marsh, by the sea pinks along the creek, by the pretty shells and seaweeds on the beach.

But perhaps you think I am quite wrong in taking it for granted that you need to "learn to see." What gives me the idea that you ought to learn any such lesson ?

Well, nine times out of ten, if I hand a flower to a child and ask him to look at it and then to tell me about it, he will stare at it, oh, very hard indeed, for some moments, and then he will have nothing to say.

Now, this cannot be the fault of the flower; for we have seen that the flower is made up of so many different things that to tell about them all takes some time. It must be the fault of the child ; or at least the fault of his eyes and brain, both of which are needed for really seeing, and which probably he does not know how to use.

It must be that he has never "learned to see." Perhaps he has used his eyes well enough, and has really seen a great many things in the flower ; but his brain may not be able to put them together in the right way, and to find the words that are needed.

If this is the only trouble, a little practice will make it all right. He will find that his brain works better after each trial, just as a new pair of scissors works better after it has been used several times.

But often the eyes do not seem to do their share of the work ; and if they do not, there is no chance for the brain to come to their help.

That is a sad state of affairs, because, if when we are young we let our eyes form bad habits, such as not seeing the things they ought to see, we are likely to be half blind all the rest of our lives.

It would be a terrible thing, would it not, to be told

that you were about to become blind, that soon you would be unable to see the things about you?

Now, while I trust that none of you will ever become altogether blind, I tell you honestly, I greatly fear that some of you are in danger of becoming partly so, — of becoming blind to many of the things about you that would please you greatly if you only saw them. And I know that this sort of blindness must take from your lives much happiness.

But still you may wonder how I know this about children whom I have never seen. How can I know whether the boys and girls who read this are in any danger of losing their power to see?

Well, the only way I know about you boys and girls, whom I have never seen, is by watching very carefully the ones I do see.

You children who live in New York, say, have never seen the children who live in California; yet you feel sure that they have eyes and ears just as you have, do you not?

And you are pretty confident that most of them like to play far better than they like to work; that sometimes they are good-natured, and that again they are quarrelsome; and that in many ways they are like the boys and girls who live near you.

In just the same way I am able to guess that you children whom I do not know are more or less like the ones I do know.

Now, among these children only a few, as I have said before, seem to have the full use of their eyes. This troubles me, because the evil is one that grows greater as the children grow older. Perhaps you know that if you stop using any part of your body, that part soon begins to lose its power of doing the things it was meant to do.

If you should not use your legs for a long time, they would grow so weak that they could hardly carry you. It would be much as if you had no legs, or at least as if you had legs that could not do the work they were meant to do.

If you stopped using your hands, you would find your fingers growing stiffer and stiffer, so that at last they could not take a good hold of things.

And if your eyes are not used for seeing clearly the things before them, they will grow less and less able to see clearly.

A COUNTRY ROAD

I HAVE taken a walk along a country road which was bright with flowers of many kinds, where lovely-colored butterflies and buzzing bees were hard at work hunting for sweet stuff, where birds were singing in the trees as they watched their nests, where a rabbit would dart from the bushes close by, and a squirrel would scold at me from overhead, — where, in short, there was so much to look at and delight in, that I could hardly make up my mind to keep on to my journey's end, instead of stopping to see if I knew the names of all the flowers, to admire the queer, bright-colored little patterns on the wing of the butterfly which was resting on a neighboring blossom, and to find out what sort of eggs were in the nest that I knew must be near at hand, for the mother bird let out her secret by her frightened clucking.

Well, I have taken just such a walk; and on going into the house I have felt as if I were obliged to put aside a book of enchanting fairy stories, or rather as if I were turning my back on fairyland itself, with all its wonderful sights and sounds and adventures.

And then what has happened?

Why, some child (it has not always been a child) has come in, and I have said, " Was not that a fine walk? What did you see along that lovely road ? "

Now, if he was a boy (for I want to be quite fair), he probably had seen the rabbit and given it chase; and it is more than likely that he had stopped long enough to chuck a stone at the squirrel; and if the mother bird had not finished with her foolish chatter, I fear he gave her some evil moments by hunting for her nest, with no good intentions. But if, fortunately for them, he had met none of these creatures, he probably looked at me in surprise, and answered by look, if not by words, " No, I thought it a long, stupid walk. I did not see a thing."

And if it was a girl, I fear the answer, silent or spoken, was much the same.

Now, I say that boy or girl must have been partly blind to have missed seeing those wonderful flowers, and butterflies, and bees, and birds, and many other interesting things which I have not time here to tell about. Certainly they were not using their eyes properly; and the longer they go about in such a way, more worthy of a bat than of a well-made child, the more useless and bat-like will their eyes become.

It is really more natural for a child to use his eyes constantly than it is for an older person. The grown-up man or woman is likely to have so many things to think about, that eyes and brain do not always work together, and so the surroundings are not noticed.

For every boy knows that if his head is full of the ball game he is going to play, he runs along without eyes or thoughts for other things.

And every girl knows that if she is on her way to some friend to whom she has a secret to tell, she is in such haste to reach her journey's end, and is so busy thinking what her friend will have to say about it all, that of course there is no time to pay attention to anything else. Her eyes may be in good working order, yet they are not of much use unless her brain is ready to help them; and that little brain just now is too busy with its secret.

No, by the people who are half blind I mean only those who much of the time use neither eyes nor brain, who can neither tell you what they have seen nor what they have been thinking about. Sometimes it seems as if such people were not only half blind, it seems as if they were only half alive.

A HOLIDAY LESSON

BUT I am in hopes that some of the children who read this book will say, " I do not think it fair to call children half blind and only half alive. I know I am not half blind. I saw all those things that Mrs. Dana saw along that country road, and " (perhaps some of them may add) "a good deal more too. I know all the different flowers by sight, and the sunny hollows where the first ones come. I know where ever so many of the birds build their nests, and how their different eggs are marked and colored. Often I go down to the little pool in the woods where they come for their bath. I know how the caterpillars wrap themselves in leaves and come out beautiful butterflies. I have peeped into the hollow of the tree where the red squirrel is bringing up its family ; and I have seen how the pretty green katydid scrapes his wings along his sides, and makes the sound, ' Katy did, Katy didn't,' and oh, so many more things that I have not time to tell them all."

Ah! that is just it. The child that knows how to use his eyes can see so much, so many wonderful things!

That is why I am so anxious that he or she should not miss through carelessness the revelations that come to the child alone.

It seems as though the woods and fields were more ready to tell their stories, to whisper their secrets, to children than to grown people. If people learn to use their eyes and ears only after they are grown, I hardly think that they will ever read quite the same stories, ever listen to quite such wonderful secrets, as if they had begun to look and to listen when they were little children.

If fairy godmothers came now, as the stories tell us they did once upon a time, to the christenings of our little ones, offering whatever gifts the parents should choose, it seems to me one of the wisest selections would be the power *to see*.

And so when I ask you children, now that you are putting by your lesson books for many weeks, to learn one lesson this holiday time, — to *learn to see*, — I am asking you to do something that will make your lives far happier than they could be were this lesson left unlearned.

THE
GARDEN OF EARTH

*A Little Book on Plant-life, Plant-growth,
and the Ways and Uses of Plants*

BY

AGNES GIBERNE

AUTHOR OF
"THIS WONDERFUL UNIVERSE," "THE ROMANCE OF THE MIGHTY DEEP," ETC.

"When Spring unlocks the Flowers to paint the
laughing soil."—REGINALD HEBER.

"O then indeed I knew how closely knit
To Stars and Flowers we are."—ALFRED NOYES.

A Sub-tropic Garden.

FOREWORD

It does not fall to the lot of most people to be able to devote much time to Botany. This book does not pretend to be even an introduction to that delightful pursuit. Given, however, a certain admiration for the beauties of the garden and countryside, Miss Giberne's book is calculated to enlarge it into a feeling of friendship for the individuals of the vegetable kingdom. The authoress gracefully draws aside the veil and shows the wind, the bees, and the flowers at play. The reader is encouraged to step among them, and to look for himself.

Any one who had been content with the usual superficial observation of Nature, and who is hereby introduced into an intimate acquaintance with the game and with its players, will have to thank this book for a new and very charming friendship with the animated but previously unnoticed world around him.

S. T. Dunn, B.A.
Formerly Official Guide in the Royal Botanic Gardens, Kew.

PREFACE

AN unpretentious little volume, on the subject of Plant-life and the ways and needs and doings of Plants, is all that my book can claim to be. It is, indeed, in no sense a Manual of Botany; and it is meant for beginners, whether older or younger, as well as for any who love and are interested in trees and flowers.

In the writing of it I have gained needed information from many different sources; more especially from *The Natural History of Plants*, by Kerner and Oliver. Also generous help has been given to me by Mr. S. T. Dunn of the Kew Gardens Staff, for which I am sincerely grateful. Nor can I refrain from a warm mention of the debt which I owe to my Father's early and unforgettable teachings on this subject.

In addition I thank Mr. Alfred Noyes, Mr. John Masefield, and other poets of the day whose names appear in footnotes, as well as their publishers, for kind permission to quote from their writings.

Many gardens, large and small, are in the world; and our whole Earth may fairly be described as one vast Garden, with its more beautiful and its more barren parts. I have tried to bring some glimpses, some visions, of that Garden and of what it really means, before the imagination of my readers.

This is intended to be a companion-volume to another

of mine, published a few months ago; nominally a reprint from a small volume of the same name, but entirely rewritten. I wonder whether, possibly, some who have read *This Wonderful Universe*, may now turn to *The Garden of Earth* with the feeling described by Mr. Alfred Noyes in one of his poems :—

" We should come
Seeking a little refuge from the light
Of the blinding terrible star-sown Infinite,
Seeking some sheltering roof, some four-walled Home,
From that too high, too wide
Communion with the Universe and God,
How glad to creep back to some lane we trod,
Hemmed in with a hawthorn hedge on either side."

Yet the marvels and the mysteries to be found in that hawthorn hedge are not *less* than the marvels and the mysteries of the Star-sown Universe, as seen and known in ever so limited a measure by us on Earth.

AGNES GIBERNE.

THE GARDEN OF EARTH

PART I—INTRODUCTORY

THE SPRING AWAKENING

I—IN THE GARDEN

SUPPOSE that you and I are going into a large garden, for the first time in our lives. It might be that we had lived always in some huge manufacturing town, where trees could not grow, and flowers could not flourish. Or—if this were possible—that our lot had been cast in far-north regions of perpetual ice and snow, where vegetation would be only of the very lowest.

What, then, should we think of a fair garden, breaking suddenly on our sight in spring? How much should we understand, how much should we grasp, of what would lie before our eyes?

Picture it to yourself, and try to realise how things would look. Come into the garden, in imagination, and make yourself see as you would see under such circumstances, with eyes unused, with a mind unaccustomed, to the surroundings. Countless marvels in this world we accept with calm indifference, only because we have always known them thus. Otherwise, we should be perpetually stirred to wonder and amazement at the sights around, the changes which take place, the things which happen.

So here we are in a country garden, you and I together, let us say, for the first time in our lives.

On our left lies a wide lawn, closely mown, but dotted with hundreds of yellow-eyed Daisies, all sprung up since the last mowing. On our right, divided off by a dry ditch, is a reach of longer and coarser grass, mingled plentifully with weeds; and it slopes downward to a meadow, from which it is parted by a belt of shrubs and bushes.

Trees grow in all directions; some small and slender, swaying in the breeze; some lofty and wide-spreading, with heavy, rugged trunks. Many are full of leaf, though not yet so full as in the height of summer; for this, though a warm and sunny day, is only spring-tide. Others have still the first tender flush of green, when the new little leaves have just begun to unfold. Many again are quite bare, holding up against the sky a lace-work of delicate twigs, branching off and off one from another, each new departure more delicate than the last.

You and I know well enough that plants and flowers grow and bloom and die; that leaves fall off the trees in autumn; that new leaves come in their place with spring; that seeds are formed which develop into fresh plants; and that those plants again produce seeds. Everybody knows all this, because such facts are a commonplace of our daily life.

But suppose we did not know it! Suppose we had never seen, had never even heard of, such alternate generations of plant and seed, seed and plant, each succeeding the other. Or suppose that, while in a sense knowing it, we had never given the matter any serious thought, had never cared to learn how such wonders come about.

For, indeed, they are wonders. And to unaccustomed eyes, the eyes of visitors who had never known aught of the kind before, they would be simply amazing.

In either case, if we had not known, or if, knowing, we had not understood or cared to consider—the first step for us to take would be to *look ;* to gaze hard, to find out what there is that is worth seeing and thinking about in the garden-world. This would not mean idleness. Real looking, real watching, real thinking, are often harder work than cutting or hammering or digging or studying. It *is* studying—trying to learn from the Book of Nature.

That great Book of Nature is more difficult to read than any printed volume; and naturally so. For the author of such a volume is a man, but the Author of the Book of Nature is God Himself.

It has easy pages, however, as well as hard ones; and it lies always within our reach. Anybody may read from it at any time. And that which we spell out for ourselves is worth far more to us than what we have been taught verbally by others.

II—MANY PLANTS

This is what we have to do in our garden. We will try to make out a few sentences from the Book of Nature, lying invitingly open; and then we will go on to learn other facts, many of which we could not find out for ourselves.

B

THE GARDEN OF EARTH

We all know that the trees around, excepting only the evergreens, have been lately as bare as the barest of those trees which still do not show any foliage.

Yet we may not have grasped the fact that each of those dead-looking branches is not only alive, but already is actively at work, putting forth a new array of spring clothing. If we did not know it, how should we guess that the tiny beginnings of leaves are now actually getting ready *inside* the buds of boughs and twigs, so as to come out into daylight at the earliest possible moment, dressing the whole tree in sweet fresh green, so giving it power to get through its summer work.

" What work ? " you may ask.

At the outset you may be sure of one thing. Not only that each tree has some definite task to carry out, but that each leaf has its own particular share in that task. Roots, stems, flowers, one and all have their appointed service. Every part of a plant has its own especial work to do, for which it is especially fitted; and no other part of the plant can, generally, undertake that duty.

Wandering onward, we reach a wide border, crammed with flowers. The rich, brown earth is damp from rain in the past night. If we had never seen anything of the kind before—perhaps if we had—we might know little about the varieties of good food for plants, found in such soil, without which they could not grow. A long wriggling earth-worm half shows itself, and scurries away. Only an earth-worm, yet a most useful person; for he too, humble though he be, has his tasks.

Plants of many kinds are crowded together in the

border. We note one that grows low, with small purple-blue blossoms, modestly trying to hide themselves among heart-shaped leaves, while betraying their presence by a sweet pervading scent. Close by are other tiny star-like blooms of bright blue, several on one stalk. Next comes a plant with crinkled leaves and rounded flowers of pale yellow, lifting their faces confidingly towards the sky.

These old friends we recognisĕ at once—Violets, Forget-me-nots, Primroses. But how wonderful they would seem, if they dawned on our vision for the first time !

Along the outer edge of the border grow many double red and white Daisies; so unlike their cheery little pink-tipped sisters on the lawn, that a stranger would not call them by the same name. A patch of tall, early-flowering Marguerite Daisies, standing hard by, really have a look of cousinship.

Tulips flourish in abundance; large red ones, single and double; little dainty yellow ones; and pure white ones with golden centres. The many-hued Polyanthus claims attention; and a silky Phlox with star-like pink blossoms; and a white-flowered Candytuft; not to speak of many more.

At the back grow bushes, laden with Lilac-blossoms, mauve and white; and a Laburnum flings its long golden tassels in the breeze; and on the hedge, behind the Lilacs, where a wild Rose grows luxuriantly, one green flower-bud has just begun to unfold itself, showing a tiny streak of coral-red.

All these we see for ourselves. And how much of them do we really understand ?

THE GARDEN OF EARTH

III—What the Plants are doing

Wandering still through the quiet garden, gazing at one plant after another, we come suddenly on the gardener, a hard-working man of the olden type. He is tying up some long trails of a creeper; and our presence seems to make no sort of difference to him. Presently we venture on a question—an attempt to draw him out. He surely knows much about these garden wonders. We try to intimate politely that he could tell us—things —if he would.

He goes steadily on with his work, not answering hastily. But after a pause, he says—

" Yes. I've seed a deal of their ways."

"Their *ways!*" That is rather a new idea. We had not perhaps thought of plants as having *ways* like human beings.

" What sort of ways? " we ask.

He takes a good while to consider. We begin to fancy that he has forgotten our question. But he straightens himself, looks full at us, and remarks—

" You just keep a look-out, and you'll see. They've got lots of ways—queer ways too, and no mistake."

" Tell us one—just one ! " we beg; for he has taken up his basket, and is on the move.

" You can see 'em a-lookin' up at the sun, and follerin' him along ! "

Then he disappears inside a small glass-house, and we exchange glances, deciding to take his advice.

That means careful study. Plant after plant, kind after kind, we examine. Many flowers, unmistakably, do not take any particular trouble to face the sun.

269

Some turn carelessly another way. Some, like the Violet, prefer to creep into shade. Some hang their heads, either from modesty or from weakness of stalk. But gradually it dawns upon us how very many do really seem to face the sun, as if of set purpose.

Reaching again the large lawn, still with our heads full of this thought, we are impressed by the fact that Daisies are among the number of sun-lovers.

Hundreds of little white faces, with their golden centres, are uplifted straight towards that part of the sky where the King of Day shines in his brilliance. We examine them carefully, first from one side, then from another; and again and again we note how those hundreds of slender stems slope in one direction, like the bayonets of a regiment of soldiers, all in the same direction.

No; not all. This begins to perplex us. A few here and there fail to follow the rule. The idea occurs that possibly those few are in weak health, which would explain the fact.

Then again, several Daisy-plants are growing under the shade of a mass of bushes, so that direct sunshine is cut off. And since they are debarred from looking up at the sun, they wisely do the next best thing in their power, which is—*to face towards the greatest amount of light*. This they practise quite as markedly as the Daisies on the open space are facing the sun himself. The slope of their stems, therefore, is different from that of the other Daisy stems.

So much at least we have discovered for ourselves in one afternoon. But later in the day, going back to the same spot, we note something else, not less interesting.

In the afternoon the Daisies were all wide awake, gazing skyward. Now they have shut up their faces, folding the outer white rays over the golden centres, for all the world as if they were going to sleep.

ANAGALLIS ARVENSIS (*Scarlet Pimpernel*) and A. TENELLA (*Bog Pimpernel*).

Another ramble round becomes necessary, to see if other plants behave in a like manner. We come across several which do. Tulips are plainly closing for the night; and a dainty little Linum has done the same. Also some tiny red Pimpernels, growing at the path-edge—only weeds, but not less pretty for that—and the bell-shaped Convolvulus follow their example.

Others might be noticed, not shutting up, but drooping

on their stalks, with faces turned away from the darkening sky. But many remain open, and one or two are actually unclosing their flowers, which all day have been fast shut.

> "Of all the floures in the mede,
> Than love I most these floures white and rede,
> Soch that men callen daisies in our toun."[1]

Ox-eye Daisy.

CHRYSANTHEMUM SEGETUM (*Yellow Ox-eye*).

IV—GROWING SLOWLY

As we go on, day after day, studying the garden, something else claims our attention.

[1] Chaucer.

THE GARDEN OF EARTH

Certain trees which were bare and brown now show a glint of green. Some which had boasted only a gentle flush of that tint, have small leaves. Others, which had displayed half-open leaves have abundance, fully open.

With lesser growths the same is seen. Plants which had carried only buds have now full blossoms. Some which had borne two or three flowers now bear many. The Rose-bud on the hedge is a bud yet, but its coral streak has so far widened that we feel any hour may see it in full bloom.

All this is only to be expected. But we begin to realise what it all means, and how wonderful are these silent changes, perpetually going on.

Why should we not watch the actual working out of such changes? Why not see with our eyes the growth of a leaf—the opening of a flower-bud? It happens incessantly, all around us. Flower after flower unfolds. Leaf after leaf expands. Can we not follow the wonder for ourselves, minute by minute, as it actually takes place?

We do our best. We sit down, and fix a steadfast gaze on the pretty Rose-bud, which seems just ready— more than ready—to burst into bloom. We look— and look—and look—steadily, persistently, till eyes and brain are weary.

And it is in vain. Not the smallest movement can be observed. Not the faintest alteration can be detected. Tired of watching, we wander away, and in an hour or two come back—to find that the bud has opened; the Rose is in bloom.

Sometimes we have tried to see the movement of an hour-hand in a small watch; and we have failed. The

BREAKING INTO LEAF.

hand does move, but so slowly, so gently, that we cannot detect its motion. So it is with plants and leaves and flowers.

In some cases growth is far more rapid than in others. A Scarlet-runner will in one night—if it is a good growing night, warm and close—become four or five inches longer. Hops are still more expeditious. A Hop-shoot has been known in a single night to add eight or nine inches to its length. Yet even then, if we sat up with a lamp, and gazed continuously hour after hour, it is more than doubtful whether we should actually detect the growth.

As Keble wrote—

> " Who ever *saw* the earliest Rose
> First open her sweet breast ? "

But it is worth while to make the attempt. Looking into such possibilities for ourselves is much more interesting than only to hear what other people may have done.

> " A Rosebud by my early walk
> Adown a corn-enclosèd bawk,
> Sae gently bent its thorny stalk,
>   All on a dewy morning.
> Ere twice the shades o' dawn are fled,
> In a' its crimson glory spread,
> And drooping rich the dewy head,
>   It scents the early morning.
>
> .   .   .   .   .   .
> So thou, sweet Rosebud, young and gay,
> Shalt beauteous blaze upon the day,
> And bless the parent's evening ray
>   That watched thy early morning." [1]

[1] Robert Burns.

PART II

I—A Good Look Round

WHETHER a garden be large or small, whether it is a town or a country garden, in any case it is sure to be full of interest.

Somebody once spoke of her little town-garden as "just the size of a pocket-handkerchief"; which was a modest way of stating the matter. But even the very tiniest scrap of a garden, if well cared-for and lovingly tended, may hold beautiful growths. And if you have no garden at all, there is still something to be done. You may have two or three plants in pots; or, better yet, a wooden window-box full of flowers. The commonest plants, the simplest blooms, are things of wonder and charm.

We all know something of plant-life. Like the visitors to a new garden, we do at least know that plants grow, and bring forth leaves and flowers; and that when the leaves die, fresh leaves come in their stead; and that, when seeds have been formed, new plants arise in time from some of those seeds.

But I wonder how many of us have begun to look on plants as *living things*—as not only having life, but having habits and ways of their own. I wonder how many of us quite realise that, as living things, they breathe, they feed, they work; that they have what seem to be likings and dislikings; that each kind of plant needs a particular sort of place to grow in, and a certain amount of warmth; that some plants do well in one soil, while others must have a different soil; that the climate which suits one does not suit another.

All this and much more is true. Plants can be said to sleep and wake. Plants live out their lives, even as we live out our lives. Plants carry on their especial tasks. Plants may have good health or bad health. Plants, in fact, are *beings*—living creatures. They are a wonderful part of the vast creation of God. And they have a marvellous work to do for Him—and for us. Without plants, without the tasks that they carry out, we ourselves could not live.

We depend upon them for our daily food. For instance, for our vegetables—for cabbages and cauliflowers and potatoes; and for far more than these. And they are such good faithful little servants. They do not fail us. We shall hear more about this later.

Our World is made up of many lesser worlds, which interlace and yet are separate. The World of Mankind; the World of Animals; these we know. And also the World of Plant-life; the World of Green Things; the vast Vegetable Kingdom.

We cannot rightly speak of the whole Vegetable Kingdom as a world of green things, because it contains many growths which are not green; such as brown and red seaweeds; and yellow and grey fungi; and countless invisible specks of life. But in this book we have to do chiefly with green and flowering plants,

THINGS GREEN AND FAIR

"There was once a nest in a hollow;
Down in the mosses and knot-grass pressed,
Soft and warm and full to the brim—
Vetches leaned over it, purple and dim,
With Buttercup-buds to follow." [1]

II—PLANTS AND ANIMALS

What is the real difference between Plants and Animals? That question comes first.

Why, of course—they are so very unlike. Animals can feel and suffer; animals can love and hate; animals can understand when they are spoken to; animals can—well, not exactly talk, but they can make us understand by signs and looks and sounds what they want. Sometimes we say of an especial pet, "That dear dog knows every word that is said to him."

But this is true only of a few among the highest and most sensible of animals. What we have now to think about is—*all* animals of every kind, from the highest to the lowest, as compared with *all* plants of every kind, from the highest to the lowest.

Your little dog may be clever and affectionate, and horses and elephants have extraordinary sense. But will an oyster understand if you speak to it? Can you win the love of a beetle? Is a cheese-mite intelligent? Could a worm do your bidding?

When we speak of a dog's powers, we are looking at the difference between higher and lower animals. What we have now to see is—the difference between *any* kind of animal and *any* kind of plant.

We can grasp in a moment the distinction between an Oak-tree and a horse; or between a Wellingtonia

[1] Jean Ingelow.

278

and an elephant. No one ever muddles up the one with the other. A man never stands gazing, and shaking a puzzled head, and saying: " Well, on the whole, I *think* the cow is an animal, and not a vegetable. I really believe that the Elm must be a plant, and not an animal."

But when we get very low down in the two Kingdoms, matters are by no means so easy.

When in the Animal Kingdom we leave behind us elephants and horses, cows and dogs, four-legged beasts of all sorts, birds, reptiles, fishes and insects. And when in the Vegetable Kingdom we leave behind us Oaks and Elms, Flowering Plants of all kinds, and Ferns and Mosses. And when we get right down to a wide borderland, just between the two Kingdoms, where the very lowest and smallest of animals and of plants are found—then perplexities begin.

For it is there that the line has to be drawn, dividing the Animal Kingdom from the Vegetable Kingdom. And that is just what is so hard to do. It becomes most difficult to say which of the minute creatures there is an animal, and which is a vegetable. Many mistakes have been made in the past.

Some tiny creatures, long believed to be animals, have turned out to be really very minute plants. And other tiny specks, long believed to be plants, have turned out to be really very minute animals.

You may think it odd that this puzzle should exist; since, after all, we are sure of one thing. Plants remain in one place, firmly rooted to the ground; while animals are not rooted, but move freely about. So that there is always one clear indication, by which to know them.

Yes; if only the rule held good throughout. Strange to say, it does not.

In that hazy borderland, between the two Kingdoms, the test breaks down. Animals and plants, living there, are very tiny, very simple in make, very much alike, and very puzzling. Some of these minute animals will fix themselves in one spot, and stay there, and behave for all the world like plants. And some of these minute plants will actually swim about in search of food, going from one place to another, and behaving for all the world like animals.

So it is not surprising that learned men should have made a few mistakes, in trying to settle which was which; or that certain learned men do not believe that any clear line at all can be drawn between the two.

III—The Parts of a Plant

We will go now for a little stroll around the garden, and find out what there is to be seen. If you cannot go into a real garden, you must picture one in your mind.

The first thing to be noticed is this—that plants, in growing, follow a regular plan.

They do not come up anyhow, in a chance fashion, so that nobody can tell what to expect. Unlike as one plant is from another, still they are more or less *built* after one general scheme.

Certain *parts* are found in the greater number. And if one asks, " Which parts are those that go to make up a full plant? " the answer will perhaps be, " Oh, that is easy enough. There are roots and stems, branches and leaves, flowers and fruits and seeds, and heaps more."

But we do not want to hear about "heaps." We want to have all the different parts of a plant brought under the smallest number of heads; under four heads. The four chief parts of a plant are—

THE ROOT;
THE STEM;
THE LEAVES;
THE FLOWERS.

And under these four headings the whole plant is embraced.

First, as to the *Root*. This is not commonly pretty, though most useful and necessary. It burrows into the earth, branching out generally in divers directions. It does the work of an anchor, holding the plant firmly in its place, and keeping it from being blown away by gusts of wind. It drinks in water from the soil, to support the life of the plant, and to keep it in good health. Water and food, I might say. But all food taken by a plant has to be liquid, or else in the form of gas. Plants in general cannot, like men, eat anything solid.

Then secondly, the *Stem*. In smaller plants it is usually green. It acts as a backbone to the whole; or rather as a body, like the body of a man. It is the pathway by which all the water and liquid food, taken in by the roots, travel upward and pass into the branches, and thence into the leaves. In most cases the main stem sends out branches or lesser stems to right and left.

Thirdly, the *Leaves*. These are all-important. If you were to do away with the leaves, you would soon put an end to the life of the plant. Just as the roots drink in water and food from the soil, so the leaves drink in food from the air.

But they do not only drink it in. They also work up and alter that which they have received, together with that which the roots have sucked up; and they make it fit for food. Food, first, for the plant itself; and then food for animals and men. Leaves are the most wonderful little *workshops*, doing what nothing and nobody else in the wide world is able to do. Without the help of leaves, no plants could live or grow : and so no human beings could live or grow either.

Fourthly and lastly—the *Flowers*. These, too, are little workshops, different in kind. They are the seed-growers.

You no doubt look upon flowers as by far the most important part of a plant, because of their beauty. But they have this other use, and a very weighty use. One chief work of a plant must always be to bring, forth fruits and seeds, from which new plants may grow.

If no fruits, no seeds, were brought into being, it would soon mean an end of most of the vegetable-life on earth. In time we should have no more herbage, no more trees, no more grasses, no more corn or grain of any kind. All the old plants would die; and no new ones would come to take their place. The world would change into a vast rocky and sandy and pebbly desert, where neither animals nor men could live.

Yet, while this is the special work of flowers, and perhaps their most important work, we need not suppose

c

it to be the only object of their existence. If it were, we might well wonder why they should be so lovely as they are, when little plain green blossoms could produce seeds just as well as beautiful and gorgeous ones. Many large trees have plain green flowers; and they carry on their task of seed-manufacturing most successfully.

True, a definite reason is known for the bright colours of flowers, as we shall find later. They are believed to act as a lure to insects, thus inducing them to do what is a very important piece of work in connection with the growth of plants.

But this does not cover the whole question. May we not confidently believe that, when Our Father in Heaven caused all these lovely forms and radiant colours to spring forth, He had a loving thought for us, and that He meant them to be a delight to His children who were to inhabit this Earth?

We know well the words spoken by Our Lord, Who Himself loved flowers, when He told His followers to "Consider the Lilies of the field, how they grow," adding that "Even Solomon in all his glory was not arrayed like one of these."

What an utterly different world ours would be, if no blue and crimson, no golden or pure white blossoms grew anywhere; no Roses, Pinks, Primroses; nothing but small insignificant seed-makers. We can hardly picture to ourselves such conditions.

Perhaps nothing speaks to us more plainly of the *kindness* of Our Father than the care He has taken to provide us with beautiful sights for our enjoyment. Just as nothing tells us more clearly of the love for beauty in the Divine Mind than do the flowers of earth in their endless and exquisite variety. Is not each one an embodied Thought of God?

> " A thing of beauty is a joy for ever;
> Its loveliness increases; it will never
> Pass into nothingness; but still will keep
> A bower quiet for us, and a sleep
> Full of sweet dreams, and health, and quiet breathing.
> Therefore on every morrow are we wreathing
> A flowery band to bind us to the Earth,
> Spite of despondence. . .
>   Yes, in spite of all,
> Some shape of beauty moves away the pall
> From our dark spirits. Such the Sun, the Moon,
> Trees old and young, sprouting a shady boon
> For simple sheep; and such are daffodils
> With the green world they live in; and clear rills
> That for themselves a cooling covert make
> 'Gainst the hot season; the mid-forest brake,
> Rich with a sprinkling of fair musk-rose blooms." [1]

IV—The Parts of a Flower

Suppose we find our way to a Wild Rose—to that one which grew on the hedge in the garden which we visited in the first chapter of this book.

Those were spring days, and now it is summer. Or, if not, let us imagine that it is. We shall find that, instead of one bud only just opening, the tree carries a mass of delicate white pink-edged blossoms.

We will pluck one of them, and look at it carefully. What you have to think about is—not the Parts of a Plant, but the Parts of a Flower.

Notice first the small stalk on which it grows—an off-shoot from the main stalk or stem, coming up straight from the root. Then see where the flower meets its

---

[1] Keats.

stalk; and you will discover what look like five small pointed leaves, green in colour, joined at the bottom into one. This is the CALYX, and the pointed leaflets are SEPALS.

Sometimes a calyx is all in one; sometimes the sepals are all separate; sometimes, as here, they seem to be half joined into one and half separate. It is this green part which covered up the bud safely before it began to open, and kept it warm and sheltered. The sepals really are *leaves*, though rather unlike the regular leaves of the Rose.

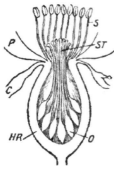

DIAGRAM OF ROSE FLOWER.

Within the green calyx we come to another circle of leaf-shaped things; not green, but white, with rosy tips; the prettiest part of the flower—its PETALS. These, too, were folded protectingly over the inner part of the bud, before it opened; being themselves protected by the sepals.

In the Wild Rose there are usually five petals. All the petals of a flower, taken together, are known as the COROLLA, or crown; and they, like the sepals, may be either joined into one, or half separate, or quite separate. They are, indeed, the crown of the flower, both in position and in beauty.

And the petals also of a flower are *leaves ;* different in shape, different in colour, from the regular leaves and from the sepals, yet neither more nor less than leaves.

They are what we call *modified leaves ;* that is altered

leaves, changed leaves; altered in shape, changed in colour; but the same in actual origin.

Within the corolla we find a number of little dainty things, standing upright, slender, and with golden tips; golden, because of a fine yellow dust on them, which often comes off when touched. They are named STAMENS; and the stamens again, though you would not think it, are *leaves ;* different once more in form and in tint, yet still leaves.

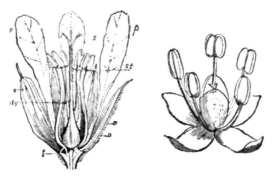

SECTION OF THE FLOWER OF HERB-ROBERT, A SPECIES OF GERANIUM : *c c*, calyx; *p p*, petals; *st*, andrœcium or stamens; *o*, gynœcium or pistil, composed of ovary *o*, style *sty*, and stigmas *s*; *t*, thalamus. FLOWER OF GOOSEFOOT.

The golden dust is called POLLEN; and no other kind of leaves, except stamens, has power to bring into being this wonderful yellow pollen.

Within the stamens, and surrounded by them as by a little bodyguard, are the tops of the PISTILS. Some flowers have one pistil; some have two or three; some have many. The Rose has several. And the pistil, like the sepal, the petal, and the stamen, is just a modified or altered *leaf*.

THE GARDEN OF EARTH

The pistils and the stamens together carry out the great task of SEED-GROWING. Stamens cannot do this alone. Pistils cannot do it alone. They have to work in company.

Perhaps you may find it hard to believe that those lovely pink and white petals, and those little soft yellow-tipped stamens, are not only one in nature with the green leaves, but also are one with each other.

This can be made more plain. The Wild Rose which

LEAF OF ROSE WITH STIPULES: *s*, apex of the sheath.

we have examined is what we call "single." But now let us get two more Roses; not wild ones this time, but a half-double Rose, and another that is fully-double.

What do we mean by "single" and "double"?

Let us compare the three. The wild one has a single row of five petals, and a large array of stamens. The half-double one has a great many more petals, and not nearly so many stamens. The fully-double one has very many more petals still—it seems quite made up of petals—and *no* stamens. They have entirely vanished.

Where can they have gone? And how is it that so many more petals have appeared? Simply this—that the stamens have *turned into petals*. Curious, is it not? Both being in their nature *leaves*, they can be made by careful cultivation to change from the one form of leaf into the other. Stamen-leaves can become petal-leaves; and petal-leaves can change again into stamen-leaves.

287

This does not mean that a single Rose-blossom can be so altered. It means that the *plant* which bears the one kind may be gradually made to bear the other kind. Any particular sort of Rose-tree can be so tended as to bring forth Roses more and more double year by year.

It is the gardener's care which causes such a remarkable transformation of stamens into petals. And if for a long while a Rose-tree bearing double Roses is neglected, and no further care is taken, then very often the Roses will become smaller and less double, with fewer petals and more stamens, each year. The plant has thus begun to *revert*, as it is called, to the old form.

Pistils also can undergo this change from their natural state into petals.

> " In misty blue the lark is heard
> Above the silent homes of men ;
> The bright-eyed thrush, the little wren,
> The yellow-billed sweet-voiced blackbird,
> Mid sallow blossoms blond as curd
> Or silver oak-boughs, carolling
> With happy throat from tree to tree,
> Sing into light this morn of spring
> That sang my dear love home to me.
>
> .   .   .
>
> Airs of the morning breathe about
> Keen faint scents of the wild wood side
> From thickets where primroses hide
> Mid the brown leaves of winter's rout.
> Chestnut and willow, beacon out
> For joy of her, from far and nigh,
> Your English green on English hills ;
> Above her head, song-quivering sky,
> And at her feet, the daffodils." [1]

[1] From *England and Other Poems*, by Laurence Binyon ; published by Elkin Matthews. By permission.

PART III

I—NAMES AND NATURES

WE will think a little now about the immense numbers and varieties of Flowering Plants that are in the world.

Though the great mass of them are made, as we have seen, after one general plan—with Roots, Stems, Leaves, Flowers—yet there is every kind of difference between one and another.

Look around in any garden where you may happen to be, and see how many kinds may be discovered almost at a glance; how many different trees, how many different shrubs, how many different smaller plants, what quantities of little weeds. And if it is so in one garden, or in one place, what must it not be in the Earth as a whole?

We may, indeed, picture our Earth as a vast Garden, with rich beds and borders of flowers, with woods and forests, and with dry and sandy parts where few things can grow.

You might come across a man who has given his entire life to the study of plants; and you would find that he feels he has only begun to understand a very little of their extraordinary numbers and kinds, their ways of growing, their behaviour, their history. The

289

more a man knows of Nature, so much the more he has learnt what an immense amount lies still beyond his power to understand.

And the true understanding of plants means a great deal more than just being able to give their names, either in English or in Latin.

It is useful to know their names, and still farther to be able to say to which Divisions or Families in botany each one belongs. But that is a small part of the question. Many people who can give names glibly enough know almost nothing of their real nature, their true history. And some others, who are not at all ready with their names, could tell you any amount about the plants themselves, and about their curious wonderful ways.

You know how, in the Animal Kingdom, we find an enormous variety of creatures, ranging from the eagle to the humming-bird, from the elephant to the mouse, from the whale to a speck of floating jelly.

And it is the same in the Vegetable Kingdom. There too, we have all kinds, all sizes. There too, we can range from the vast Wellingtonia and the wide-spreading Banyan, down to invisible vegetable-specks, living their own tiny lives; and from huge flowers, a yard across, down to blossoms so minute that they can only be seen with a magnifying-glass.

Not all plants are equal; not all have the same powers; not all are beautiful. And no two kinds of tree, no two kinds of herb, no two kinds of flower, are alike.

More than this, though one might not think it, no

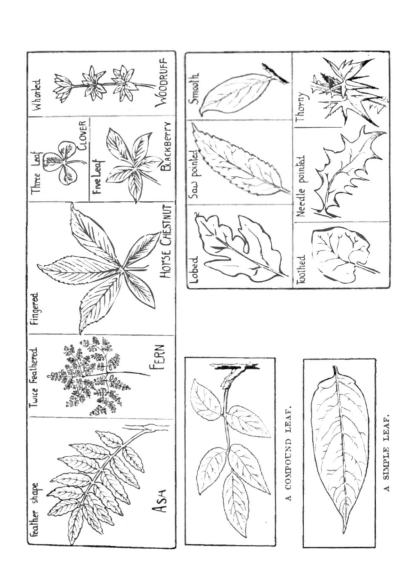

Feather shape | Twice Feathered | Fingered | Three Leaf | Whorled

ASH | FERN | HORSE CHESTNUT | CLOVER | WOODRUFF

Five Leaf | BLACKBERRY

Smooth | Saw pointed | Lobed

Thorny | Needle pointed | Toothed

A COMPOUND LEAF.

A SIMPLE LEAF.

two flowers on one plant, no two leaves on one tree, no two blades of grass in one field, are absolutely the same.

Here, again, is something which anybody may prove for himself. Next time we go for a walk, or out into a garden, we might try to find two Oak-leaves, or two Elm-leaves, or two Rose-leaves, or two Grass-blades, which are precisely the same; the same in size, in shape, in markings, without the very smallest difference.

It will not be an easy task. And when we think we have succeeded, we must put the question to the test by looking at both through a magnifying-glass, or under a microscope. If then we can still detect not the tiniest difference, we shall have done something to be proud of. But I hardly think we shall succeed.

All the leaves of an Elm will be alike; very much alike; just as the brothers and sisters in one family are sometimes very much alike. Yet generally each leaf will be slightly unlike all the other leaves, just as each child in a family is different from all the rest.

II—Such Numbers!

We have been thinking so far mainly of the higher kinds; those known as Flowering Plants; and we shall go on thinking mainly about them.

But before making any farther advance, it is as well to picture to ourselves, in some small degree, what is really meant by the whole Vegetable Kingdom; the vast World of Plant-life.

To do this we have to begin very low down, and to go steadily upward. We have to make a start far below the level of Flowering Plants. It will be like climbing a long ladder. Only, instead of a ladder standing by itself, we must picture in our minds a ladder surrounded on all sides by enormous numbers of vegetable growths. As we mount, step by step, we shall see one kind following another; beginning with the smaller and simpler sorts, and going on with those that are larger, less simple in make, more complex and finished.

At the very bottom we find ourselves in the midst of swarms upon swarms of those tiny vegetable-specks, spoken of earlier; specks so minute as to be invisible except under a microscope. Among them a great number of varieties are known; but in them all we find no trace of root or stem, of leaf or flower. In very many cases each one is a mere tiny cell of living jelly; and when they increase in numbers, it is done by the cell dividing into two—the halves going off in different directions as a couple of plantlets.

A whole book might be written about these specks of vegetable life alone; their number · is so great. Only two or three kinds can be named here.

Sometimes on snow-clad mountains a curious sight is seen in the shape of a patch of *red* snow. That snow is not in itself red; for the colour is lent to it by multitudes of minute plantlets; millions and millions of them mixed with the snow; each one far too small to be seen by the naked eye. And even their red tint is borrowed from something else that is present; it is not actually their own.

You may have heard of the famous little Diatom-plants—exceedingly small, but important because of their multitudinous numbers. Mere specks of life, they are so tiny that if a hundred of them were sprinkled on a piece of clear glass, and you were to hold up that glass against the light, you would see nothing. Yet the Diatoms would be there.

Real living water-plants are they; each one enclosed in a minute case or box, made of a flint-like substance, in two halves which exactly fit one another like a box and lid. The outside is decorated in all sorts of patterns; one kind having one pattern, and another kind another pattern. About two thousand different species are known; each particular species being marked with its own special design, unlike all the rest. The beauty and finish of these ornamental markings are marvellous.[1]

For thousands of years nobody knew anything about the Diatoms and their wonderful little boxes. It was not till men had learnt how to make microscopes that the Diatom-cases could be seen at all.

Somehow these living specks travel about; and probably it is by means of very fine lashes—called *cilia*—put out through little holes, and used like oars for rowing themselves along.

A step or two higher up the ladder brings us to the small and dainty Volvox plant, which may be found in many an English pond. It is greenish in colour, and globe-like in shape; and it too moves about like an animal, rowing itself along by means of little arms or *cilia*. It really is not one plant only, but a whole colony of plantlets, all pressed together and joined into one, and surrounded by a kind of envelope.

[1] For illustrations of these Diatom-cases see *The Romance of the Mighty Deep*, by the same author: opposite pages 154, 156.

THE GARDEN OF EARTH

III—A Ladder of Life

Now as we climb we have to leave behind us these lowest and simplest forms of Vegetable life. Passing up two or three more rungs, we find ourselves soon among the company of Lichens.

Many a time, when looking at some old cottage or barn, we have noticed on the roof a curious yellow

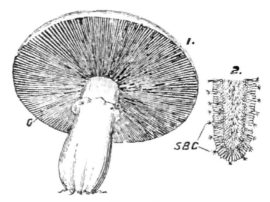

1. MUSHROOM, SHOWING "GILLS."
2. GILL PLATE IN SECTION, showing spore-bearing cells SBC.

colouring. Also on some aged wall we have seen a number of different tints, brown or grey or reddish, looking like stains. All these were due to Lichen-plants, and were actual vegetable-growths, flourishing where no other kinds could find sustenance.

Sometimes in a wood we light upon a piece of grey Lichen, looking much like a dried seaweed, and seeming as if it were dead. But it is not a seaweed, and it is not dead.

As we continue to mount the ladder, rung by rung,

we pass innumerable Fungus-growths—Mildew and Blight, Toadstools and Mushrooms—some of which are poisonous, and some have unpleasant smells. But all are in their nature vegetable.

Nor must we omit to note, in passing, the vast array of Seaweeds; real plants these also. Most of us know well the pretty little branching red ones; and the wide brown ribbons; and the slimy green kinds; but enormous numbers besides are found in other parts of the world.

All these — Lichens, Fungi, Seaweeds—belong to the great Lower Division of Flowerless Plants.

So also do the Mosses, farther up; and the huge brotherhood of Ferns, higher up still.

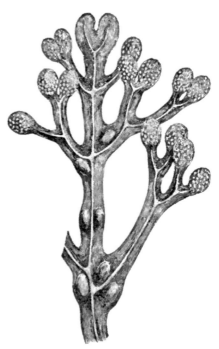

FROND OF COMMON SEAWEED
(*Fucus Vesiculosus.*)

But when we get to the Mosses and Ferns, we see that we have made a very important advance. They come much closer to the Higher Division; for they have roots and stems and something very like leaves. Practically, the fronds take the place of leaves, and also they take the place of flowers.

THE GARDEN OF EARTH

At certain times of the year we may see on the back

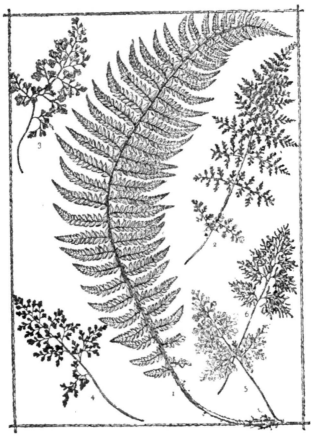

1. HARD PRICKLY SHIELD FERN (*Polystichum aculeatum*) (Upper Side).
2. ALPINE BLADDER FERN (*Cystopteris regia*) (Under Side). 3. ANNUAL
MAIDENHAIR (*Gymnogramma leptophylla*) (Upper Side). 4. ANNUAL
MAIDENHAIR (*Gymnogramma leptophylla*) (Under Side). 5. PARSLEY
FERN (*Allosorus crispus*) (Barren Frond). 6. PARSLEY FERN (*Allosorus
crispus* (Fertile Frond).

of a fern-frond curious raised brown markings, arranged
in rows. This is known as the " fructification " of a

fern. In other words, it is the " spore-growing " part of the plant; and, like a flower producing seeds, it produces " spores."

LEAVES OR FRONDS OF MOUNTAIN FERN.   LEAF OF OAK.

These spores are very tiny, and are much more simple in make than seeds; but they serve the same purpose. Their task is the same. They have to provide, not only

D

new ferns, but also new mosses, new fungi, new lichens, to take the place of the old when the old die. Thus the Earth is kept supplied with fresh generations of these various growths.

And now, as we still mount our ladder, we find a marked change, and we come to a new Division.

All the plants which we have so far noticed in our upward progress belong to the vast Lower Division of FLOWERLESS PLANTS. But at last we have reached the great Upper Division of FLOWERING PLANTS.

At the very beginning of this Division we come across the large Grass Family, sometimes called the Grass Order. There are many such big Families or Orders or Tribes; and they include often such enormous numbers of distant cousins, that really they are more like Scotch " Clans " than Families.

Here we see the plan followed of a regular structure, built up out of Roots, Stems, Leaves and Flowers. Not always pretty flowers, or brightly coloured, but still flowers of some description, producing seeds.

All the Grasses belong to this Family; little low ones and tall rank ones. The highest kinds in Britain seldom rise above a man's waist; but in tropical countries they are often over his head. Wheat and Barley, Oats and Rye, Rice and Indian Corn and the Sugar Cane, are included in the same clan.

Presently we find ourselves in the midst of hordes of Flowering Plants, such as grow in meadows and hedgerows, on hills and downs, in valleys and by rivers, in gardens and parks; wild flowers and cultivated flowers; plants that we all know, and plants which none of us

WELLINGTONIA.

have ever seen; thousands and thousands of them; some beautiful; some curious; some sweet-smelling; some interesting. But, indeed, we may say that in one way or another all are interesting; and that very few are without some touch of beauty.

And the Trees; first the Pines and the Firs—cone-bearing—and the multitude of Palms. And then the immense varieties of Forest trees; not perhaps most of them really higher on the Ladder of Life than many flowering plants of a smaller growth. Yet they are so tall and stately that we might wrongly place them at the top. Can anything be more beautiful or more grand than an ancient Oak; or a great Beech, sweeping its branches to the ground; or a splendid Cedar of Lebanon; or a gigantic Wellingtonia with a trunk so huge that a dozen people might sit down to dinner within its bark; or a vast Indian Banyan-tree, with its numberless root-trunks?

Think of the extraordinary difference between one of these and a rolling invisible speck of jelly in a pond. Yet both are alive; both grow; both belong to the same Vegetable Kingdom.

> " Large streams from little fountains flow,
>   Tall Oaks from little acorns grow." [1]

> " I know a bank where the Wild Thyme blows,
>   Where Oxlips and the nodding Violet grows;
>   Quite over-canopied with luscious Woodbine,
>   With sweet Musk-roses, and with Eglantine." [2]

[1] David Everett.
[2] *Midsummer Night's Dream.*

A WIDE WORLD OF PLANT-LIFE

IV—Some Curious Differences

We have learnt now a little about two great Divisions in the world of Plant-life. Certain Subdivisions must also be mentioned.

With the very first beginnings of growth from a Seed sown in the ground or in a pot, we may notice that two humble small green leaflets creep quietly up above the soil. They are the *Cotyledons* or *Seed-leaves*; so-called because they are the first to spring from the seed. Each day they get a little taller; and soon other leaves grow up from between the two. In time the first pair, having done their share of work, fade quietly away; and the later leaves are often unlike them in shape.

Great numbers of plants begin life thus, with the two leaves. In some cases, however, as with the Oak and other Forest trees, we do not *see* them, for they remain underground, and the leaves which first appear are not true " Seed-leaves." Still, the fact is the same that most of our trees, such as the Oak, the Beech, the Elm, the Birch, the Sycamore, actually do begin their careers with a pair of such leaves. And thousands of lesser plants do the same.

A very unimportant matter, you may perhaps think. What does it matter?

Well, in one sense, perhaps not much. But a good deal that is interesting goes with it.

Sometimes, in place of those two leaves a plant begins life with only one Seed-leaf; and that makes a considerable difference; or rather, a considerable difference goes with that arrangement. Plants which spring from bulbs may be said to have only one Seed-leaf. The

THE GARDEN OF EARTH

Lily-of-the-Valley and the Narcissus grow thus; as also do Rushes and Grasses and Orchids.

If this distinction of either One or Two Seed-leaves stood alone, it might be of interest, though we could hardly count it to be worthy of much attention. But the number of Seed-leaves is not the only sign which marks off one big Subdivision of Flowering Plants from another.

It is a curious fact that most of the One Seed-leaf plants seem to grow—or, as one may say, to be built up—in *threes*. Their flowers, for instance, have usually three sepals and three petals, or else twice or three times three; that is, six or nine of each.

But the Two Seed-leaf plants are hardly ever thus. They are commonly found to be in fours and fives— or in twice four or five, as the case may be.[1]

Any of us may put this to the test. We may count the sepals and petals of a Lily and a Narcissus, and then those of a Buttercup and a Primrose. And usually these rules will be found true—that the Threes go with the single Seed-leaf, and the Fours or Fives with the double Seed-leaf. Once in a way a flower seems to have made a mistake, and to have its numbers wrong; but this is rare; and we have to examine several of a kind, noting what the greater number are like.

[1] These lesser Divisions of Flowering Plants are known as Mono-cotyledons and Di-cotyledons; by which is meant Plants with One Seed-leaf, and Plants with Two Seed-leaves. There are also Plants which have several, called Poly-cotyledons, and Plants which have none, called A-cotyledons. "Mono" means One; "Di" means Two; "Poly" means Many; and "A" means "No." But we need not trouble our heads with the two last.

A third distinction helps to mark these Subdivisions as apart each from the other.

With a Two-Cotyledon plant, if we study the leaf carefully, we shall nearly always find its markings—its ribs and veins—to be *netted*. There may be a main rib running up the middle, and there will be many lesser ribs or veins branching off sideways towards the edges. When we try to tear this leaf, it will not tear straight, but only in a jagged way along the branching side-ribs. This can be seen with an Oak-leaf or a leaf from a Rose-tree.

But if we get a Lily-of-the-Valley leaf we shall at once find that it is not netted or branched. A number of long lines run all the way from the stalk to the leaf-tip. And if we try to tear it, we shall see that it tears smoothly down its full length. It is the same with other Mono-cotyledon plants.

And yet again a fourth difference exists between these two big Subdivisions.

If an Oak or an Elm is cut down, and we look at the cut end, we may notice many lines running round, circle within circle. These lines show the age of the tree. Each year a fresh growth or layer takes place, between the outer wood and the bark; and so the trunk gets steadily larger year by year. That is the way in which Di-cotyledon plants grow (see page 74).

But the Mono-cotyledon plants increase in quite another fashion.

They do not grow by added outer layers. The wood of a Palm-tree, for instance, when cut down shows no circles. It does not increase by layer added to layer.

THE GARDEN OF EARTH

Its wood grows in bundles of fibre, scattered through the trunk. Palms have slender smooth trunks, not rugged and massive like so many of our forest-trees.[1]

But if somebody asks *why* straight-veined leaves, stamens in threes or sixes, and inward-growing stems, should belong to the single Seed-leaf—and *why* branching-veined leaves, stamens in fours or fives, and outward-growing stems, should belong to the two Seed-leaves—no answer is possible. No sufficient reason has been found. We can only say that we do not know.

We do know, however, that whether they begin life with one cotyledon or with two cotyledons, it makes no difference as to the sweetness of the flowers, the beauty of the trees, or our enjoyment of them.

> "Between the erect and solemn trees
> I will go down upon my knees;
> I shall not find, this day
> So meet a place to pray.

> " Haply the beauty of this place
> May work in me an answering grace,
> The stillness of the air
> Be echoed in my prayer.

> " The worshipping trees arise and run,
> With never a swerve, towards the sun;
> So may my soul's desire
> Turn to its central fire.

> " With single aim they seek the light,
> And scarce a twig in all their height
> Breaks out, until the head
> In glory is outspread.

[1] These Divisions are often spoken of also as EXOGENS or outward-growing and ENDOGENS or inward-growing plants.

A WIDE WORLD OF PLANT-LIFE

" How strong each pillared trunk; the bark
That covers them, how smooth; and hark,
    The sweet and gentle voice
    With which the leaves rejoice !

" May a like strength and sweetness fill
Desire, and thought, and steadfast will,
    When I remember these
    Fair sacramental trees."

J. D. C. PELLOW.[1]

---

[1] From *Georgian Poetry*, 1918–1919, published by " The Poetry Bookshelf." By permission.

PART IV

I—Put into Classes

In a small book of this kind it will not be needful to say very much about the way in which Plants have been sorted or classified by botanists. Still a few clear ideas on the subject, before going on to the make and the ways and the habits of plants, are desirable.

Plant-lovers recognised that certain groups more or less closely resembled one another; and it became convenient to have names for such groups, so that the nature of any particular one might be quickly conveyed to gardeners or botanists. If these groups could be arranged in some definite order, it would then be fairly easy for a gardener to make a methodical list of his stock, and for another to find any given plant in that list. He would look for it under the name of the group to which he knew it belonged. The question was—How to carry out such an arrangement?

Suppose we wished to classify Mankind into divisions. We might make one class of tall men, another of short men. Or one class of stout men, and another of thin men. Or we might sort them by the colour of their hair; those with black hair, those with brown, those with red, those with yellow.

307

FAMILY RELATIONSHIPS

This would not be a good mode, because in other respects the men in one class would often be so utterly unlike. A far more sensible plan would be to sort them by their *descent;* by Race and Relationship. Many points of real resemblance—of inherited likeness—would then be found in large numbers of men, belonging to one family or to one race.

Several different methods were tried for plants, without much success. Then a learned Swede, named Linnæus, took the matter up.

His scheme [1] was a very simple one. He placed all the Flowering kinds in Classes by means of their stamens and their pistils. First came ten classes : of plants with one stamen only in each flower, plants with two stamens, plants with three stamens, and so on up to ten stamens. Then a class with many stamens; and then some classes with stamens growing in particular ways. All these were again divided into lesser classes by means of their various kinds of pistils.

People were delighted with the plan; it was so easy to grasp; and it was taken up far and wide.

But in time botanists grew dissatisfied. The scheme was not good enough. It was too much like classifying men by their height and size, or by the colour of their hair. Such utterly diverse kinds came into one class, only because they happened to have the same number of stamens, when perhaps hardly another point of resemblance could be found in them.

Gradually that simple system fell out of general use, and another took its place.

This other is known as the Natural System; and in

[1] Known as "The Linnæan System."

it plants are arranged according to what seem to be their actual relationships. They *appear* to be related, because of their marked likeness one to another, not in one respect only, such as the number of their stamens, but in many respects; such as the way in which they grow, the forms of their leaves, the manner in which they produce seeds, and so on.

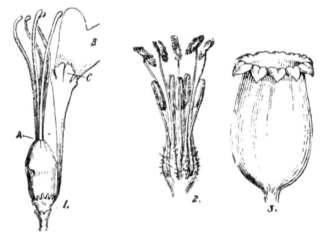

DETAILS OF RED CAMPION.

1. Pistil and Styles. *B.* a petal to show attachment and Corona *C.*
2. Stamens. The anthers of the long ones have opened to shed the pollen.
3. Capsule.

By " relationship " we commonly mean descent from the same more or less recent ancestors. This we know to be true with men. And though we cannot absolutely declare that it is true with groups of plants, there is every reason to believe that it may be the real explanation.

It seems to be with them as with ourselves. Some

people are very nearly related, such as brothers and sisters. Others, such as first-cousins, are not so near; and others, such as second and third cousins, are more distantly of kin. Many more, again, are united only by the tie of belonging to the same race, the same country; while countless numbers can only be called connected because they all belong to the great Family of Mankind in general.

We have already heard something of the first main division of all plants into two very large classes—Flowerless Plants and Flowering Plants. Our business now is with Flowering Plants only; and chiefly with those which begin life with either one or two little Seed-leaves. These are separated into lesser classes, under various titles, as follows—

All Flowering Plants are divided into NATURAL ORDERS, sometimes called FAMILIES.

Each of these Natural Orders or Families is divided into groups called *Genera*. One such group is called a *Genus*.

Each Genus is divided, again, into different *Species*. This word is the same in the singular and in the plural. We speak of *a* species and of *many* species.

Lastly, each species may be divided into many *Varieties ;* more or less alike, yet with differences.

The word " Tribes " is sometimes used as a title for a lesser division or class belonging to one of the Natural Orders. And, as stated above, the relationship here spoken of is believed to be a real thing; to come from actual descent. Plants which we look upon as near of kin are, in all probability, descended from one common ancestor.

II—Roses and their Relatives

"Loveliest of lovely things are they
On earth that soonest pass away.
The Rose that lives its little hour
Is prized beyond the sculptured flower." [1]

We have noticed earlier the make of a Wild Rose. It was white, with pink tips; and it had five green sepals, partly joined into one, and five tinted petals; and many delicate gold-tipped stamens.

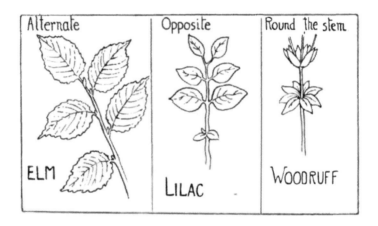

We might have seen that the leaves of the plant grow *alternately*; not in pairs, just opposite, but first one on one side, then another higher up on the other side. Also we might have noted the tiny leaflets, called Stipules, growing at the bottom of each leaf-stalk.

Now we will look at a very near relative of the Rose; a first-cousin. This is the Strawberry Plant. If we examine the flower, we shall find not indeed only five,

[1] W. C. Bryant.

but twice-five sepals and five white petals, and a great many stamens; also stipules, but not alternate leaves.

Another near relative we might find, if it is the right time of the year, in the hedge-rows. Its name is Potentilla or Cinquefoils; and it has a pretty little pale yellow flower, with again ten sepals and five petals and many stamens. One kind has soft white undersides to its leaves.

These all belong to a great Order or Family, named ROSACEÆ; and that Order is divided into three Sub-families: the Rose Sub-family; the Pear Sub-family; and the Almond Sub-family. Sometimes the whole large Order is spoken of as the ROSE FAMILY. But while each of the Sub-families really is rather like a very big Family of innumerable cousins, the whole Order is more like a huge Tribe or Scotch Clan.

And think what a useful Tribe this is to us. What should we do without the Strawberries, the Raspberries, the Blackberries, the Cherries, the Apples, the Pears, the Almonds, the Plums, the Peaches, and many other fruits, which its different members manufacture for our use?

Or, again, what should we do without the multitudes of lovely Roses, and of numberless other beautiful flowers, belonging to it?

We have already seen some of the general signs by which we may recognise many members of this very fascinating clan. One other characteristic must be mentioned: that, with hardly an exception, its members do *not* manufacture anything hurtful or poisonous to man.

The question of their seeds is interesting, because from them come many of our favourite fruits. And though they are so nearly related, they differ oddly in the manner in which those fruits grow and ripen.

For instance, with the Strawberry flower. Within its clustering stamens are several pistils, each of which

FRAGARIA VESCA (*Wood Strawberry*).

has its own stigma, its own style, its own ovary, the last-named holding one tiny beginning of a seed.

As time goes on, the petals having done their work fade and drop off, and the sepals close in around the young fruit. This fruit really is the *receptacle* of the flower; a sort of tiny cushion, from which the pistils grew. It begins to swell, and gets gradually larger and larger. Later on it also gets rosier and rosier.

Meanwhile, those parts of the pistil which contain each one its little seed get harder, but not bigger. And as the berry increases in size they slowly separate, going farther and farther apart, till at last they are scattered all over the crimson surface, as you will see in any ripe strawberry. Those small, yellow, seed-like things are really dried-up pistil-remains, each having its own seed inside.

The Raspberry follows quite another plan. Here we find not ten, but five sepals, and also five petals. And here again—as with many flowering plants—there is the receptacle from which the pistils grow. But in this case it is not the receptacle which swells into a luscious fruit.

If you look closely at a ripe Raspberry you will see, rising from its rather lumpy surface, a number of tiny threads. They are the remains of the pistil-styles; and so the ripe parts of the Raspberry are actually the *pistils*, which have changed into this soft state, pressed closely together. And the hard part within, from which you pull the ripe berry, is the dried-up remains of the receptacle, which has given up all its juices to feed the growing fruit.

With Apples and Pears we have again a different structure. In their flowers also are found the five calyx-divisions, and the five petals, and the many stamens. When an apple is fully ripe, you see at the end farthest from the stalk a dried-up something, which is just the remainder of part of the sepals. But *part* of those same sepals has united with the pistil, to grow into a beautiful and refreshing fruit, in the

E

middle of which—if you cut it open carefully—you may find five divisions, and one or two seeds hidden snugly in each.

Then, again, there is the mode followed by stone-fruit trees, belonging to this Family : such as Plums and Peaches, Apricots and Cherries.   These also have their five sepals, their five petals, and their many stamens. But with them we find only one pistil, which grows and changes into a soft eatable fruit, containing inside a single seed, shut firmly up within a hard protecting stone.

Countless lesser differences run through the numberless varieties of this great Order, to which we owe so much.   We have gone more fully into the " ways " of the Rose Tribe than will be possible with others.   But it is well to gain a clear notion of what is generally meant by such an Order or Family, and by its Subfamilies and relationships.

It might make us think of the Tribes of North-American Indians, which in olden days used to wander over the country; each separate Tribe being divided into Families, the members of which were closely related, while the whole Tribe was connected, but more distantly.

> " Ye Violets that first appear,
>   By your pure purple mantles known,
> Like the proud virgins of the year,
>   As if the spring were all your own—
>   What are ye when the Rose is blown ? " [1]

> " What does it take to make a Rose,
>   Mother-mine ?
> The God that died to make it knows;
> It takes the world's eternal wars,

[1] Sir Henry Wotton (A.D. 1600).

FAMILY RELATIONSHIPS

It takes the moon and all the stars,
It takes the might of heaven and hell,
And the everlasting love as well,
                    Little child." [1]

III—" BUTTERCUPS AND DAISIES "

Next we have to think about two or three more such Orders or Families in the Kingdom of Plant-life.

Suppose we begin with a Buttercup. If it is spring or early summer, and if a field happens to lie near, we may easily find one. In examining flowers a small magnifying-glass is very helpful, though much can be done without it.

About half-way down the flower-stalk one or two little leaves will be found, not unlike the other leaves, only not so large, and these are called *Bracts*. Many plants have no bracts.

We shall see once more five small green sepals, and five bright yellow petals, and many stamens; and in the centre, growing up from a little cushion-like receptacle, several pistils. In these points a Buttercup is much like the flowers of the Rose Order. But there are differences.

The stamens of the Buttercup—and of many other plants belonging to the same Order—grow from close *below* the ovary, instead of, as with many of the Rose Family, from around or *above* it. This may seem to be a very slight matter, yet with it appears to go a distinction which is far from slight.

The plants belonging to the Rose Tribe manufacture

<hr>

[1] This and other quotations from Mr. Alfred Noyes in this volume are from his *Collected Poems*, published by William Blackwood, and are used by permission.

with hardly an exception only food that is good and wholesome. But plants belonging to the Buttercup Order have, in many cases, fruit that is very unwholesome and even poisonous; and in their stems are sometimes found acrid and burning juices.

We do not in the least know *why* wholesome fruit

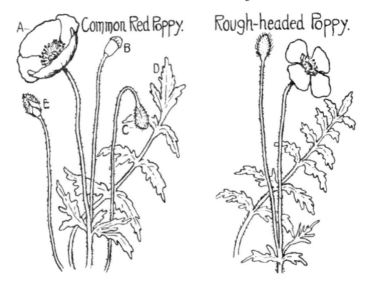

Common Red Poppy.   Rough-headed Poppy.

should go with stamens that spring from above the ovary, and unwholesome fruit with stamens that spring from below the ovary. We only know that so it is. Many travellers with some knowledge of botany, when going through a wild and strange country, have trusted to such tokens as a means of telling safe from unsafe fruit, and have found the plan to answer.

The Buttercup Order, often spoken of as " The Crowfoot Family,"[1] contains many flowers familiar

[1] Order, RANUNCULACEÆ.

to us all, such as the Anemone, the Hepatica, the Larkspur.

In some respects the Poppy Order or Family,[1] comes rather near to it. Many of the plants in this Order also manufacture fruits unwholesome and even hurtful in kind. From the Poppy itself comes that stupefying and deadening Opium, which works such terrible harm in Eastern countries.

A Poppy flower has many stamens, but only two sepals and four petals. Its pistils are joined together, and do not grow separately, as with a Buttercup. Its juice is often milky in character.

Now let us turn to one of our oldest and commonest and dearest little friends, the Daisy, beginning with what a poet of to-day has said about it—

" I know why the Daisy is white, my dear, I know why the skies
        are blue ;
    I know that the world is a dream, my dear, and I know that
        the dream is true ;
    I know why the Rose and the Toadstool grow, as a curse and
        a crimson boon—
    *Hey ! diddle, diddle, the cat and the fiddle, the cow jumped over
        the Moon.*" [2]

With which unexpected ending we will take a Daisy in hand and examine it.

The golden centre is there, which we often call the Daisy's " eye," because with it the flower seems to gaze so cheerfully upward. And around this golden centre—which you might take for a mass of stamens—are pure white rays, or white rays tipped with crimson,

[1] Order, PAPAVERACEÆ.   [2] Alfred Noyes.

standing out in a circle, and you might suppose them to be the petals of a single flower.

But the golden centre is not made of stamens, and the outer rays are not ordinary flower-petals. We talk of the Daisy as " a flower," yet really it is not one flower only. It is a whole bunch or collection of tiny flowers or " florets," as such minute blossoms are called. And only in a sense can we speak of the whole as one flower.

Those tiny, yellow, stamen-like things in the centre

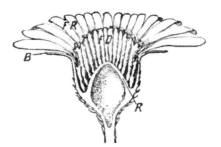

are florets; each having its own corolla and stamens and pistil. And the white rays surrounding are florets also, different in shape, yet each again having its own corolla and stamens and pistil. Altogether there are

SECTION OF FLOWER HEAD OF DAISY.

between two and three hundred of them in a single Daisy.

The florets have no green sepals of their own, however. Instead of this, there are little, green, sepal-like leaves surrounding the entire collection of yellow and white florets. These we might call the " calyx," though the right word for them is *Involucre*—a word something like *envelope*. They really do " envelop " or cover up the young Daisy bud.

A Daisy is a Composite Flower, for it is composed or made up of many florets, all growing together and behaving like a single flower. It belongs to the " Composite Order," [1] sometimes spoken of as the " Sunflower Family."

We all know the big Sunflower, with its soft central cushion of yellow florets, and the large outstanding yellow rays. This is an important member of the Family; and, indeed, a great Sunflower looks as if he had an extremely good opinion of himself.

Then we have Dandelions, and Thistles, and Chrysanthemums, and China Asters, and many more; though it must not be taken for granted that every plant with " composite flowers " belongs to the same Tribe. Other marks beside those already named distinguish its members. But we have not space to go farther into the matter here; though I think we may spare room to quote what our northern poet of past days had to say about a Daisy-plant, which stern duty forced him to demolish.

> " Wee, modest, crimson-tippèd flower,
> Thou's met me in an evil hour;
> For I maun crush amang the stoure
>   Thy slender stem;
> To spare thee now is past my power,
>   Thou bonny gem.
>
>   .   .   .   .
>
> " Cauld blew the bitter biting north
> Upon thy early, humble birth;
> Yet cheerfully thou glinted forth
>   Amid the storm;
> Scarce reared above the parent earth
>   Thy tender form.
>
> " The flaunting flowers our gardens yield,
> High shelt'ring woods and wa's maun shield,
> But thou, beneath the random bield [2]
>   O' clod or stane,
> Adorns the histie [3] stibble-field,
>   Unseen, alane.

---

[1] Order, COMPOSITÆ.   [2] Shelter.   [3] Dry.

THE GARDEN OF EARTH

"There in thy scanty mantle clad,
   Thy snawy bosom sunward spread,
   Thou lifts thy unassuming head
         In humble guise;
   But now the share uptears thy bed,
         And low thou lies!" [1]

Another plant, neither pretty nor sweet but very common, may have a moment's attention, the Wild Parsley. It grows in fields and waste grounds, and a second name for it is "Fools' Parsley." It looks so like real Parsley that children have sometimes eaten and have been made ill by it or even poisoned.

The manner in which this plant grows should be noticed. Several flower-stalks branch outward from one centre, and often lesser stalks branch outward again from these. In each case the stalks, springing from one spot and bearing tiny white flowers at their tips, stand out somewhat in the fashion of an open umbrella held upside down. So the Order to which the Wild Parsley belongs is described as " Umbel-bearing." [2] The flowers are said to " grow in umbels," like an umbrella.

To the same Family belong the Carrot, the Parsnip, and Celery, also Hemlock, which is poisonous. It is curious that Celery which when cultivated we find so good to eat, is unwholesome when in a wild state.

Certain plants, branching out much after the same fashion, such as the Elder-bush and certain Geraniums, do not belong to this Order.

These few examples will be enough to give some little idea of what is meant by Orders and Families,

[1] Robert Burns　　　　　[2] Order, UMBELLIFERÆ.

and also of the way in which plants are grouped in Classes.

But the subject is such an enormous one that it has

CAUCALIS ANTHRISCUS (*Upright Hedge-Parsley*).

to be studied by itself. There are numberless books, large and small, written about the Divisions and Classes.

It is a good plan to hunt out the various flowers

which may be found in one's neighbourhood; and then, with the help of a book about wild flowers, to learn all that one can about them. Not only their names, but the principal marks by which they may be known again, and by which some of their near relatives can be recognised. All this, as one goes on, becomes exceedingly interesting.

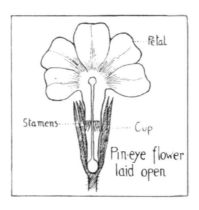

Pin-eye flower laid open

PART V

I—WHAT SOIL IS MADE OF

WE all know from early childhood that plants grow out of the earth, for it is a fact constantly before our eyes. But not everybody thinks seriously about what he sees, and not everybody considers and wonders *how* a plant thus comes; what is in the ground to make it grow; why it should appear; and why, having appeared, it should continue to gain in size and height.

People are so used to these marvels, so used to having small plantlets push their way up through the soil, and bring forth leaves and flowers and fruits, that they take it all as a matter of course and forget to feel any surprise.

Yet it is by no means a matter of course!

Why *should* plants come up? And why *should* they increase in size? And why *should* they bear leaves and flowers, and produce fruits? If we did not know that things are so, we should never have expected such extraordinary happenings. For though they seem to us quite ordinary, they would not be so to one who had never before seen anything of the kind.

What can there be in the soil which does so much?

It does not do all, for air and rain and sunshine all share in the work, but it does a great deal.

You have noticed often the different kinds of soil found in different places. Here it is yellow and sandy; there it is white and chalky. Here it is red; there it is grey. Here it is coarse and stony; there it is fine and

GRAND ST. BERNARD IN WINTER.

soft. And if we go to the top of a high mountain we come upon great spaces of solid rock, with no soil at all worth mentioning.

At the Grand St. Bernard for instance, in Switzerland, where the monks live and go out with their big dogs to hunt for travellers lost in the snow, it is all hard granite rock with no covering of earth. Nobody can dig there, for you cannot dig rock.

325

THE WORK OF ROOTS AND STEMS

Earth's soils are largely made from rocks. The hard rock has first to be split and broken and crumbled, and then gradually mixed with other materials; and at length soil is formed, in which plants can grow.

More powers than one go to this work of soil-making. It is tremendously important work, and it takes a good deal of time.

First King Frost steps in. He splits the rocks, and breaks up the stiff earth-clods, and does no end of good. Where a little water happens to lie in a crack, it presses the sides of the crack as it freezes farther apart, and so begins to demolish the mass. Bitterly cold weather, though unpleasant, is much needed each year for the soil.

Frost acts quickly and strongly; but another power, which is gentle and slow in its methods, does as much if not more in its own way. This is—Rain. One would hardly suppose that small falling raindrops could help to destroy solid rocks; to " decompose " them is the right word, and to " decompose " simply means to " unmake."

That which gives raindrops this power is the presence of certain gases, such as nitric and carbonic acid gases, in the water. If enough of these is present it can eat its way gradually through the hardest rocks. At the same time, such gases unite with other substances found there, to form *salts* which are required for the growth of plants.

When the soil is so far ready that certain of the simpler kinds, such as lichens and mosses, can begin to grow in it, and when spores have been brought by wind or water or animals, then such plants themselves will soon lend help. Their roots creep down quietly into the cracks and force the sides more widely apart, and as they die and decay they become part of the soil, fitting it for use.

Then as the soil goes on improving, and plants of a higher make can thrive there, these also shed their leaves and the leaves decay, and by and by the plants die also. All this enriches the earth more and more.

Soil that is formed only or chiefly of broken and crumbled rock may be spoken of simply as " earth " or " earth-mould," but when a large amount of leaves and dead plants have been added it becomes " vegetable-mould." It is then of far greater value.

Many different kinds of food required by plants— such as potash, soda, magnesia, lime—are found in soils; and each particular kind of plant must have its own especial kinds of food, to keep it in good health. What suits the constitution of one will often not do at all for another.

II—The Work of Worms

A curious fact comes in here about the manner in which earth is changed into good mould. Some way back it was remarked that worms have a certain work of their own to carry out, and very important work too.

Many of us have perhaps looked upon worms as ugly slimy, useless creatures, unpleasant to handle. Well, they may be ugly, and they certainly are slimy. But useless they are not.

It is believed that they have no power of sight, though light does faintly affect part of their bodies; so far as is known, they have no means of hearing;

their sense of smell at best is very feeble; and they do not seem to have any great amount of sense. So we cannot look on them as gifted creatures. Yet they have their task to do, and they do it perseveringly.

A part of it is the dragging of fallen leaves underground. Have you ever remarked how the piles of autumn leaves gradually disappear? They are not *all* swept up and carried away by gardeners. In a garden or a park this may account for a good many, but not in fields and woods. Yet there, too, in time they silently vanish.

And the worms have a hand here. They are believed to swallow a certain amount of the softer parts of leaves; and they draw goodly supplies into the soil for stopping up the holes of their burrows. If you keep a look-out you may sometimes find a twisted leaf sticking out of the ground only half pulled under by a worm.

Besides supplying the soil with dead leaves to serve as manure they take in large quantities of the soil itself as food. And this is all cast out again by them, enriched and improved and fitted for use. It has been said, indeed, that the whole of the soil in a garden or a field passes in time through the bodies of the worms, being thus prepared for its work.

One would never guess what numbers of worms are in the ground; sometimes as many as tens of thousands in one acre, or in one garden or field. Birds are perpetually after them, yet still multitudes remain.

One day I saw a blackbird that had just found a long fat worm. He had, no doubt, four hungry little ones at home, for he proceeded scientifically to cut the worm into four pieces, all the same in length. Then he tried to get the four into his mouth to carry away. The first two were easy enough, and the third was not difficult. But with the fourth he had hard work, for his beak really was too small. Perseverance, however, won its reward, and at length all four were firmly gripped, sticking out on either side like huge moustaches. Then he flew happily away to his family. But what the worm may have thought of the proceeding—if a worm can think !—is another question.

III—Growing Up and Growing Down

A Root taken out of the ground seems a plain, dull, brown thing, not attractive. The leaves of a plant are pretty, and the flowers are often beautiful, and the fruit may be good to eat. But the root—who cares for the ugly root, buried out of sight ? Useful, no doubt, since a plant without a root could not grow. But interesting—no !

Yet roots in their way are just as wonderful, and just as interesting, as any other part.

To give in few words the difference between a Root and a Stem is not quite easy. The stem comes from the root; and the two are so joined together that at a certain spot they are one. Often it is difficult to say exactly where the one ends and the other begins.

Some one may say, " Oh, that is easy ! A root is brown and a stem is green." But many stems of trees are brown, and some roots are green—such as those of certain Orchids which grow in the air, and never go under ground.

It has been said that stems may be known apart

because they send out buds which grow into leaf-bearing shoots, while roots cannot do this. But here again the distinction fails. It is commonly true; yet roots are known, though they are rare, which do produce such buds.

Or again, we may say that a root is under ground and a stem is above ground. Only, as we have just seen, some roots grow in the air. And some plants—especially ferns—have their stems under ground. What you see in a fern is usually *not* the stem with leaves on it, but the leaves alone. And you might easily take the underground stems for roots.

These, however, are exceptions. More frequently we do know a root when we see it; and we seldom make the mistake of supposing a root to be a stem, or a stem to be a root. A botanist knows that the two are quite different in their actual make.

Have you ever thought how singular it is that the roots should always go creeping under the soil, while the stems always rise upward into air and light—with just those few exceptions?

Why should they do so? Why may not the roots sometimes for a change try to come above ground, or the stems once in a while try for a change to go burrowing below ground? We never see this happen, with all the hundreds and thousands of garden-plants and forest-trees known to us. Such a thing is unheard-of. And why?

No explanation can be given except that which has been offered before : that it is their nature so to grow, and that He Who gave them life gave also to each its own particular nature and character.

F

THE GARDEN OF EARTH

" The earth bringeth forth fruit of herself; first the blade, then the ear, after that the full corn in the ear."

Those words, spoken nearly two thousand years ago, still hold mystery. We have been trying to see something of how the soil is first made ready, by one means and another, so that it may be able to " bring forth " plant-life. But—like the roots growing under ground— we are still feeling our way very much in the dark with such difficult questions. We see what takes place, we " know not how " it happens. Only so much as we do see is full of interest.

Most of us can recall how Tennyson, studying a tiny plant, touched on these mysteries—

> " Flower in the crannied wall,
> I pluck you out of the crannies;
> I hold you here, root and all, in my hand;
> Little flower—but *if* I could understand
> What you are, root and all, and all in all—
> I should know what God and man is."

IV—Tips and Hairs

And now we have to think again about how roots behave under ground.

As they climb cautiously downward, into the dark moist earth, they send out branching side roots. When we pull up a plant we seldom fail to find such branching rootlets growing from the main root.

And if we examine them closely we may be able to make out a few tiny hairs near the tips of the rootlets; though most likely these could only be seen with the help of a magnifying-glass.

331

THE WORK OF ROOTS AND STEMS

It is very largely through these hairs that the roots take in food from the soil. All the young soft tips drink in moisture, but it is the tiny hairs which do most of the work.

A great deal of food is needed by the growing plant, and especially a great deal of water. You would hardly believe what a quantity of the latter has to be taken in. Those plants which live entirely in water have really very little that is solid in their make; and even with land-plants at least half of their substance is in most cases water, and often as much as three-quarters. So we can easily imagine what supplies of it a plant must drink to keep itself going.

In fact, a plant can in its way be just as hungry and thirsty as a man; and if food and water fail or become scanty it droops and gets limp and weak, just as a human being would do. This drooping of leaves and stem is often called " wilting."

Sometimes only a few root-hairs are to be found. Sometimes such numbers of them are crowded together, round about the root-tip, that it seems to be clothed in a kind of thick velvet. Their business is to suck up water, and at the same time they receive whatever of solid substances may be dissolved and floating in the water.

Root-hairs are really *cells* on the outside of the root-tip, and it is when need arises that some of the cells lengthen into hairs. Not only do they become long and thin, but also they gain a curious power to *suck*, so that they can draw away water and salts clinging to specks of soil: clinging, indeed, so fast that force is often needed before they can be dislodged.

THE GARDEN OF EARTH

We have already heard something about living cells, in connection with the lowest forms of vegetable-life, and more must be said later.

Just now it is enough to observe that a cell is a very minute bag of living liquid. We could not by any possibility *see* one, unless in a most powerful microscope. But the whole root and all the smaller root-branches are simply made up of masses and masses of such cells—as, indeed, is the entire plant. They grow and change and alter their shapes, and gain fresh powers, and do different kinds of work, as may be required.

A word here about the food of plants found in the soil. Some mention was made earlier of "mineral salts," as they are called, which a plant must have if it is to carry out its proper work, and some of the most needful of such " salts " contain soda and potash, iron and phosphorus. These substances, taken in through the roots in liquid form, are worked marvellously into the living substance.

Among the pressing needs of all plants—we are thinking now of the higher kinds, such as grow in field and wood and garden—they *must* have a large amount of carbon, and they *must* have a large amount of nitrogen.

The carbon they get out of the air easily enough. And one might expect that they should get their supplies of nitrogen from the same quarter, since enormous quantities of nitrogen float in the atmosphere, much more than of any other gas.

But, strange to say, they cannot take and use nitrogen straight from the air. They cannot feed upon it at all when it is in what we call a " free " state—that is, by itself alone. They can only feed on it when it is *united with some other substance.* And plants in general have no power to bring about this union.

So the work has to be done for them. The "free" nitrogen is made ready for their use in the soil by numberless tiny specks of living creatures—the very lowest and smallest and simplest kinds of life, either vegetable or animal. They are called "Bacteria," and weak and tiny as they are they have this task to carry out. They have to capture the nitrogen gas, and to unite it with some other substance, so that it may become fit to be food for plants and animals.

It is only certain kinds of these minute "Bacteria" which have the power; and more particularly certain kinds that feed largely on the roots of beans and clover and other growths belonging to the same family, though not on those alone.

So the living specks of which we are thinking, hidden away in the soil, are doing two things. They are feeding on the roots of bean-plants or clover-plants; and at the same time they are busily making ready the food which those bean-plants and clover-plants must have to keep them in health.

You see now what an important question it is— what kind of soil we put seeds into, year by year, whether in gardens or on farm-lands.

And now to come back to roots in general.

The root grows downward away from the light, and as it does so, gradually lengthening, its *tip* travels gently round, hunting for food like a live thing. And, of course, it is a live thing. The plant has life.

THE GARDEN OF EARTH

All parts of the soil are not alike. Here may be found more water; there, less water. Here are more of such salts and other foods as are needed, dissolved in water; and there are smaller quantities. And the business of the root is to find out where it can get just that kind of food, and just that amount of water, which the plant must have if it is to grow and be in good health.

So, as the root gets longer and longer, its tips go steadily circling onward, making their way towards what is wanted.

If a root-tip touches a part which has the wrong sort of food, or not enough water, what do you suppose it does? It simply turns aside and tries elsewhere.

And when it draws near to a part where there is abundance—what then? Why, it goes in that direction, and the tips on arriving at the place send out tiny root-hairs to suck in food and water.

Far away in the cold north the ground is always hard-frozen a little way below the surface, not only in the winter, but all the year round. Many shrubs and fir-trees manage to flourish even under such difficult conditions, helped by the sun. And the roots of these plants start off just as do others farther south to travel straight *downwards*.

But before long they come near to the hard frozen under-soil. What do you think they do then? Would you expect them to go steadily, doggedly, boring onward into the ice?

Not they! As soon as they get near to the frozen soil, and before they reach it, they make a sharp bend, and journey along keeping to the same level, going no deeper down, and so remaining in ground which, through the summer, is not frozen hard.

V—A Plant's Brain

In all that we have been discussing with regard to the roots of plants, one thing is clear, that they certainly behave *as if* they had some sort of dim sense, or at least as if the plant as a whole had.

More than this we can hardly venture to say, for it is a very difficult question altogether. But so wonderful are the roots in the way they go prowling under ground, not only hunting for food, but apparently choosing just the right food for their own particular growth, that they have even been named "The Brain of the Plant." So a plant's brain seems to be, not as with us at the top of the structure, but down at its feet.

We need not, indeed, imagine that a plant can really think and understand. All we know is that it certainly has *wants* ; and that it can respond to—can turn towards —that which will satisfy those wants.

When root-tips are spoken of as travelling round and round, no rapid movements are meant. If we were watching ever so long and so carefully we could not *see* those movements. They are real, but they are very slow, very gentle, very gradual.

Now what do you think becomes of all the water and liquid food sucked in by the roots?

It passes first through the hairs into the side roots, then on into the main root, and thence it journeys upward by way of the stem or trunk. Its name at this stage is "raw sap" or "crude sap." It is thus far only the "raw material," not yet fashioned into what it is meant to be. It has to go higher still before it can be altered and moulded and shaped.

And here we come to one of the chief uses of the stem or trunk—the "body" of the tree. Just as your body is used for the carrying of blood to every part of it and of its limbs, so the trunk of a tree is used for the carrying of raw sap to every part of it and of its branches; and, later, for the carrying also of the manufactured and finished sap to wherever it is needed.

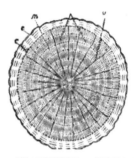

TRANSVERSE SECTION OF AN OAK BRANCH, SIX YEARS OLD : *m*, pith or medulla; *c, e*, bark; *r*, wood; *b*, medullary rays.

While winter cold reigns over the land the life of a tree is at a low ebb, and all outer active growth has come to a standstill. But this does not mean complete idleness. Within the trunk, and within the branches, preparation for spring has not only begun, but may be far advanced. If leaf-buds and flower-buds are not actually formed—and each kind of plant does differently in such respects—they are slowly taking shape, and they will be ready in time for warm spring sunshine. For the present all is quiet, and growth is sluggish, and the roots have not nearly so much to do as they will have by and by.

It is very much the same with a tree in winter as with ourselves when we are asleep at night. All day long while we are on the go, actively employed, we need plenty of food and water; but in bed we can sleep for many hours wanting neither. Yet all night long we are alive, and the beating of our hearts and the taking in of air by our lungs go on as usual, though the body is quiet.

All through the winter a tree is alive, and work is going on inside it, though it needs little food or drink. Not till the beginning of spring, the first arrival of mildness, are active growth and change seen by us; very early in the spring with some kinds of plants, and not till almost summer with others, but always with the coming of sun-warmth.

Then, indeed, the root-hairs start upon their task with energy; and quantities of liquid are sucked in to find their way upward through the roots into the trunk and branches.

And thus comes about one of the greatest marvels known in Nature. But of this we must speak in another chapter.

> " Full many a glorious morning have I seen
>   Flatter the mountain-tops with sovereign eye,
>   Kissing with golden face the meadows green,
>   Gilding pale streams with heavenly alchemy." [1]

> " Lo, here the gentle lark, weary of rest,
>   From his moist cabinet mounts up on high,
>   And wakes the morning, from whose silver breast
>   The Sun ariseth in his majesty:
>   Who doth the world so gloriously behold,
>   The Cedar-tops and hills seem burnished gold." [2]

[1] Shakespeare.　　　　[2] *Ibid.*

PART VI

I—THE RISING OF SAP

At the end of the last chapter we had just come upon one of the greatest wonders known in Nature.

All the water that is drawn in by the roots of a tree does not stay there. It passes from the hairs into the root-branches, and then by way of the main root into the trunk. After which it mounts up and up, through tiny channels, till it gets to the lower boughs.

And it does not stop there. It sends out a side-supply into each bough in turn as it passes; while still the chief amount goes on, climbing higher and higher, till the top of the tree is reached and every part has had its share.

Sometimes the sap—as yet in its " crude " or unfinished state—has a long journey. Many of our forest trees are fifty feet, eighty feet, a hundred feet high, and often much more. Trees in other parts of the world, such as the Wellingtonia in America and the Eucalyptus in Australia, rise to a height of two hundred or perhaps even three hundred feet. Yet the supplies of sap rise to the very topmost twigs.

Think what a marvel this is, this steady upward climb of the raw sap which takes place each springtide in every plant that lives and grows, in each herb,

GOVERNOR ODELL AND PARTY PASSING THROUGH A WAWONA
TREE, CALIFORNIA.

each shrub, each tree, in garden and field, in wood and
forest, throughout the whole world.

THE GARDEN OF EARTH

We know that things are so. But how does it come about? That is no easy question to answer.

Water and all liquids pour downward, never upward. Not once in our lives have we ever seen a stream running uphill. If we tried to any extent to make it travel thus we should fail. For the strong attraction of our Earth, perpetually at work, draws everything towards the ground, from higher to lower levels; and water because of its fluid make responds quickly to that pull. So it always flows downward to lower levels.

Except in this case! And here we find just the opposite. Here we have water in large quantities, taken in by the roots, mounting steadily to the tops of the highest trees, going as it seems to us right in the teeth of that tremendous earthward pull which we call "Gravitation" or "Gravity."

No easy matter this to account for. Many explanations have from time to time been given, but even when taken all together they cannot be said to explain fully what goes on.

It was long believed that the rise of sap was due to a certain form of attraction which is found in very small tubes. If you hold upright in water a tiny glass tube, you will see that the water *inside* rises just a little higher than the water *outside*. For the sides of the tube, attracting the water inside, draw it slightly upward. With a very minute tube indeed, the water would rise much higher.

Now a tree-trunk contains millions of most slender tubes. Some of them may be as much as two or three feet in length, and they lie *up and down* the trunk, not across it. Such tubes have been named " channels " and " water-pipes " and " water-mains," because of the quantities of water filtering through them.

In a tree which has begun its growth with two small seed-leaves these delicate water-pipes lie chiefly between the bark and the wood. But in a tree which has begun its growth with only one small seed-leaf they run throughout the whole trunk.

It was argued that the sap, reaching each of these tubes in turn, would be naturally drawn upwards by this particular kind of attraction, which is known as " Capillary," from the Latin word for " hair." Each of our hairs is really a tiny hollow tube. But though, no doubt, there is truth in the explanation, it is not enough by itself, not nearly enough, to account for the mystery.

II—Other Suggestions

A different idea, more lately put forth, is less easy to make clear. It has to do with the " make " of the cells and tubes of a tree.

Both cells and tubes, little round cells and long slim tubes, are clothed in a most fine and delicate skin, which is called by the same name as the thin outer skin of our bodies—the " cuticle." And the tubes are not open at either end like a glass tube. All these cells and all these tubes are closed at both ends.

As the sap rises in the tree it has to make its way right *through* this skin before it can go from one cell or one tube to another. It finds no tiny open doorways. The whole tree-trunk is divided into millions and millions of little compartments, and in every few feet of its upward journey the sap has to pass into and out of countless multitudes of them. This is a very different matter from a clear run through one long channel, and it is impossible fully to explain.

The subject as a whole is far too difficult to be gone into here. All I can tell you is that the sap does so journey from cell to cell, from tube to tube, filtering gently through the enclosing skins. Not only in spring-time upwards to the leaves, but later on, when it has been fashioned into the completed sap, it travels again in like manner, away from the leaves to all parts of the tree, both above and below, wherever it may be needed.

One other fact, which bears on this question of the rising sap, is easy to grasp. You have heard how the roots suck in liquid and send it upward. Such constant pressure from below of more and more sap ever rising must, it is thought, help the forward move-ment of that which is in front, very much as people in a dense crowd are pushed on in front by the pressure from behind.

Also the constant giving off by the leaves of quantities of water is believed to lend some little assistance. Water vapour is poured into the air from tiny leaf-passages, and as it goes, more and more water is needed from below to take its place.

So we may say that probably both the roots and the leaves do, to some extent, lend their aid in the upward journeying of the raw sap. But with all these proposed explanations it cannot be said that the rise of the sap is fully understood.

Perhaps hardly anything is more surprising than the

energy with which the small root-hairs suck in water and despatch it on its upward climb. Still, one naturally asks *why* this remarkable energy, begun in the roots, should last unbroken until the mounting sap has gained a height of one or two hundred feet or more above the ground? Why does it not die down, long before then, under the ceaseless drag of Earth's attraction? And again, what is it which gives such energy to the tiny hairs?—a force which, it has been said, goes beyond that of a boiler in a steam-engine!

One great cause, and one alone, may be spoken of as meeting the entire difficulty. Not as explaining it, not as showing precisely how the work is done, but simply as stating to what it is due.

All this wonderful energy, this force of movement, this persistency of work, this growth and change and development, spring from the LIFE of the tree. That Life is in its very nature active, energetic, aspiring— which means that it must climb upward. It cannot rest content where it happens to be. It must strive after something ahead. It works and it must work, just because it is Life.

But we can no more explain fully the " how " than we can tell exactly how it is that the life in your body keeps your heart and lungs working, day and night unceasingly, without any effort of your will. We only know that things are so.

In the same manner we know that the life of a tree— the life that is in the tree—accounts for the work of the roots, for the energy of the root-hairs, for the rise of the sap, and for countless other wonders.

THE GARDEN OF EARTH

III—How Many Leaves?

The sap, having reached the boughs, passes into the twigs, and thence onward into each separate leaf.

For this purpose it has climbed the trunk—that it may get to the leaves. They have a great task to carry out, which they could not possibly do without the raw sap to manipulate.

Each leaf by itself may be regarded as a small workshop; this has been said earlier. And the " crude sap " brought to it by the channels of trunk and branches is as the " raw material " brought to a manufactory.

" Pig-iron," for instance, is taken to great ironworks, to be there transformed by many complicated methods into all kinds and varieties of iron and steel goods. Or, again, a different class of raw materials may be conveyed to a soda manufactory, and after many processes the finished article, soda, is produced for uses innumerable.

In like manner the raw sap is brought to the leaves of a tree, to be transformed into many diverse substances, needed by the tree itself for its own use, and needed also by human beings.

These " workshop " leaves are always green, except when they first open out in early spring and when they fade in autumn. In the spring many of them show pink and salmon tints, but that is before they begin their real business. And in the autumn they often turn yellow or red, but that is when their task is done. The life of a leaf is both short and busy. No idlers are they, these useful little friends of ours.

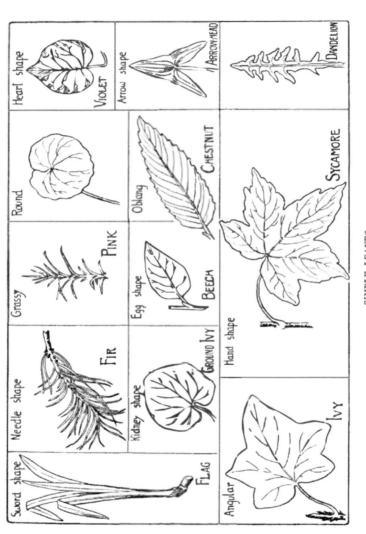

SIMPLE LEAVES.

THE GARDEN OF EARTH

They take in hand the raw materials, which are dissolved in water and brought to them from the soil, together with the gases which they receive from the air; and they work up these materials and gases into what is known as " *Organic Substance* "—that is, into such a substance that LIFE CAN WORK IN AND THROUGH IT.

Life cannot work through all kinds of substance. It cannot, for example, through marble or granite. But when the leaves have prepared this " organic substance " it has become fit for food of animals and men, for Life can enter into it and can use it.

Each day with early dawn the toil of the green substance of leaves begins. At night, in hours of darkness, it rests; but no sooner does sunlight return than it is once more hard at work.

How many leaves would you imagine to be on a tree? Counting is no easy matter with one of any considerable size, they cluster in such dense masses. But a reckoning was made with an Oak, probably a large tree, for the result gave about seven hundred thousand leaves! What, then, must be the multitudes in a wood, in a forest, in the whole world?

Not only are their numbers enormous, but their kinds and shapes and varieties are endless. Some are large, some small; some are thick, some almost transparent; some are strong, some fragile; some are long and narrow, some short and broad; in fact, every imaginable description of make may be found.

And they grow so differently: some in pairs, one opposite another; some alternately; some in circles or " whorls " around the stem.

THOSE LITTLE WORKSHOPS

A few years ago, when I paid a visit to the Kew Gardens, I came across remarkable leaf-specimens.

Near the main entrance was a bed of plants, standing about eight or ten feet high, with very big substantial leaves, handsomely veined and ribbed, many of them measuring a good two feet across and the same in length. This was the " Kiri " plant. But others go far in size beyond those of the Kiri.

In one of the houses was a lovely fern from the tropics, the " Dicksonia." It has a woolly protective covering for its stem, and graceful fronds or leaves, fully ten feet long.

And yet another great tropic plant—the " Cohune Palm "—boasted a leaf actually *thirty feet* in length. It was deeply cut down to the mid-rib, but still the whole was one leaf.

Such a specimen can hardly be spoken of as a small workshop. It is more like a large manufactory.

" The leaves of the winter wither and sink in the forest mould,
 To colour the flowers of April with purple and white and
  gold." [1]

IV—The Make of a Leaf—

Now as to the *make* of a leaf: how it is built up or put together.

It is said to be in three parts : the Blade, the Footstalk, and the two Stipules, which look like small leaflets, just where the footstalk begins. But often no stipules are found; and often, too, is seen no footstalk. The really needful part, without which we should have no

[1] Alfred Noyes.

leaf, is the blade, the wide green portion. This reminds one of an oar, the chief part of which is called " the blade."

A leaf, like all the rest of a plant, is formed of countless tiny cells, pressed and growing together; and the mass of these, green in colour, is known as the " cellular tissue " of a leaf. This word " tissue " means strictly " that which is woven "; and here it stands for the kind of substance which may become part of a living body, either of plant or of animal.

The ribs and veins of a leaf—its skeleton—are also formed of cells; but these cells have hardened into a tough substance, which is fit to act as a strong frame-work for the soft tissue. And over the whole is a fine transparent skin or cuticle, both above and below, through which the green tint can be clearly seen.

In this skin are numbers and numbers of extremely minute openings; tiny pores or holes, so formed that they can open or close according to the needs of the plant. They are indeed so tiny that they cannot be seen at all without a powerful microscope. If you were to prick a hole in paper, with the point of the very finest needle, that hole would be simply huge side by side with a single leaf-pore.

By far the greater number of them are on the *under-sides* of leaves. No doubt this is because the under-side is the more sheltered, and not nearly so much exposed as the upper-side to rain and wind and dust. And each of them is the doorway to a minute channel or passage, leading to and from the inside of the leaf.

No one would guess how great is the number of these

little pores—or *stomata,* as they are called. A single
Oak-leaf, for instance, was reckoned to have on its
under-side alone more than *two millions.* Some of the
largest known are on the leaves of Orchids, and some of
the smallest are on the leaves of Water Lilies. But all

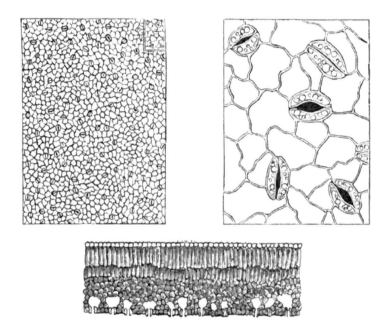

STOMATA.

are tiny. They are most useful, most necessary, for
the life of the plant. They have to let in and to let
out supplies of both air and water-vapour.

A plant—any kind of plant—must do three things,
not unlike what we have ourselves to do. It has to
breathe. It has to *digest.* It has to *transpire.* This

last word means that it has to get rid, through its skin, of water not wanted for its own use.

Would you have thought of a tree being obliged to breathe? But indeed it must. It cannot live without breathing. Like a man, it must have oxygen gas, or it will die of suffocation; yes, of actual slow suffocation. A tree breathes day and night; summer and winter.

A man breathes by means of his lungs. But a tree has no lungs; and it breathes in all its parts that are actively alive—its roots, its green stems, its seeds, its fruits. If the roots cannot find enough air in the soil, then the whole tree suffers. It also breathes by its leaves.

When a man's lungs receive the air which he has drawn in, they make use of it for his body. A kind of *burning* goes on within him, much as when fire burns away wood. The oxygen of the air is united with some of the carbon of his body, to make carbonic-acid gas; and this is poured out again into the atmosphere. It has to be got rid of quickly; for if not, the man would die.

And the same thing goes on in a tree, in any kind of plant. There too, the oxygen of the air, which has flowed in through countless little pores, is united with some of the carbon of the tree, and carbonic-acid gas is formed, ready to be poured forth into the atmosphere.

V—AND THE WORK OF A LEAF

Thus far the tree does much the same as we do. Here we come to a difference.

It has to *digest*, as well as to breathe. That is, it has to take in food, and to make that food a part of itself.

351

Like ourselves again ! But a man digests his food by means of his stomach; while a tree digests by means of its leaves.

So the leaves have to carry on two separate tasks at the same time. In breathing, they capture air with its life-supporting oxygen, and get rid of carbonic-acid gas. But in digesting, they again capture air, and do just the opposite. They keep for food the carbonic-acid gas—which is more strictly known as *carbon-dioxide*—and they get rid of the oxygen. Green plants and all green portions of plants feed very largely on carbonic-acid gas; for it is much needed in building up the substance of a tree.

Both men and plants in breathing make the air around less healthy, because they keep taking away from it oxygen gas, and adding to it carbonic-acid gas. And if this went on perpetually, with nothing to undo the harm, our whole atmosphere would in time become impossible for us to breathe.

But there is a something, and a very big something, to undo it. There is the work of leaves, of grasses, of countless millions of them in all parts of the world, taking in carbonic-acid gas as *food*, and pouring out enormous quantities of oxygen gas, so needful for life. While they breathe like ourselves, thus helping to render the air unfit for us to breathe, they also by their digestion set the matter right, and keep the atmosphere pure and good.

They are doing it always; but not all plants in the whole world incessantly. Day after day, and month after month, they carry on this work in relays. Each plant works thus only in daylight. The *breathing* of a plant goes on, as with us, both by day and by night. The *digesting* takes place only while it is light. After dark, it stops. The tree then just breathes as we do; keeping the oxygen of the air for its own use, and getting rid of the carbonic-acid gas.

And so soon as morning light returns, they are once more at their useful work; and while they still breathe out carbonic-acid gas, they catch it up again as it leaves the little pores, and use it anew as food for the plant to which they belong.

You would never guess what accumulations of that important but suffocating gas are being manufactured, day and night, through breathing. Putting aside what plants and animals do, and reckoning only what is done by men and women and children throughout the world, it is said that each day more than *one million tons* of carbonic-acid gas are poured into the atmosphere.

So no wonder the daylight task of plants is needed, to undo the mischief which we ourselves are perpetually working.

> "Small service is true service while it lasts;
>   Of humblest friends, bright creature, scorn not one.
>   The Daisy by the shadow that it casts
>   Protects the lingering dewdrop from the sun." [1]

Something has already been said about a tree having to transpire. This really is a kind of perspiration.

When a man perspires, drops of water are seen on his face; water that has oozed out through tiny pores in his skin. When a plant "transpires" the water escapes through *its* skin-pores, as invisible vapour. But

[1] Wordsworth.

a man really transpires, as well as a tree. All day long water-vapour is escaping through the pores of his skin —about as much as one pint in twenty-four hours. This is sometimes called "insensible perspiration," because we do not see or feel it.

Plenty of water, as you now know, taken in by the roots, mounts upward by way of the tree-trunk into the leaves. And in each drop there may be, at the least, a few specks of some other kind of substance, needed by the tree.

Such tiny specks !—the very smallest that we can imagine !—so minute, so light, that they float in the water unseen, and can pass with it through the delicate skins of the cells and tubes. Yet, tiny though they are, the tree must have them, if it is to carry on its work.

As they pass they are caught hold of and kept back and made use of by the leaves. And all the water that is not wanted is sent on to the leaf-pores, to escape as vapour into the outside air.

This is yet another work done by the leaves. Not only do they help to make the air more pure, but also they help to keep it well supplied with moisture. Here, too, we have to do with large quantities. Immense amounts of water travel thus, from the soil upwards through the tree-trunks, then out by way of the tiny leaf-pores, into the air which we breathe.

It has been reckoned that a well-grown Apple-tree, in the course of a single spring and summer, may part with something like two hundred and fifty pounds' weight of water. If we count the trees growing in one large orchard, we can soon find out how many tons of water are poured through them in a year. The total is astonishing—all the more if we picture to ourselves the weight of a single ton.

And since one orchard alone can do so much, what must be the supplies which are in this manner got rid of by all the orchards—all the gardens—all the woods and forests—in our country? For not only are trees engaged in the task, but plants of all descriptions as well, including grasses, ferns, and mosses.

VI—GREEN LEAVES

We have now seen that these little "workshops" have their "raw material" brought to them in two ways. First, from the roots upward through the stem; and second, by the leaves themselves inwards from the air. First, water, with invisible specks of many kinds floating in it; and second, air, with its mixture of different kinds of gases.

From these two sources the leaves are able to work up or to manufacture many "finished articles," as we may call them; such as sugars and starches, and fatty and oily substances, perpetually needed by men; many of which can be obtained in no other way.

Two wonderful powers work together for this end; each helping the other.

One of the two is in the leaf itself. It is, the Life in that leaf. We have noticed earlier the extraordinary vigour found in life; and here we find it again—the power to work, to grow, to *do*.

Throughout the whole tree, in all the active cells of which it is or has been made—"has been" because parts are always dying as fresh parts grow—in these active cells a certain *something* is found, the presence of which means the presence of Life. Where that something is, that part of the plant is alive. Where it is not, that part is practically dead.

This *something* is also in those specks of vegetable-life, the very lowest kinds known, of which you heard some time back. Each little plantlet by itself may be only one single cell; a mere bag of liquid. But it has in it this mysterious substance—soft, slimy, colourless. It holds the germ of life; and so it is a living, breathing plant. And every active cell in every plant has in it the same; without which it would not be alive.

Such living cells, whether each one is a separate plantlet or whether it is part of a larger plant, have power to work, and to shape and mould other substances. As has been said of them—they not only " provide the building materials, but they are themselves the builders."

And what marvellous building it is !

Plants by millions throughout the world, all of them living, growing, working. Yet each plant, no matter how great, has always begun its life as one tiny cell. From that cell came others, shaped first inside itself, and from each of those more and more cells, till at length a seed has taken form; and from the seed comes a new herb or tree.

And now to go back to the leaves; our busy little workshops.

They, too, are built up of multitudes of cells, each of which is lined with this living substance. But now we touch upon something else, not always found with it.

THE GARDEN OF EARTH

For here are numberless tiny *green* specks, which lend their colour to the leaves. All through the green leaves of plants, and the green blades of grasses, and young green stems and shoots, they float in vast hordes. They are found also, to some extent, in the petals of flowers, in seeds and fruits, and even in roots; but not nearly so abundantly.

And it is *only* where these little green specks congregate, that the work can be done of which we have been thinking—that particular work which is given to leaves; the taking up of lifeless materials from earth and air, and so changing and fashioning them into new substances, that they are fitted to become food for animals and men.

A curious fact is that the living cells in a leaf first *make* this leaf-green; and then, having manufactured it, they use it for their tremendously important work.

"How can they possibly do all this?" you may ask; and indeed you may well ask it! In one sense I can give no clear answer. In another sense I can. For here comes in the second great power; and that power is—Sunlight.

Sunlight and leaf-green work together in a happy comradeship. Without the Sun, the leaf-green could do nothing; and without the leaf-green [1] the Sun could not carry out this task. Each apart from the other is powerless to break up the carbonic-acid gas of the air, keeping the carbon for the building up of the tree, and setting loose the oxygen for us to breathe. Each, apart from the other, is also powerless to provide in

---

[1] The "leaf-green" is known by the name of "chlorophyll," from two Greek words for "green" and "leaf."

enormous quantities that "finished material" without which neither we nor animals could feed and live; without which the whole world would soon become one vast desert of death.

But why, and how, and in what precise manner, the great blazing Sun and the tiny invisible green granules work together to bring about such grand and world-wide results, no man living can fully explain.

> " We on this earth are servants of the Sun,
> Out of the sun comes all the quick in me,
> His golden touch is life to every one,
> His power it is that makes us spin through space.
>
> .   .   .   .
> What we may be, who knows ?   But every one
> Is dust on dust, a servant of the Sun."

[1] From *Lollingdon Downs*, by John Masefield, published by W. Heinemann.   By permission.

PART VII

I—FLOWERS IN SUNSHINE

YOU remember how the Daisies on the lawn lifted up their faces towards the Sun. And Daisies do not stand alone in their seeming love of sunshine. Many other flowers depend even more upon it.

For example, Sunflowers are looked upon as great Sun-lovers. Some of them really are too huge for beauty; such thick yellow masses! The name was given to them because of their devotion to light. It has been said that no Sunflower is ever seen with its back to the Sun.

This perhaps is not quite correct; for if the plant were not in good health, and if in consequence the stalk were weak, the flower might not be able to carry out such movements. But no doubt it would do its best.

A gardener told me that, one day many years ago, he saw in Kew Gardens two great beds of these flowers, in full bloom. And among them all, large and small— some plants standing ten feet high—he found not one single bloom that did not face the Sun.

The same thing may be seen with the curious rolled leaves of an Onion-plant—not a Shallot.

If we should examine a row of them in the evening, towards sunset, we should probably find the greater

359

number of leaves pointing towards the *west*, where soon the sun will go down. But if we pay them another visit next morning, not too early, when the Sun has been some hours up, a change will have taken place. Many if not most of the tube-like leaves will have probably managed to turn over more or less towards the *east*,

Ray floret   Central floret

where the Sun arose. Generally there are a few weakly or sickly ones, not able to do this.

For plants, like men, are by no means always in good health. They suffer from weakness, and from various diseases, partly due to bad air or bad water or not enough food, just as with ourselves.

The same apparent love of sunshine is shown by other kinds also. Some time ago I came across a Viola-plant in a garden, growing in a narrow bed which ran beside the drive. It was fully in bloom, with a crowd of pretty mauve-blue faces, turned smilingly upward.

They were marvellously arranged, so that each one might obtain as much light as possible. No attempt had been made to follow the Sun in his journey across the sky; for it would have been useless. The hedge behind, and a wall in front, cut off much of the direct sunshine, except at one certain time of the day. But the plant had plainly done its best so to place its blooms that, when the sun did come, they could make the very most of him. And when he was gone, they would still be in a position to get all the light that might be obtained in that position.

It was so cleverly managed ! Of all the seventy or eighty flowers—I forget the exact number—not *one* lay behind another.

Many were touching at their edges, because there was not too much space for them all. But they had so spread themselves out as to find enough; making a lovely pattern of delicate blooms, side by side or one above another, close together, yet each one clear of the rest. Only in one spot, I think, did I find a single small corner of a petal behind the next flower, and that was because it really could not be helped.

And all this was worked out by the plant itself. Is it not wonderful?

Of course I do not mean that the plant *thought* it out, as you or I might do. It is more like what goes on perpetually in our own bodies—the living, the growing, the putting-on of flesh, the breathing, and so on, without any conscious effort of our own wills to bring it about.

THE POWER OF SUNLIGHT

A plant cannot think, or reason, or resolve what it will do. But certainly it does often act as though after a fashion it knew what is good and needful for its growth and health. The way in which it manages to gain all possible sunshine for flowers and leaves, and the way in which it takes in and uses materials gathered from earth and air and water—are very marvellous.

It was pretty to see how gently matters had come about in this particular instance. If a party of human beings were all together, wishing to be in full sunshine, and if the space in which they could move were small, they might be tempted to think first of themselves, and to push others into the shade.

But the Violas had done no such thing. They had just spread themselves softly out, as far as they could, without any pushing. It really did look almost as if each one had tried, not only to get plenty of light for itself, but also not to hinder its neighbours from doing the same.

On one other occasion I remember noticing this eagerness of Violas for sunshine. It was on Sunday, in the country and in early morning. On my way to church, I saw a little grave in the churchyard full of them, in full bloom. And though it was so early, and the Sun had risen no long time before, yet each little face was turned towards the east, right upwards in his direction, as if rejoicing in his beams.

> " The heart that has truly loved never forgets,
>   But as truly loves on to the close—
> As the Sunflower turns on her god, when he sets,
>   The same look which she turned when he rose." [2]

[1] Thomas Moore.

H

362

THE GARDEN OF EARTH

II—How the Work is done

It must not be supposed that all plants need the same amount of sunshine. Just as with ourselves, that which is good for one is not always good for others.

Some can hardly have too much, while others droop quickly under heat and glare. Some flowers, like the Viola, lift their faces upward towards the Sun, while others, like the Violet, creep under sheltering leaves. A Viola is more like the sunshine-loving Heartsease.[1]

But, taking the question as a whole, we may say that plants in general undoubtedly do need, not only light, but sunshine also. Without warmth there can be no growth; and more warmth, though not too much, means usually more rapid growth. For the special work of green leaves, sunshine is particularly needed.

As with flowers so with leaves, you may note if you will how carefully they often seem to arrange themselves, that they may get the greatest possible amount of light. In a plant it can be seen frequently that the leaves—like the Viola blossoms—have most of their upper surfaces turned towards the Sun, spread out level to catch his beams.

With a large tree, where the foliage grows in dense masses, many parts must be more or less in shade; yet the same result is here aimed at. Each leaf at least tries to obtain its share of sunlight.

Something else is worth noticing, in the way that leaves are arranged. Very commonly they grow in a

---

[1] All three are species of Viola.

kind of pent-house style, sloping gently outwards, one above another, so that rain, pouring on them, is guided away from the trunk.

A reason for this may be conjectured. Do you remember that it is the soft *tips* of the roots, where they are clothed with hairs, that suck in moisture from the soil? But in a tree, with its widely spreading roots, those tips are far away from the trunk, often many yards distant. Rain, falling close to the trunk, is not needed; while at the root-tips it is much needed. So when the sloping leaves throw it outwards, it falls where it is wanted.

At times we may see leaves doing the opposite. If on a rainy evening, after a dry day, you pass a patch of potato-plants, some of the leaves may be tilted up, standing on end and twisted as one might twist a piece of paper, to form a channel for water. Thus again they guide the falling drops to the roots, which in a small plant are not far from the stem.

However, this curling of the leaves *may* arise from another cause. Many leaves, which all day long have turned their upper surfaces broadside to the sun, will droop and curl at the coming of night.

For at night heat pours quickly away from the ground, and from all upturned surfaces; and the leaves in that position might suffer from cold. So, perhaps, it is mainly on this account that they no longer face upwards. Such drooping and turning away has been called "the Sleep of Leaves."

It is not real sleep with them, as with us. It is simply a movement, placing the leaves—often also the flowers—so that they may keep a little of their warmth until the morning. Yet their so doing may be of use to the plant in the two ways named above.

Leaves, as we have seen, are called upon to carry out many and varied tasks. But of all that they have to do, not one is more necessary for ourselves than the wonderful way in which they transform the raw sap into all kinds of food and other useful substances.

A very remarkable part of the matter is that each kind of plant should always make its own especial material, and should always go on making it. Through years, through hundreds of years, still plant after plant, shrub after shrub, tree after tree, manufactures always and only its own particular " brands," and never any others.

Different plants may grow side by side, using the same air, the same earth, the same water; and yet the "finished article " turned out by each is not the same.

One kind brings forth poisonous berries. Another brings forth a delicious fruit. Another brings forth a remedy for illness. Another brings forth something of use in our household work. Another brings forth that which we need for clothing. But always, always, the same thing is made by the same kind of plant.

And this means that each plant uses for its work exactly the right materials. It chooses out those substances, from the various supplies which travel to it in air and in water. It refuses the wrong ones and keeps the right ones, handing over the latter to the leaves— its small workshops. And the leaves, busily toiling through the few months of their brief existence, always turn out that particular article which they and their kind alone are able to produce.

The make of the soil is thus of great importance. It may be good or bad for the plant. It may be too dry or too damp. It may be lacking in just that description of food which is necessary for the particular manufacture of that plant. If the soil be good, the plant will be healthy, and will work with vigour; if bad, then the plant must become sickly and feeble. But still in every case each one produces, and can produce, only its own especial materials.

> " Ask me why I send you here
> This firstling of the infant year;
> Ask me why I send to you
> This Primrose all bepearled with dew.
>
>   .   .   .
>
> Ask me why this flower doth show
> So yellow, green, and sickly too;
> Ask me why the stalk is weak
> And bending, yet it doth not break;
> I must tell you, these discover
> What doubts and fears are in a lover." [1]

III—PLANT MANUFACTURES

By far the greater part of this complicated work is carried on by the Green Leaves of plants, though not the whole of it.

One exception is in the matter of Wood. Our larger trees contain masses of wood. In the trunk is the softer sap-wood, close to the bark, full of tiny channels through which the sap journeys. And also there is the heart-wood, filling up the centre with hardened remains of channels, through which the sap no longer passes; and that part is nearly dry.

[1] Thomas Carew (about A.D. 1600).

THE GARDEN OF EARTH

" How does the wood come to be there at all ? " one may ask; and perhaps you would answer, " Why, it *grows!* It *is* the trunk itself." Yes, it is; but it has to be made. It has to be built up, year by year, within and by itself, layer upon layer. And even there, though in a sense the leaves do not carry on the work, it is more or less due to them. For if they did not faithfully perform their share, by changing the raw sap into finished sap and sending it back through countless channels to nourish every part of the tree, no wood could grow.

Other materials, such as rubber, are made in the stems of trees, and not actually by the leaves; and the same may be said of seeds and fruits, formed in and by the flowers. Yet in all these cases the leaves lend a hand.

From early morning till evening they are at it incessantly; gathering air and water; choosing the materials that they need; working all up under the sun's rays; and turning out in the end that which it is their duty to produce.

Then at last the completed sap is ready. And the different uses of it, made by different plants—the varieties of substances brought forth—are simply amazing.

Some serve for the food of the growing plant itself. Some are meant for the support of young plants in the future. Very many are food for animals and men.

Indeed, the greater amount of food, upon which our lives depend, comes to us in this way. We get it straight from plants by eating fruits and vegetables, roots and stems, either cooked or uncooked. We get it by eating bread and pastry, cakes and puddings, made from the flour of wheat or oats or other such growths. We get it by eating animals which have lived on vegetable-food. We get it by eating animals that have fed on other animals which have lived on vegetable-food.

So again and again we come back to the work of leaves. Such numbers of substances, needful for the support of life, have to reach us thus!

For neither we ourselves, nor animals in general, have any power to take food-materials out of the soil, or out of the atmosphere, and to use them as food. Until they have been worked up by plants, and made ready, we simply cannot use them. We depend entirely on the Vegetable Kingdom to prepare them for us.

IV—The Food that We eat

Let us think of some of the different things that we commonly take at breakfast or dinner, and try to find at least one or two that have *not* been made ready for our use by any plant.

Somebody may suggest, " Salt ! " And we do get that out of the sea or from rocks in the earth, ready made. But though salt is good, we can hardly call it " food." No one could *live* on salt for even a very short time.

What about Bread? That comes from Corn. The raw materials, gathered out of earth and air by millions and billions of Wheat-plants, are worked up by each one separately into nourishing grains; and these are ground to fine flour, and the flour is made into loaves of bread. But if the Wheat-plants failed to do their part, we might cry out in vain for bread.

What about Butter? That comes from the milk of cows, churned into butter by man. And cows feed largely on grass and hay; either green grass, each blade of which has worked up the raw materials from earth and air into a form which cows can digest; or hay, which is simply dried grass.

SUGAR-CANE.

What about Beef and Mutton? Just the same. Cattle and sheep live mainly on grass. Without it they would die, unless some other vegetable-food should take its place.

What about Cheese? That, again, is made from milk or cream. Without the right vegetable-food for cows we should have no milk, no cream, no cheese.

What about Sugar? Immense supplies of it come

from a kind of grass, the Sugar-cane, which grows to a height of from eight to fifteen feet, with thick jointed stalks. In these stalks the sugar ripens, being manu-

[Photo: *J. da Luze Perestrella*.

BANANAS AND THE SUGAR-CANE ON CANARY ISLES.

factured there by the plants themselves. A large amount also is made from " Sugar-beet " plants, nearly related to Beetroot; and we all know what a sweet vegetable beetroot is.

THE GARDEN OF EARTH

What about Rice? One of the most important of foods; not so much in Europe as in Eastern lands. The Rice-plant, like the Sugar-cane, is a kind of Grass; and it grows in water, and only in very hot countries, such as India. Its work is to manufacture those small grains, which we know well in puddings. Enormous supplies of Rice are needed; for it is the principal food of the people of India, China, and elsewhere. It has been said that more than half of the people in the world are fed mainly on Rice. And each tiny grain, of all these enormous quantities, is made and shaped separately by the Rice-plant.

COCOA.

What about Tea? It also is grown largely in India and in China. Two or three hundred years ago tea was a luxury, used only by the very rich. Now everybody, even the poorest, must have his or her cup of tea. And it comes to us entirely through the work of leaves. In fact, as we know, tea *is* leaves.

What about Cocoa? The Cocoa or Cacao plant grows in warm countries, especially in Ceylon and the West Indies. It has clusters of small flowers, growing straight from the trunk, or from the larger branches, not from twigs or stalks. When the fruit ripens, a large pod, several inches long, hangs where the flowers were; and this pod holds rows of seeds or " cocoa-beans."

What about Fruits? Apples from the Apple-tree; pears from the Pear-tree; oranges from the Orange-tree; dates from the Date-palm; bananas from the

371

Banana-plant; strawberries from the Strawberry-plant; currants from the Currant-bush; plums from the Plum-tree; peaches from the Peach-tree;—but the names are endless. All these and many many more are the work of the Vegetable Kingdom.

Then, too, the vegetables that we eat—potatoes, cauliflowers, turnips, carrots, cabbages, beans, peas, asparagus, onions—are numberless, and each one is manufactured by its own kind of plant, and by no other.

COTTON.

Nor is this all. When we turn to clothing, we find the same thing over again.

What about Cotton? Huge supplies of cotton are used by mankind, woven into all sorts of materials. Where does the cotton come from? Why, from the Cotton-plant, which grows abundantly in the plains of India and in other sultry regions. The cotton itself is a sort of soft down or fine hair, clinging to the seeds when they ripen.

What about Wool? We make from it all kinds of warm stuffs for winter wear; cloth, flannel, merino, also blankets and shawls, coats and comforting wraps of every description. The raw wool comes to us from the backs of sheep; and those sheep have fed on vegetable food. But for that food, but for the work of each small grass-blade, the wool would never have grown.

THE GARDEN OF EARTH

What about Silk? It is woven by the Silkworm, which feeds entirely on green leaves. What about Linen? It comes from the Flax-plant. And the list might be widened to any extent in other directions. What about Bass for the use of gardeners? It is procured from the Lime-tree. What about Camphor? It is distilled from the wood of the Camphor-tree.

So we see, just a little, what an immense debt we owe to the manufacturing work of plants. And I have not named a hundredth part of the whole; no, nor a thousandth part.

Not all useful to us, you may say. Very likely not. Man is not the only being on Earth to be considered. Certain growths, which are useless for ourselves, may have other uses, not known to us. At the least, when they die they help to enrich the soil.

And some which we might hastily condemn, counting them worse than useless, are not really so. There are plants which manufacture berries full of deadly poison; and if a child eats one or two of those berries, he will die. Yet that same poison, given in very tiny quantities at the right time and in the right manner, to some one who is dangerously ill, will act as a powerful medicine, and may save his life.

V—OCEAN FOOD

One thing more. How about Fishes, Crabs, Lobsters, Shrimps? Do we here owe anything to our vegetable friends?

Yes, a great deal; though we cannot speak in quite such certain terms with regard to ocean-creatures as with regard to land-animals. Ocean-life is so enormous, so different from life on land, that we are only beginning to understand a little about it.

So far as we know, however, the creatures there also which belong to the Animal Kingdom are not able, generally, to get their food straight from air or water or soil. They too must—generally—wait until it has been worked up for them by beings that belong to the Vegetable Kingdom. Only we cannot venture to say that with them it is *always* so.

You may smile at the idea of a fish having to do with air or with soil. But there is air in the sea, or a fish could not breathe. And there are soils at the bottom of the ocean, where hordes of animals live; many and curious kinds of soil.

On dry land animals feed largely on vegetables. But in the sea very few fishes feed on seaweeds. Just a small number do; while by far the greater number live entirely on animal-food.

The strong devour those that are weaker; and the weaker prey on those that are weaker still. So, stage by stage, we get down from the larger inhabitants of the ocean to those that are known as the " lower animals " of that vast region. Numberless hordes of small live things throng the middle and upper reaches; many of them of the Crayfish kind; very many only the young of bigger creatures dwelling below. And these serve as food for teeming millions of fishes; perhaps especially for such as herrings, which again nourish the larger kinds.

And on what do these " lower animals " feed—these multitudes of little restless beings ? Do *they* depend on vegetable growths ?

THE GARDEN OF EARTH

Not on such seaweeds as we all know. But the whole ocean, down to a certain depth, is thronged with immense supplies of another kind of vegetable—tiny tiny specks of life, which were spoken about earlier in this book.

Do you remember the Diatoms, and their minute ornamented shells? Small as they are, and invisible to our eyes, they yet are true plants, real vegetables. Being plants, they can only live where some amount of sunlight is able to reach them. Deep below, where utter darkness reigns, they cannot exist. But in the upper reaches of the ocean they throng in hundreds of billions, serving as food for untold myriads of animals, both small and great.

It has been curiously said in a recent work that: "Diatoms are the pastures of the seas;"[1] that, in fact, they take that place in ocean life which is taken on land by "the grass of the fields." And not Diatoms only, but many other kinds of tiny one-celled plantlets help to crowd the ocean.

But how about lower depths still, the floor of the deep, where all is darkness? Diatoms cannot live there; yet sea-creatures flourish.

As Diatoms die, their little bodies in tiny shells sink by millions to the bottom, and there form a fine " ooze " or mud. And the creatures that live on and near to ocean's floor are believed to swallow quantities of this muddy ooze, which is largely made up of Diatom remains. So in this way they also may come in for vegetable food.

Only—once more—we cannot say with the sea, as

[1] *Conditions of Life in the Sea*, by J. Johnstone, p. 77.

375

with the land, that it is always thus. Some odd creatures are known to exist there—animals—which seem to have the power to prepare food for themselves, just like plants, out of the " raw materials." And they actually have in their bodies some of those curious little green particles, which on land are found in plants alone.

Other such instances may in time become known to us also. But on the whole, in the sea as well as on land, men and animals owe a heavy debt to plant-life.

PART VIII

THE WORK OF FLOWERS

I—WHAT FLOWERS ARE FOR

Now at last we come to Flowers, and to their work in life. All that we have heard so far about Roots and Stems and Leaves leads up to those lovely blooms, which are—at least in our eyes—the crowning part of the structure. Not that they can be looked upon as its highest aim; for it is they who have to work out that aim; it is they who have to bring about the *chief* end and object of the plant's being.

We love them for their beauty, their wonderful forms, their colouring, their delicacy, their tenderness, their grace, their perfumes. They seem to belong to us; to be what S. Francis of Assisi would have called " Our little Sisters."

Great as is the variety found in kinds and sizes and shapes of leaves, the variety in flowers is even more astonishing.

They range in size from some so tiny as to be almost invisible, to others which are enormous. Some of these huge specimens are never to be seen in Britain; a fact that need not trouble us, for the largest are by no means always the most beautiful.

In the tropical parts of America grows a plant[1]

[1] An *Aristolochia*.

which bears balloon-like flowers, so big that children sometimes draw them over their heads, for fun, like caps.

But the one which carries away the palm for size is a " Rafflesia "[1] found in the island of Sumatra.

RAFFLESIA FLOWER.

This plant is a parasite; it does not draw its nourishment from the soil, but sends its roots into the trailing stem of a vine, and feeds on it. Living upon another is not a fine manner of life; and we all speak with contempt of " parasites."

The flower blooms close down on the Vine-stem, with no stalk. It is very thick and fleshy; and is said to

[1] *Rafflesia Arnoldi.*

be in shape not unlike an enormous Forget-me-not blossom. When fully open it measures *three feet across.* It has a most disagreeable smell; and we should hardly care to have one in our rooms.

One day, when walking on the Surrey Downs, I caught sight of a minute floweret at my feet, growing low in the grass. Plucking it, I had a good look through a magnifying-glass; and in a moment the wee thing, so tiny and insignificant, had changed into an exquisite flower, delicate and lovely, with pure white petals, beautifully marked, just like some grand hot-house bloom.

It is strange what shoals of lovely things are all around us in Nature, which we do not notice; which indeed often we cannot see without help from a micro-scope. And yet, no matter how small or how hidden away such things may be, their make and their finish are perfect. Nothing in Nature is ever "scamped" or done anyhow in a hurry, because "nobody will see!"

Between these two extremes among flowers, the very big and the very little, lie immense numbers of kinds, far beyond our power to reckon.

If we began only to talk of their shapes, their colours, their markings, we might go on for hours. And then their scents! Not all sweet, certainly. But many are delightful—such as those of Roses, Carnations, Violets, Lilacs, Heliotropes, Jessamines, Mignonettes, Lilies-of-the-Valley.

At least five hundred different scents are known, one and all manufactured in little Plant-workshops.

It seems clear that Flowers are *meant* to be a joy to

us. Though it is by no means only for admiration that they exist, since they like the leaves have an especial work to carry out—still they might have done that work without being so beautiful as they are. Many flowers which are not beautiful do the same work as their fairer sisters, and do it well.

But what a different world this would be, if we had no sweet little " Sister-blooms " to love and tend; if we had all that we need in the way of food and clothing through the Vegetable Kingdom, but nothing to satisfy the craving that is in our minds for beauty of form and of colouring.

> " There in a meadow, by the river's side,
> A flock of nymphs I chancèd to espy,
> All lovely daughters of the flood thereby,
> With goodly greenish locks all loose untied
> As each had been a bride;
> And each one had a little wicker basket
> Made of fine twigs, entrailèd curiously.
> In which they gather'd flowers to fill their flasket,
> And with fine fingers cropt full feateously
> The tender stalks on high.
> Of every sort which in that meadow grew
> They gathered some—the violet, pallid blue,
> The little daisy that at evening closes,
> The virgin lily and the primrose true,
> With store of vermeil roses,
> To deck their bridegrooms' posies
> Against the bridal day, which was not long;
> Sweet Thames; run softly, till I end my song." [1]

II—PISTILS AND STAMENS

In an earlier chapter we heard about the different Parts of a Flower. They were : the Flower-stalk; the

[1] E. Spenser.

THE GARDEN OF EARTH

Calix or Sepals; the Corolla or Petals; the Stamens, with their Pollen; and the Pistils.

Stamens are usually in two parts; the Filament and the Anther. The word "filament" is from the Latin for "thread"; and the filaments or stamen-stalks are often so fine and delicate as to be very much like threads.

But the really important part of a stamen is the anther; precisely as the really important part of a leaf is the blade. A leaf is still a leaf, though it has no footstalk and no stipules. And a stamen is still a stamen, though it has no filament. But a footstalk without any blade would not be a leaf; and a filament without any anther would not be a stamen.

Inside the Anther is the Pollen; and without this curious golden dust the flower could not do its work.

A Pistil, like a stamen, has more parts than one; generally three—the Stigma, the Style, and the Ovary. Some plants have only one pistil to each flower; others have two or many pistils; but each pistil may have these three parts.

By the *style* is meant the little stalk. The *stigma* is on that stalk; and the *ovary* is down at the bottom of it, often embedded within the flower, out of sight. That small hollow ovary is one of the necessary parts of the whole. It and the stigma are as important as the stamen-anther.

Sometimes a pistil has no style; and that does not matter. What does matter is that there *must be stamens and pistil*. Without these two the flower—nay, the plant itself—would be a failure. They need not, however, be always on the same flower. The pistil may grow on one flower, and the stamen on another. But both are needed.

Sepals and petals have their task to do, in sheltering and protecting the stamens and the pistils. Yet without either sepals or petals the flower might still be a flower.

And why?

Because the true work of a flower, that for which it lives, is—not merely to be beautiful, not merely to give forth a sweet scent, not merely to win admiration, but— to bring forth fresh life, to start new plants, which in time may take the place of the old ones which die.

Seeds, it is true, are not the only mode by which plant-life can be carried on. A gardener is able to produce new plants by other means. A slip from a Rose-tree, cut in a certain way and put in soil of the right kind and carefully tended, will send out roots and in time will become a Rose-tree. Or a leaf-bud may be taken and put into the stem or branch of another kindred tree, and it will grow there, sending forth a shoot, and in time bearing roses like those of the tree from which it was taken.

Such modes are called "growth by cuttings" and "budding"; and "grafting" is another plan, not unlike the last.

But these are and must be the work of a gardener. No plants can carry out such methods for themselves. In a wild state their only way of bringing fresh plants into existence is, generally, by seeding. So the manufacture of seeds really is the prime work of flowers. It is that for which they are made, and that for which they die.

Yes; they not only live for it, but also they die for it. Until the flower fades and falls, the seed has no hope of beginning its life as a new plant.

You may remember what Keble wrote, on the subject of the work of flowers, when describing a day in early November—

> " Why blowest thou not, thou wintry wind,
>   Now every leaf is brown and sere,
> And idly droops, to thee resigned,
>   The chaplet of the year ?
>
> .   .   .   .   .   .
> " Now quiet shows the woodland scene;
>   Each Flower and Tree, *its duty done*,
> Reposing in decay serene,
>   Like weary men, when age is run."

So each tree, each leaf, each flower, may be looked upon as just *doing its duty*.

III—How the Seeds grow

Inside the small ovary of the pistil are tiny bodies, called Ovules; sometimes many, sometimes only one or two. And since it is they that are meant to grow into seeds, the question of new young plants depends on them.

The word " ovule " means " little egg "; and an ovule is, in a sense, as much the beginning of a future plant as a bird's egg is the beginning of a future young bird. The ovary is a kind of case which holds the ovules.

Each of these has to begin life as a single small cell, with its lining of living substance. That cell has power to grow other cells; and when they are formed, the one divides into two, and each of those two again into two more. As the numbers thus increase, they remain firmly pressed together, gradually taking shape as a tiny living ovule.

Next, the ovule has to grow into a seed. But the pistil cannot manage the whole of this work alone. It must have help.

True, it has help already. There is the eager Life of

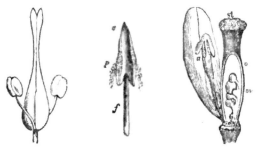

FLOWER OF THE COMMON ASH.
A STAMEN OF THE WALLFLOWER: f, filament; a, anther; p, pollen.
VERTICAL SECTION OF THE OVARY OF THE BARBERRY : o, ovary; ov, ovules attached to a projection called the placenta; st, stigma; a, anther.

the Plant. There are the air and water and food, taken into roots and stems, and worked into condition by the green leaves. There is the great sun, shining down by day, and giving that warmth without which no seed could ever come into being.

Yet these are not enough. Something else must happen, if the ovule is ever to become a real seed; a seed which shall have in it, not only life, but exactly that kind of life which may grow later into the same kind of plant as the one in which the seed itself grew. Sunshine, and water, and air, and food, and the prepared sap passing through the plant—all these must fail, unless a certain *something* takes place.

A little of the golden pollen from one of the stamen-anthers *must* somehow reach the stigma of the pistil, and *must* send a slender tube-like growth down the style or stalk, to reach and touch the ovule below.

And then, from this meeting, this union, of a pollen-grain with an ovule, a seed is formed; and in time, under right conditions, a new young plant—child of the old plant—may be expected to spring from it.

It might at first sight seem rather curious that, while this union of the two is so vitally needful, all sorts of difficulties seem to be put in the way of its coming about.

Matters would be so easy, if only the stamens of a flower were always nicely arranged just around and over the pistil of that flower. Then, when the pollen is ripe and the ovules below are ready for it, and the anthers are opening, a passing breeze and the swaying of the plant would shake down some of the loosening golden dust upon the pistil-tip, exactly where it is wanted.

But that is by no means what usually happens.

Perhaps the pistil grows very tall, standing up and away from the stamen-tips. And when the pollen falls, it drops down below, wide of the stigmas, and is blown away by the wind.

Or the stamens themselves grow long, leaving behind the short pistil-tips, and the plant droops over on one side; and again, when the pollen escapes it does not touch the pistil.

Sometimes a plant has two kinds of flowers growing

on it; one kind having stamens only, and no pistils; the other kind having pistils only, and no stamens. This is the case with Pines; and with them the pistil-flowers grow high up, the stamen-flowers low down. So the pollen as it falls, is likely to be borne away by the breeze, and none of it may reach the pistils above.

When, as often is the case, the stamen-flowers grow on one tree, and the pistil-flowers on another tree, the difficulty becomes still greater.

Yet all this is only perplexing until we find the true reason for it. A right good reason exists.

The main object throughout is clearly that pollen should reach the pistils. But—*not the plant's own pistils.* That makes all the difference.

For the sake of the plant itself; for the vigour of the seed; for, if I may say so, the growth of *character* in the plant-race—we know it to be better that a plant should not use its own pollen, but should receive some from another plant of the same kind. And who may assert with authority that " character " is not a thing aimed at in the life of plants, even as in a far greater and higher degree it is aimed at in the life of human beings? True, in their case it is perhaps character rather of the type than of the individual. Yet even with them there *is* individuality; since no two plants of the same kind and under the same conditions ever grow precisely alike, or respond in precisely the same mode to their surroundings and their opportunities.

Therefore, deliberately and purposefully, and not by chance, all kinds of difficulties are put in the way of a plant using its own pollen; so that, for its own good, it is driven to seek some from elsewhere.

And since it is tied to one spot, and cannot possibly travel for what it needs, it is compelled to make use of other means. How this is done will come later.

Many years ago the Variegated Laurel was introduced into our country from Japan; but only the pistil-bearing kind came. So none of the bright red berries, admired by travellers, were seen here. After a while the other and stamen-bearing kind was brought too; and speedily red berries made their appearance all over England. This illustrates the absolute necessity for pollen, before the pistils can produce seeds.

IV—Plant Storage

As the young seed grows it needs food; and the parent-plant has to see that the hungry young ovules and seeds are properly supplied. Shut up as they are inside the ovary, unable to get out, they can do nothing for themselves. So the roots and leaves must keep them going.

Three different kinds of plants are commonly known : those which live one year only and then die, called Annuals; those which live two years and then die, called Biennials; and lastly those which live many years, called Perennials.

The two first are alike in a single respect, that they flower only once. But the one-year kinds have a much shorter time in which to complete their task; so they are obliged to " hurry up " with it.

All that they have to do must be done in one season— the growth of the plant itself from a seed; the forming of roots, of stems, of leaves, of flowers, of seeds. The roots have to gather in food; and the leaves have to prepare it; and the finished sap has to make its way through cells and channels to every part, that the tiny beginnings of seeds may get their full share. And at the end of the summer the plant dies, quite worn out. But the seeds remain alive, ready for the next spring.

Two-year plants manage differently. In their first season they grow roots and short stems and leaves, but no flowers. They are indeed much too busy, laying in stores, to have any leisure for flowering. Thus far, their work is one of preparation. They are gathering together a supply of nutriment, ready for use in the year following; food for the flowers, food for the seeds.

With some plants much of this food is piled together in the roots, as with a Radish; the long red root of which we all know so well. But the plant did not mean it for you! It meant that nice little reserve-store for its own use next year—if we may say that a plant in any sense " means " anything—and you have spoilt those plans, by stealing the deposit.

When nobody interferes and the plant is left to its own devices, it goes on with its preparations through the first summer. And when the following spring arrives, it begins to bud and flower. Then the root slowly shrinks and gets thinner, as its carefully husbanded provision is used for present needs.

With many plants the *bulb* may be said to take the place of a seed; as in the case of Crocus bulbs, Snowdrop bulbs, Hyacinth bulbs and others, which begin life with only one small seed-leaf. These bulbs also are packed full of hidden provender, enclosing the little bud from which the new plant will spring. And as the young plant grows, the bulb will gradually give up its stored supply, becoming smaller and smaller.

Sometimes the storage is in the leaves, instead of in roots or bulbs. We find this with a very commonplace though useful plant—the Cabbage. You know what large strong leaves it has, and how wholesome they are said to be. No wonder!—for the leaves are real reserve-stores of food, laid by for the plant's own use.

In other cases, again, the storage is in the stem, instead of roots or leaves, as with the brown " tubers " of the potato-plant. Many people suppose them to be roots, because they are dug out of the earth. But they are really more in the nature of swelled portions of underground stems, as they have buds—the " eyes." They are big with a fine hoard of starchy nourishment, which would later have been most useful for the plant itself, if some one had not stepped in and eaten the " potato."

SNOWDROP. (Showing stem, flower and root.)

These storages are found, not only in biennials, but in plants of longer life. And there are also special little stores, carefully put by for the feeding of the seeds when they begin to grow.

By that time the seed will have separated itself from the parent-plant, which may or may not have died. But the living seed has its own little private store, packed neatly inside its hard outer coat.

Sometimes the stock of food is in the " cotyledons," and usually it is folded close about the tiny beginning of life in the seed. Either way it is at hand, ready for use, so soon as it may be wanted.

> " Fair Daffodils, we weep to see
>   You haste away so soon;
> As yet the early rising sun
>   Has not attained his noon.
>   Stay, stay,
>   Until the hasting day
>   Has run
>   But to the Evensong;
> And having prayed together, we
>   Will go with you along.
>
> " We have short time to stay as you,
>   We have as short a spring,
> As quick a breath to meet decay
>   As you or any thing;
>   We die
>   As your hours do, and dry
>   Away,
>   Like to the summer's rain,
> Or as the pearls of morning dew
>   Ne'er to be found again." [1]

V—Making Ready for Summer

Even in the cold dark days of winter, when growth is more or less at a standstill, when the plant is in a kind of chrysalis state, when nothing seems doing, even then we must not suppose that the seed is perfectly idle.

Inside that hard outer coat, preparation is going on. Through the winter months the seed is living, breathing,

[1] Robert Herrick (about A.D. 1600).

getting into the right condition. Changes are taking place in its make, without which it would be unable later to carry out its appointed task.

This silent winter-work of seeds, of bulbs, of plants in general, is very wonderful. All outside looks dead and lifeless. No one would imagine how much activity lies beneath.

Some plants are more asleep—more like a chrysalis, in fact—than others. We know how all but lifeless a chrysalis may seem; yet it is not dead. It is only preparing for a happier future. And in the same manner the trees are not dead; the bulbs and seeds are not dead.

Many among them are already at work, very quietly, very noiselessly, yet not less truly. Down in the dark earth with some, inside the dead-looking boughs with others, leaf-buds and even flower-buds are being manufactured, are being shaped and put together, in readiness to burst out joyously when the right hour shall arrive.

By some people winter is counted a rather sad season. Not by girls and boys who do not mind cold, who can race and slide and skate. But for older people, and for lovers of gardens, it does perhaps seem rather melancholy.

Yet it is not really so. It is only Nature's night; and night is needful for those who work hard. Winter is Nature's time for rest in her Vegetable Kingdom, and for gaining fresh strength to work anew. The world around may look grey and dull and chilly; but actually it is full of hidden life, full of hope, full of growing readiness for the lovely time coming.

THE WORK OF FLOWERS

Bulbs look very dead when taken out of the ground, and placed upon a shelf, or put back into the earth. Either way they have to wait, silently and patiently. To wait for what? Why—for the coming of the Sun in his power, that he may call them to a new life.

Meanwhile, though buried, they still live. They are being made ready for the presence of the Sun. They are growing, under ground, their new and glorious spring garments. When spring is here, they will be ready to respond; ready to say to the Sun : " Yes, here I am —waiting ! " ready to send forth new roots, new stems, new leaves, new flowers.

This work of preparation, which goes on under ground or above ground, with seeds and bulbs and branches, takes time. Certain alterations, certain developments, inside the seed or bulb or branch, have to come about before the new growth can begin to show itself.

It was at one time thought that bulbs and seeds might start growing much earlier than they do, if only they were in the right soil, and had the right amount of warmth and moisture. It was supposed that they waited for the spring, *only* because of the checking cold of winter.

But this, with the greater number, was found to be a mistake. The experiment was tried; and they did not respond. They would not begin growing until the spring.

Much the same was noted with potatoes. Some potato-tubers were dug up in the autumn, and were put in a warm sheltered cellar, where the air remained always at about the same degree of warmth. For many months, through mild autumn days and cold days following, they lay there quietly; doing nothing that could be seen. Then spring came. In that sheltered cellar no sunshine could enter; and the air was found to be actually colder than it had been through the winter. Yet, strange to say, those tubers began to sprout, began to send out slender shoots, bearing leaves.

Now why and how was this? If they grew then, when there was no added warmth to make them, why should they not have begun earlier?

Simply because *they were not ready!* They needed the winter months for all that had to be done first; for the changes that had to go on in them, before such growth could become possible. Warmth at the right time would help them. But warmth before they were ready to sprout was useless. They *had* to get through their preparatory work; and then—and not till then—could they carry out those tasks in life, which would be their duty to do.

It is the same with hundreds of plants, which scatter their seeds on the ground in autumn days.

There the seeds lie, to be gradually washed into the soil, where they often find at once plenty of warmth and moisture; quite enough, one would think, to make them " germinate " without delay. Yet they do not. They send no roots downward, no leaves and stems upward. They lie hidden; making ready for their future.

And perhaps a cold spring comes, much colder than the autumn was. Such cold must and does hinder advance. Yet, in spite of it, many seeds and bulbs start active life, though slowly, and begin to send forth leaves, sometimes even flowers. For now they are ready; they have had their time of preparation; and that makes all the difference.

In this, as in other respects, plants vary greatly. Some seeds take much longer than others in preparing. Some are more readily affected by warmth. Some will spring up at almost any time, like Mustard and Cress, under certain conditions. And the above is true of bulbs, as well as of seeds.

Spring is really a time of Resurrection.

Each bare and lifeless tree, which in the autumn " seemed to have died," [1] has only been asleep; and now, with the coming of spring sunshine, it leaps into a new and glorious life. Each bulb which " seemed to have died " and was buried in the earth, forces its flowers upward to a fresh and lovely existence. Each little seed, which looked so cold and lifeless, is found in some new form of beauty and fragrance, while still remaining *itself*. The individuality is unchanged. If that seed had never been sown, that plant would never have grown.

Nature holds for us many symbols, many parables, if only we will read them, as surely we are meant to do; and none more striking than this. Perhaps the most wonderful part of it is that, while so buried, while still so seemingly " dead," the bulbs and the seeds are actually at work, fashioning their own resurrection bodies in readiness for the coming springtide. May we not find here a suggestion, if not an actual prophecy, full of promise for our own future, and for the future of those who still belong to us, though out of sight—who are " not lost, but gone before "?

[1] Wisdom of Solomon, iii. 2.

K

THE GARDEN OF EARTH

VI—Seed-Scattering

A few words must come in here about another part of
the matter; and that is—the way in which seeds are
scattered about and carried from place to place.

It is easy to see that if the plant—any plant—had

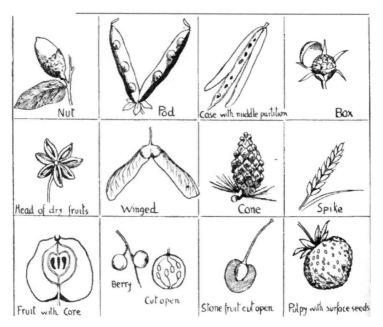

VARIETIES OF FRUIT.

to manage this work alone and unaided, failure might
commonly result. The seed, on becoming ripe, would
just fall from the flowers to the ground, close at hand.
How could they do otherwise? Then, when the young
plants grew, they would crowd round about the old plant,
and would soon choke one another to death.

THE WORK OF FLOWERS

Imagine what would happen, if *all* the acorns of a great Oak were to drop down within a few yards of the trunk, and *all* were to take root and grow up. Hundreds,

FLOWERS OF OAK.
♂ Male.   ♀ Female.

if not thousands, of young Oaks might be fighting for life at one time, under the shadow of the parent-tree. And they could not thrive. Space and light and food would all be lacking. Fortunately, acorns do not so easily find a footing. But with many other plants "germination" is a quicker and more easy matter.

Thus the pressing need comes in that seeds should somehow travel or be taken elsewhere. And then arises the necessity for help from outside.

All do not need such help equally, since many plants can do a good deal for themselves. A large number come under the heading of "Sling-fruits"; a name used for those that possess a curious "expulsive force," by means of which they can sling or fling their seeds to a distance. With some, the seeds are jerked away; or they are shot off as from a catapult; or the enclosing envelope, when it breaks open, does so with an energy that tosses the contents violently to right and left.

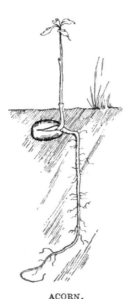

ACORN.

Many plants, however, are gifted with no such clever mechanical devices, and they have to depend on outside assistance.

The winds of heaven step kindly in, and make themselves useful, especially with smaller and lighter seeds, easily carried about. Not a few are so formed as to float in the air; and one of these we all know—the Dandelion-seed, with its soft downy "attachment." Dandelion "clocks" as the children call them will rise high and fly fast before the gentlest breeze.

Seeds of this description may travel to almost any

distance; and there are many others more or less like
in kind. Some have light growths of hair, serving the
same purpose; some have tails or wings or feathers;
all making it possible to rise lightly and to journey far.

Water lends a hand in the work, though not so
largely as wind. Naturally, the seeds of water-plants

Seed head.

Dandelion.

TARAXACUM OFFICINALE
(*Common Dandelion*).

are carried off by currents; and land-plants sometimes drop theirs into a river. Swept down towards
or into the ocean, they may voyage to a distant shore,
before finding a soil in which to root. But this can only
happen with those which have an outer coat hard
enough to keep the inside perfectly dry, from the beginning to the end of their excursions. Cocoa-nuts floating
in the sea have been known to travel to far-away resting
places.

Animals also give some help. When sheep and cows and many smaller beasts press against bushes and hedges in autumn days, seeds are apt to cling fast to their hairy or woolly or furry coats, and to be carried to a good distance. Ducks, disporting themselves at the edge of a pond, and becoming half-clothed with mud, will bear away seeds in that mud, to deposit them elsewhere. Even birds flying—even some insects—give their aid in much the same fashion; one and all helping to scatter seeds broadcast.

PART IX

I—POLLEN TO THE PISTIL

SINCE anthers really are transformed leaves, and since pollen is manufactured in the anthers, these again may perhaps be called small workshops; different in kind from the green-leaf ones, yet not less important.

At one time pollen was often spoken of as " Flower-dust "; a pretty name! But with many plants, in place of being a fine powder, it was found to be sticky and in lumps, far too tiny lumps to be seen as such without a microscope.

When ripe and ready for use, the pollen has to make its escape; and this comes about in many ways. Frequently a tiny slit or hole appears first in each small sac; and the pollen-grains are no longer imprisoned. Yet even then, though the prison-door is actually open, they have no power to walk out; so they must wait for something else to happen, completing their release.

And here we touch on a very interesting matter; that of CROSS-FERTILISATION.

In an earlier chapter something was said about the difficulties put in the way of a plant supplying its own pistils with pollen " made on the premises,"—pollen from its own stamens; and about the need that it should

400

not, for its good, for the sake of its health and vigour, be allowed to do this. It is in every way better that the pollen which reaches its pistils should come from some other plant of the same kind. If not from one of precisely the same variety, it must at least be a very near relative; otherwise the golden dust or sticky little lumps will be useless.

And just as plants, because they are fixed in one place and cannot possibly travel about, have to use outside help in scattering their ripened seeds, so at an earlier stage, they must from the same reason use outside help in exchanging their pollen, one with another.

We sometimes hear of what is called "Crossing" by gardeners. That is to say, the gardener takes pollen from one plant—from an Orchid, for instance—and puts it on the pistil of a second, not precisely the same in kind though closely connected. And from the union of these two may spring a third Orchid, partly like the one and partly like the other.

Cross-Fertilisation on the contrary is done, not like Crossing by gardeners but by the plants themselves, with outside help. Such help is commonly given by Winds, by Water, and by Insects.

A child may accidentally share in this important work, though it happens rarely. You may have seen a little boy thrust his nose into a Tiger-lily, with its gorgeous striped petals; and when he moves away—if it is the time of ripened pollen—he may have a yellow tip to his nose. Then if he should go to another Tiger-lily plant, and should put his nose into a second flower, he would probably leave a little of the yellow stuff there, on a pistil-tip.

So, unconsciously, he would have given his tiny help in the world-wide work of Cross-Fertilisation.

One of the chief friends of plants, as just stated, is Wind.

In some trees the catkins or stamen-flowers, with their stores of pollen, grow long and hang low; while the pistil-flowers, with their ovules, are perhaps higher up; so that the pollen from the former would not easily reach the latter. And the reason why it should be so we know. It is *better* for the trees that each·should pass on its stores of golden dust to other trees, and should receive what is needed for its own use from those others. It is better, in fact, that each tree should not live a self-centred and selfish life, merely to supply its own needs, but that all should " freely receive and freely give."

As their pollen is very light and dust-like, the most gentle of breezes can lift the whole supply above the tree-tops. Then, when it slowly descends, all the pistils have a fair chance of capturing enough for their requirements; while no tree is likely to receive pollen of its own manufacture, since that would soon have been borne away by the breeze.

Pollen-grains are very tiny; and the amount contained in each stamen is small; therefore naturally we do not realise what huge supplies are grown every year. In the majority of cases it quits the little enclosing sac in so gentle and unobtrusive a manner as to draw no attention.

But when a great number of trees of the same kind grow together, and when they all shed their " dust " at the same time, the effect is much more in evidence.

For example, in a vast Pine forest, immense clouds of pollen may be seen, swept along by the wind, not only through the forest itself but far beyond, falling like a fine golden rain on trees and grasses. Of such abundant quantities only a few specks here and there may arrive on the waiting pistil-tips of kindred trees; few, that is

CATKINS OF THE OAK.

to say, compared with the tens of millions which drop where no pistil-tips are waiting. They sink to the ground, unwanted; useless failures, one might say. The matter may, however, be viewed from another standpoint.

Suppose that only just enough pollen were manufactured each year to meet the needs of all pistils, not allowing for failures. Much of it still would not reach the right spots; and this would mean many less seeds

403

brought to perfection, which in time could hardly fail to diminish sorely the numbers of our forest-trees. We usually find in Nature this wonderful fulness of supply; far more of each kind of growth than may seem to be

STAMINATE AND PISTILLATE CATKINS OF A WILLOW.

actually needed, so as to make sure that there will always be enough.

It means something else that is beautiful. It means that Our Father in Heaven gives with a Royal abundance. He gives like a King.

Large numbers of our trees depend almost though not quite entirely, for this work of scattering pollen, on the help that is given them by Wind. One curious instance is that of the Hazel-tree, the pollen of which is not ripe at the same time that the stigma is ready for it. So the pistils' only chance is the bringing of pollen from other Hazel-trees by friendly winds—from stamen-flowers which happen to have ripened a little earlier.

Oaks and Beeches, Poplars and Birches, Walnut-trees and Plane-trees, most of the Conebearing-trees and most of the Palms, have their pollen conveyed in this way from one to another, with very little other assistance. The same may be said of Grasses generally, of Rushes and Reeds, of Wheat and Oats and Barley. All these manufacture pollen fine enough and dry enough to be carried with ease by moving air.

On a warm and fairly still evening in late summer, at a time when pollen is ripe, clouds of it may sometimes be seen floating over a meadow; the stigmas being then ripe to receive it. Each kind of grass must have its own particular kind of pollen; and when supplies are dealt out thus by the breeze in wholesale fashion, they naturally get a good deal of the wrong kinds. But this does not matter; for when the wrong kind is dropped on a stigma it simply takes no effect. Some of the right kind is pretty sure to find its way thither also.

Each passing breeze, as well as stronger winds, takes a share in the task; helping first to stir the flowers, thus loosening the imprisoned powder; and then carrying it where it is wanted. The number of different kinds of plants, thus regularly assisted by the winds, is said to be as much as ten thousand.

But Wind is only one of the kind friends which come to the help of plants. We have next to think about the doings of INSECTS.

THE WORK OF WINDS AND INSECTS

" We were a million grasses on the hill,
   A million herbs which bowed as the wind blew,
   Trembling in every fibre, never still;
   Out of the summer earth sweet life we drew.
Little blue-flowered grasses up the glen,
Glad of the sun, what did we know of men ? " [1]

II—How Doth the Busy Bee

The story of Cross-Fertilisation, through generous offices of Bees and other Insects, reads curiously like a tale of friendly co-operation between them and Plants. Between Plants, earth-bound, fixed immovably in one spot for the term of their natural lives; and Insects, free to range hither and thither at will.

Plants require help in the work of supplying their pistils with the right pollen; and Insects require food for themselves and their young. So plants manufacture and offer tempting supplies of honey and pollen; while insects, creeping or flying in to secure that food, give the needed assistance by carrying pollen from one plant to another.

Books to any extent might be written, and in fact have been written, on that one topic alone. In this small volume no more can be attempted than to point out the general mode pursued, with a few slight instances given as examples of what goes on perpetually at flowering-time throughout the world. The subject is one well worth studying.

For, indeed, it is a marvellous story of mutual intercourse and mutual help; unconscious, we may say, on both sides; though that which is done often looks

[1] From *Lollingdon Downs*, by John Masefield, published by William Heinemann. By permission.

strangely—like many other things in insect-life and even in plant-life—*as if* both insects and plants knew in a manner, dimly, what they are about.

In any case, one fact becomes clear with daylight clearness, that all the vast work of Cross-Fertilisation is part of a great plan—a Divine plan—not, as once was imagined, putting needless hindrances in the way of success, but working steadily and systematically towards beautiful ends and ever fuller developments. The reading of it recalls to mind certain words spoken in earliest days of our world's history—" *And God saw that it was good !* "

That each helps the other is a truth undeniable. A plant cannot stir; but it *can* manufacture food. A bee can flit to and fro with ease, but it cannot manufacture the sweet stuff which forms the foundation for real honey. The raw material is in the flower; and the hive-bee has in its own little body a small apparatus which can transform that raw material into food for itself and for human kind.

So the plant does all it can to attract the bee—and other insects. And the bee does its utmost to satisfy its own needs, while performing friendly offices for the plant.

Most of us must often have watched a big humble-bee bustling from flower to flower; diving in and out of blossom after blossom; blundering into this one and that one in her eager search; till one is almost forced to the belief that bees are not quite so clever as one had imagined. She keeps forgetting which flower she has tried before, and she rushes again and again into the same, coming out with what sounds like a " buzz " of indignation at not finding what she expected. Whether all are equally dense it is difficult to say; but certainly I have at different times watched several acting thus.

Sooner or later she generally meets with success. Then she remains for some seconds, gathering the nectar that she loves. And while so occupied, something else

POLLINATION BY BEE.

is apt to happen. If the pollen is ripe, part of it sticks to her legs, and probably to her body as well. This she carries away to the next flower into which she plunges; and as she buzzes and squirms about, a little of it is rubbed off, to remain on the pistil or pistils of the second flower.

Such is the mode in which bees and numberless insects carry on the work which winds undertake with grasses.

They, too, are helping forward " fertilisation," not knowing or caring about that object, any more than do the winds, but intent only on getting their food.

Through all the warm fine days of summer months this goes on. Humble-bees, honey-bees, insects in countless numbers, fly or creep and dive into flowers of all descriptions; and as they search for what they want, they carry off the loosened pollen, and give it over to other plants.

What the hive-bees want and search for is not always the same. Two especial needs have to be supplied : pollen, for what has been called " bee-bread," and sweet nectar, to be made into honey. When the workers leave their hive in the early morning, they seem to be " told off " for different tasks. One goes in search of pollen; another in quest of a supply of nectar; but never both at the same time.

A pollen-gatherer loads her little baskets—a curious arrangement of stiff hairs on her back pair of legs—and often gets her whole body covered as well with the golden stuff, before she returns to the hive. No light weight this, for so small a creature. Yet so soon as she is relieved of the burden by her sister-workers, she is off again for more.

But a nectar-gatherer has a lighter task. Her little baskets are useless when she goes hunting, not for honey, but for that which is to be transformed into honey. We all talk conventionally of insects getting " honey " from flowers. But honey, as we know it, is a " manufactured article "; [1] and the " nectar " which the

[1] Tickner Edwardes.

bee procures is a thin, sweet, watery liquid, only the raw material on which she has to work. The manufactory which does what is necessary is within her little body.

She has two small stomachs—so-called—one being the true stomach, while the other is a minute reservoir or "honey-sac," into which the sweet nectar which she sips is passed through a tube traversing her body. When she goes home with her sac full, having probably by the way used some as food, she gives over the contents to the empty sac of another bee; and by the latter it is stored in a cell. During such transferrings certain changes take place in its make, altering it from the original thin liquid into genuine honey, good for food of men.

In both these expeditions, which the bees are said to undertake by turns, perhaps on alternate days, they constantly help forward fertilisation, bearing pollen from plant to plant.

The question has been asked, "How is it that bees always carry away the right kind of pollen?" It naturally stirs up a counter question: "Do they, always?" At all events, they sometimes carry home honey-dew, instead of the right kind of nectar, for honey.

Authorities are not quite at one about this pollen-gathering. It has been confidently stated that they always carry one kind only at a time, and never mix different kinds; and that during a single excursion a bee will visit only one kind of flower, passing by all others. But a precisely opposite statement, founded on personal observation, is made in another and most weighty quarter. Again, in one direction we are told that, when they reach the hive the various kinds and colours of

L

410

pollen are still kept separate in the cells; while in another direction we are informed that all the care of the bees is useless, since the different kinds of pollen are packed indiscriminately together in the cells.

A suggestion may perhaps be hazarded here that bees, or rather communities of bees, *may* not all follow the same plans. Some possibly may act in one way; some in another. It would be interesting to know if any evidence could be found of this.

In an earlier chapter something was said about the beauty of flowers, and the reasons why they may have been made so beautiful. Of one reason we need feel no real doubts; which is, that they might bring gladness and joy to us who live on the Earth.

But another and a very important reason, if not for their actual loveliness, yet certainly for their gay colouring, is that they may draw the attention of insects. If no insects came to visit them, we should have a sad dearth of pollen where it may be most urgently needed.

Though we can hardly suppose that insects love beautiful things as we do, simply for their loveliness, they are no doubt attracted by bright tints. Some of them are believed to possess what is called a " colour-sense." In other words, they seem to know blue from yellow, pink from green. More than this, they even show signs of preferring one colour and disliking another.

It is said that a honey-bee loves a deep violet-blue, and has no objection to green or yellow, while she shows a marked avoidance of scarlet or orange-red. Whether any feeling of actual distaste is in question cannot be known with certainty. All we can be sure of is that, for some reason, she does not usually tackle flowers of those tints, but seems to keep away from them.

Somebody has suggested, as a possible explanation, that bees may suffer from " colour-blindness." Men are often more or less " colour-blind," and cannot distinguish certain hues, such as red from green. Possibly bees may have some such defect of vision, so that they cannot *see* red or orange-red blossoms; in which case, naturally, they would not go to them.

In a general way gay flowers do undoubtedly draw many insects. It is interesting to notice that those trees which depend chiefly on winds to carry about their dusty pollen, and which therefore do not need the help of insects, have usually small and dull flowers, easily overlooked. While plants which depend mainly on insect-visitors, have generally larger and brighter blooms.

Bees seem long ago to have discovered that what they want is more often to be found in the gayer flowers. How far this really has been due to " finding out for themselves," and how far to simple " instinct," it is impossible to say.

With most insects a large amount of instinct is found. By this we mean a kind of knowledge which is born with them, inherited by them, and not knowledge which is gained later through experience. But with such possession is also found a certain amount of power to learn from observation and practice. To decide in any particular instance exactly how far action has arisen from blind instinct, and how far from " finding out," is very difficult.

THE GARDEN OF EARTH

Perhaps the only case known of Cross-Fertilisation being carried on by a warm-blooded animal, not an insect, is that of Humming-birds.

III—Curious Contrivances

Thus it becomes clear that, in the various plans found in Nature for the carrying of pollen from stamens to pistils, a good deal may be seen of hindering and of helping : of hindering the pollen from getting to the wrong pistils ; of helping it to get to the right ones. That a flower should be fertilised by its own pollen is bad ; therefore hindrances are placed in the way. That the pistils of one plant should be supplied with pollen from other similar plants is to be desired ; therefore helps are provided.

A certain plant belonging to the south of Europe grows abundantly in ponds or in shallow waters of a lake ; and with it may be markedly seen both the hindering and the helping. Like many others, this—the *Vallisneria spiralis*—has two kinds of flowers, the pistil-bearing and the stamen-bearing. Its pollen is of a very sticky nature.

In mud at the bottom it has its roots ; and long slender leaves grow upward, still under water. There too, the flowers quietly take shape ; both kinds, pistil-flowers and stamen-flowers, being sheltered safely inside sacs or bladders. Each pistil-flower is alone within its sac ; and on a lengthening stem it rises and rises till the surface is reached. Then it opens out, with large petals and wide-tipped hanging pistils, to wait for the pollen which has to be brought to it.

413

After quite another fashion behave the stamen-flowers.
They also take shape out of sight far below, encased in a
bladder through which no damp may penetrate. But
instead of only one flower, the sac contains many;
and when they gain a certain stage, the enclosing sac
opens to set them free. Then, in place of growing
upward on a long stalk, they break short off and spring

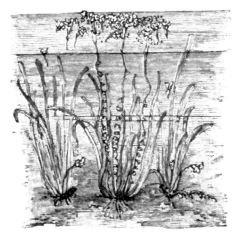

VALLISNERIA SPIRALIS.

to the surface, at the time when their pollen is just
ripe.

On first arrival at the surface they are fast shut,
and rounded like little globes; but soon they open, to
float as tiny boats on pond or lake. Wonderful little
boats, too—three flowers joined together forming one
boat—supported by three outspread sepals, and so
constructed as not to overturn even when blown
about somewhat roughly. They have power to right

414

themselves, and so to keep their precious pollen dry for use.

For use—but *not* for the use of those pistil-flowers which were grown on the same plant with themselves. In time these triple-boats, only two of the three having out-standing ripened anthers, as they are wafted about or even if no breeze stirs, are sure to gather round some of the pistil-flowers standing out of the water. Floating objects always do tend thus to draw together, through mutual attraction.

Some of the pollen-grains on board a tiny boat will then come into touch with one of the long drooping pistils, and will reach a waiting stigma; and, being sticky, will remain on it. Thus the needed work is done—so gracefully done too!—and Fertilisation is secured.

Nor is this all. We have seen how the pistil-flower grows upward from the bottom to the surface of the water, that its needs may be met. That being accomplished, its presence above is no longer called for. So the long stalk acts in an extraordinary manner. It shortens, coiling in a spiral, till the flower is again close to the bottom; there to ripen its seeds at leisure for the next year.

Did you ever watch a humble-bee trying to make her way into a Calceolaria flower? The entrance is rather complicated; but the bee, quite naturally, sits on the lower lip, and opens a door to herself by light pressure against the upper lip. A hidden " nectary," with plenty of sweet juice, then springs to view, " presented to the humble-bee, just like a spoon." When she has had enough and departs, " the lower lip snaps to, and the nectary disappears from view." [1]

But here also something else is pretty sure to happen. If the pollen within is ripe, she will be dusted over with it, and will leave some in flowers of a neighbouring plant.

We need not imagine that the bee understands the make of the flower, or knows that a certain pressure will cause the store of sweet stuff to come within her reach. Matters are so planned that she, taking her position at the entrance and trying to get in, will naturally exert such pressure. Still, when she has done it often, it is not impossible that she *may* remember how she got in before.

In much the same manner bees creep into the flowers of Foxgloves and Snapdragons. With the Wild Mustard a curious scheme is followed. The anthers are first bent *towards* the pistil; which might seem all right for the depositing of pollen on the stigmas. But when the pollen is nearly ripe, the stamens very curiously twist themselves round, till their faces are turned *away* from the pistil. Could speech say more plainly, " No, my pollen is *not* wanted there : it must go elsewhere, and pollen from some other plant has to come here " ?

A second reason exists for this singular behaviour of the stamens. When a bee comes in for food, it so happens that the anthers as now placed—after the turnabout of the stamens—will brush her back with pollen. But if they had remained as they were before, she might have failed to carry any away. So the golden stuff which may not go to the pistils close at hand is borne away to other plants; and more bees, going first to those plants,

[1] Kerner and Oliver, ii. 228.

416

will bring some here instead; a very fair and wise exchange.

The Butterfly Orchis grows its pollen in two tiny lumps, close together. When a butterfly enters to feast on the sweet nectar, it oftens happens to press its forehead against these little lumps, which, being very sticky, remain attached like a new-fangled head-dress. But the visitor does not keep this burden long. Going into other flowers, it is pretty sure to press soon against a pistil-tip, leaving there part at least of the head-dress.

In all such Cross-Fertilisation work, done by winds and insects, as in the " Crossing " work of gardeners, not only is ordinary fertilisation carried on, but also the growth of fresh varieties is advanced.

Not that " Crossing " or " Cross-Fertilisation " will always account for such fresh varieties. Differences do appear from time to time, with no apparent reason; differences in size, in shape, in the form and colouring of flowers, in modes of growth. Plants are perpetually producing slight variations in their offspring; and the power to do so seems to be inborn. Fresh kinds, fresh types, are from time to time found in them, suddenly and unexpectedly.

This brings us naturally to a recollection of Darwin's favourite thought—" *The survival of the fittest*,"—by which he meant the survival of the strongest, of the healthiest, of the best-fitted to make their way in life. Such " survival " depends mainly on the plants' power of response and of self-adaptation to surroundings. A slight illustration of how this power works may be offered here.

THE WORK OF WINDS AND INSECTS

Suppose that among a mass of Viola-plants growing together, one in particular has a greater capability than the rest to grow longer flower-stems; and that in consequence fuller sunshine is gained by its flowers than by those of any other plant in the group. As a result, those flowers will be more visited by insects, and will receive fuller supplies of pollen; so that, in the course of generations, this particular form of Viola will become more abundant than other and weaker kinds. Here at once is a very simple form of such "survival." The wonderful power seen in plants to adapt themselves to varying conditions seems sometimes to draw very near to actual animal-intelligence.

Gardeners can do a great deal for the producing of new forms; not, like insects, without understanding, but with deliberate intention. Countless new and lovely kinds have thus come into existence; and each year we have more and more of them.

Many years ago only the red form of the common Poppy was known. But the owner of a garden, where a bed of them grew, found one day among the rest a single blossom of a different hue. He at once marked it; and when it seeded he kept the seeds and sowed them apart. Then, when the young plants grew, he watched carefully till more of the unusual tints made their appearance; and again he marked these, kept the seeds, and grew fresh generations of plants, with pink and striped flowers, never seen before. They were named "Shirley Poppies," from the place where the selection occurred.

This probably was simply a natural development, a " Freak of Nature," not due to any " Crossing."

THE GARDEN OF EARTH

" Evening rose from a bed of pain,
  And out of the west day dawned again;
  With outstretched fingers of falling light
  She touched the tree-tops and made them bright;
  And under the leaves, a-spark with dew,
  The cry of the blackbird sparkled too;
  And every hillock and glade and tree
  Was filled with the makings of melody,
  As the dying light streamed miles along
  Through murmur of water and leaf and song." [1]

" And murmuring of innumerable bees." [2]

[1] From *The Heart of Peace and Other Poems*, by Laurence
Housman, published by William Heinemann. By permission.
[2] Tennyson.

PART X

I—PLANT MOVEMENTS

THE movements of plants, and of their various parts, are very curious. These alone would be enough to prove that they *live*. Things without life do not move and stir and turn round of themselves, any more than they grow or change in shape.

Something of the above we found in earlier chapters. We saw how a leaf or a flower will try to follow the sun in his daily journey across the sky; and this is true, not only of a leaf or a flower, for the whole plant generally is inclined to bend towards the sun, or towards the best light it can find. If we keep one in a window, and never turn the pot round, it will grow all to one side, and its shape is spoilt.

Again, we noticed how leaves and petals droop and close in dull weather, or when night is near. Not all in the same manner or to the same extent; for different kinds are as unlike in their ways as different people are unlike in theirs. Still, more or less and in one fashion or another, they all have their own little movements, regularly carried out.

Also, we saw how roots move, how the delicate tips circle about in their hunt for food. And it is the same with other parts.

420

THE GARDEN OF EARTH

The stems, for instance—of some kinds certainly, and it may be true of all—go gently round and round, pointing a little towards the east, towards the south, towards the west, towards the north, and then toward the east again, so completing the circle, over and over again, day after day. And not only the main stem, but lesser stems which branch out from it, are believed to follow the same plan.

These movements are so very slight, so very slow and quiet, that they cannot be *seen*. They can only be made out by most delicate and exact measurements. Such measurements have been taken by those who have given their lives to the study of plant-life.

It is supposed, though not yet known with certainty, that each separate leaf may likewise carry on its own tiny movements, daily, in circles. Though we speak of " circles," the actual movements are believed to be, more strictly, not exact circles, but ovals—or what is known in Astronomy as " ellipses."

This fact, which probably is true of all plants, is much more markedly seen with Climbing Plants. If we examine one of them, we shall see how it twists in and out of a trellis-work or round and round the stem of another plant. And it does this in a most curious way. As the stem lengthens, its *tip* travels round and round in the air, hunting incessantly for something to lay hold of. Then, finding a support, it bends around that support, embracing firmly its new friend.

If you happen to live near a Hop-garden, you can, at the right season, study the growing Hops, and can see how they gradually mount and hold hard and hang in graceful festoons. Or you may find in the hedge a wild " Clematis,"—the " Traveller's Joy "—and again you will see much the same.

But such plants as the Bryony have extra help in climbing, for they grow *tendrils*, delicate spirals, which unwind and wind anew, and cling fast as they rise. The tendrils, like stem-tips, are ever going round and round, very gently, ever on the watch for a new support; and when they have come across what they need, they take resolute hold and refuse to let go.

While all stem-tips circle in this manner, they do not all move in the same direction. Those of the Scarlet Runner and of the Bindweed circle from west to east by the *north ;* but those of the Hop and of the Honeysuckle circle from west to east by the *south.* It is practically the same difference as when the hands of a watch move forwards, or are made to move backwards.

Why this difference should exist we cannot say; we only know that so it is. And each plant keeps steadily to its own manner of moving, and will not consent to go the other way round, not even if it is so fastened as almost to force it to change. This has been tried; but the victim rebelled, and insisted on following the mode to which it was used.

Climbing Plants generally go upwards. They do not care to travel along a support laid flat on the ground. Some Creeping Plants grow thus; but a real Climber, if compelled to do so, gets out of health and sickly; for the life then lived is not natural to it. Mounting upward is its true nature ; the nature of the life that is in it.

We may safely say that the tendrils, like other parts, are often, if not always, *modified leaves.*

THE GARDEN OF EARTH

II—Sensitive and Meat-eating Plants

That all Vegetable Growths are more or less sensitive is pretty clear. They are sensitive to sunshine, to heat and cold, to moisture, to changes of climate and weather. We know how quickly they open their flowers to greet the sun, and how soon they droop from lack of water or of light and warmth.

By this word " sensitive " is meant generally *the power to receive and to respond to impressions*. It means with ourselves the power to receive light-waves, sound-waves, and any manner of touch; and to respond by the sensations of sight, of hearing, of feeling. Such sensations are often outwardly expressed by speech or movement; and a plant can respond by movement, though not by speech. These movements show us, not that the plant can actually see or hear or feel, but that it is in some way affected, that it is *touched*—disturbed or checked or helped—by outside influences.

A dog is standing in the road, and a motor-car spins suddenly round the corner. Instantly the dog jumps aside. That is his response to what suggests to him danger. The dog has brains and can think. He knows why he has hurried away.

A plant responds, but does not think, does not know why, which makes a very great difference. Still, the fact remains that it does respond. It is not like a rock or a stone. In its degree, it is sensitive to outer influences, to what goes on outside it and apart from itself.

And as some human beings are more sensitive, more easily stirred or startled, than others, so some vegetable growths are more quickly affected than others. A

423

certain particular class is known by the name of "Sensitive Plants," because of their especially rapid response.

With one kind, a gentle wind blowing on the leaves, a few drops of rain, or even the touch of a finger, will cause a hurried folding together and drooping; much as other leaves will do *slowly* at the approach of night. A particular species, growing in India, is so excessively sensitive, that even a touch is not needed.[1] It is enough for a man simply to come near; and the slight stir of air caused by his movements will make the leaves shrink and fall, as if in alarm.

Years ago I saw in Kew Gardens a singular example. It was the Telegraph Plant from Bengal,[2] a small thing in a pot, with slim pointed leaflets. Outward touch had no effect, but as we stood looking one leaflet here or another there would suddenly *drop*, like a railway signal falling to announce a train. Then, I was told, each would gradually rise to its old position soon to drop again. No cause was known to which these movements could be traced, but they were found to be more frequent with greater heat.

Many sensitive plants grow in tropical countries, and one of them, a Mimosa, has delicate leaves, which respond prettily on the smallest provocation. First the leaflets droop, then with speed the whole leaf-stalk falls limply. In such cases we do not find the slowness of movement common in plant-life.

By far the greater number of these curious growths belong to foreign countries. But the little Wood-sorrel

---

[1] *Oxalis sensitiva.*   [2] *Desmodium gyrans.*

of England shows the same tendency. Its leaves will shrink slightly with rough handling, or if touched in a certain manner with the blade of a penknife.

" A Sensitive Plant in a garden grew,
And the young winds fed it with silver dew,
And it opened its fan-like leaves to the light,
And closed them beneath the kisses of night.

" And the spring arose on the garden fair,
And the Spirit of Love fell everywhere;
And each flower and herb on Earth's dark breast
Rose from the dreams of its wintry rest.

" But none ever trembled and panted with bliss
In the garden, the field, or the wilderness,
Like a doe in the noontide with love's sweet want,
As the companionless Sensitive Plant.

" The snowdrop and then the violet,
Arose from the ground with warm rain wet,
And their breath was mixed with fresh odours, sent
From the turf, like the voice and the instrument.

" Then the pied wind-flowers and the tulip tall,
And narcissi, the fairest among them all,
Who gaze on their eyes in the stream's recess,
Till they died of their own dear loveliness.

.   .   .   .   .   .

" And the hyacinth purple and white and blue,
Which flung from its bells a sweet peal anew
Of music, so delicate, soft and intense,
It was felt like an odour within the sense.

.   .   .   .   .   .

" Each and all like ministering angels were
For the Sensitive Plant sweet joy to bear,
While the lagging hours of the day went by
Like windless clouds o'er a tender sky.

" And when evening descended from heaven above,
And the earth was all rest, and the air was all love,
And delight, though less bright, was far more deep,
And the day's veil fell from the world of sleep.

425

SOME REMARKABLE WAYS OF PLANTS

" The Sensitive Plant was the earliest
Upgathered into the bosom of rest;
A sweet child, weary of its delight,
The feeblest and yet the favourite,
Cradled within the embrace of night." [1]

Another kind is marked by another sort of sensitive-ness, by what looks very much like sense. There are plants which actually feed on solid animal-food. This is a remarkable exception.

In the chapters on Roots and Leaves we saw that " vegetables " in general, using the word in its widest sense, are able only to take in liquid food, or food in the form of gases. Not one of them could receive or digest anything solid. Yet here we find that rule apparently broken.

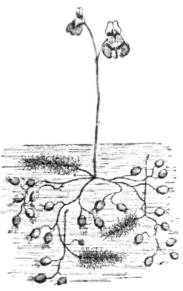

BLADDERWORT.

No less than five hundred kinds are known, in various parts of the world, which more or less live on animal-food, taken in the solid form. They are often called " Insectivorous Plants," because they subsist largely on insects; and also sometimes they are described as " Flesh-eating."

Such food is captured by them in many ways, and only two or three can be mentioned here.

[1] Shelley.

M

A large number belong to the group of Bladderworts.

UTRICULARIA VULGARIS (*Common Bladderwort*).

They live in water, and have curious little bladders, which in springtime rise to the surface, and there float, acting as traps for the unwary. Each bladder has one tiny opening, closed by valves, and it can be entered from outside, but not quitted from the inside.

Small creatures, such as the young of gnats and worms, force their way in through protecting bristles, perhaps out of curiosity, perhaps in search of food, perhaps only to escape pursuing foes—and once in they have to stay, for the valves cannot be opened from within. They may live in their prison for hours, or even for days, but in the end they die, and are digested.

Then there are the remarkable Pitcher-plants of

California, and other tropical parts. Beautifully shaped hanging pitchers grow on them, partly filled with liquid. These, too, act as traps. Creatures fall, or fly, or creep into them, to be caught and held fast until they die, when again they are slowly digested.

PITCHER-PLANT.

One of the commonest and best-known of such plants is the Sundew,[1] widely spread through North Europe and North America. It grows usually on exposed moorlands, and also in some very cold regions.

Here it is the leaves which act as traps. Each leaf lies flat on the ground, in shape slightly "trough-like" and very sticky. Any small insect alighting there is caught and held firmly, despite all its struggles.

At the first touch of a victim the leaf begins to pour out juices from the little glands, which have power to manufacture such juices, and its edges turn slowly and ruthlessly up, curling over so as to imprison the unfortunate prey—once more to

[1] *Drosera.*

428

serve as meat for the plant. About twenty-four hours later, if it is a quite small insect, the leaf uncurls and is ready for another victim, though digestion often takes much longer.

DROSERA ROTUNDIFOLIA (*Round-leaved Sundew*).

A tiny scrap of meat placed there will be treated in a like manner, taken captive, well soused in juice, and gradually disposed of. Midges, ants, beetles, and small butterflies, are perhaps the commonest items of Sundew fare, though, as we have seen, it seems to like variety.

429

Often seeds and pollen-grains are wafted thither, for the same purpose.

If a dragon-fly happens to be captured, that is a grand haul. One or two more leaves will then come bending over to help the captor, for extra strength is needed to hold such a vigorous captive, and more juices for his complete subjection than a single leaf can supply.

Yet another Insect-eating plant is the " Venus' Fly-trap," a native of North America. Here again the leaves are the traps. Sharp spines grow on them, and when an unfortunate insect alights there, it is caught at once by the sticky outflow. Then it is closed in upon, slowly, pitilessly, the sharp spines crossing till its imprisonment is complete. Sometimes the leaf will remain tightly shut for a week, a fortnight, or even three weeks.

And these are only a few of the extraordinary " Flesh-devouring Plants " now known to botanists.

III—The Health of Plants

We often speak of plants as being healthy or unhealthy, just as we speak of human beings; and it is the simple truth that they, like ourselves, may be either well or ill, either feeble or vigorous. They suffer from illnesses and diseases, much as we do, and often from the same causes.

It may be bad air which upsets them, or want of good water to drink, or insufficient food in the soil, or not enough sunshine, or too much heat or too much cold. One kind needs what another cannot stand. So with us —" one man's meat is another man's poison."

Mention has been made earlier of growths which do not root in the ground, but drain their nourishment from some other plant upon which they live. Parasites of various kinds are common in the Vegetable World, and they are usually looked upon as hurtful, as bringing disease, if not death, to the tree or herb attacked.

The smallest and most abundant of these unwelcome guests are the Bacteria—tiny invisible hordes ! We spoke of them as among the very lowest on the rungs of a ladder of vegetable growths. It is not certain that all the Bacteria are " vegetable " in nature, for some may be " animal," but at least very many of them are. And their numbers are simply enormous, far beyond our power to reckon.

Not much has been said, so far, about the quantities of *Seeds*, which can be produced by a flowering plant in one season. These quantities differ immensely, for some plants bring forth very few, perhaps one or two seeds only to a single bloom. But they are rather rare, and with others matters are widely the reverse.

For instance, a single plant has been known to grow ten thousand seeds in a year; another sixty thousand; another a hundred thousand; another seven hundred thousand; and so on.

And if each of those thousands of seeds should produce next year another ten or a hundred thousand, and each of those again the same amounts in the year after—think what it would all come to. Naturally, they do not, because many seeds must always fail, from want of water or of room to grow or some other cause.

So much for the manufacture of seeds by flowering plants. But when we go down the ladder to the swarming Bacteria, these numbers are far surpassed. Here we find nothing in the shape of seeds, but more generally growth by each individual dividing into two.

And very quickly it comes about ! You would hardly believe, unless you already know it, how rapidly these tiny atoms of life get through what we describe as " growing up." When careful watch had been kept over some of them—of course through a microscope—it was found that *in twenty minutes* they had so reached maturity as to divide again.

With human beings a " generation " is supposed to last about thirty years. But with these minute beings a " generation " seems to last less than half-an-hour. And this, at such a rate of increase, means that in the course of about eight hours some sixty millions of them might come into existence, all descended from one small ancestor.

So no wonder that there are plenty, and more than plenty, of them !

Plants suffer from many different kinds of disease. But when we use the word " suffer," we do not mean that they actually endure pain. The plant, as a plant, loses health and vigour and beauty. Whether it is in the very faintest degree conscious of its loss is another question.

We all know of the Potato Disease, and many among us can remember the terrible famine in Ireland, which followed its outbreak. For at that time the poor of Ireland lived mainly on potatoes, and when they failed nothing remained.

Most of us, too, are familiar with the small round objects called " Oak-apples." But they are not apples,

They are a disease of the Oak-tree. Such gall-growths are found on other plants as well, and they are usually due to a small living creature getting inside the stem, or branch, and staying there, while an unhealthy lump forms round it.

Often we see upon the trunk of a tree a large unsightly swelling, and this again means disease. With a tree, happily, it does not mean pain, as any such growth would with a man, but it does mean that the health of the tree is not what it should be.

One well-known parasite is an odd little red plant, called the "Dodder," which goes creeping over others, sucking its food from them, and never taking the trouble to send a root into the earth. One may often see the Dodder crawling over bushes on a common.

And though usually we look on such parasites as hurtful to the plants upon which they fasten, yet it may not be so in every case. For, with regard to the "galls" just mentioned, it has been found, curiously, that in growing thus they have sometimes caused the *single* flowers of the plant attacked to become *double;* the stamens altering into petals. You know how the single flowers of a Wild Rose may become double through cultivation. Here the same thing is believed to come about, not through a gardener's care, but through that which is more in the nature of a disease.

And this does not stand alone. A botanist, who studied the matter closely, found in certain instances that a parasite, preying on the roots of a plant, instead of doing it harm seemed actually to do it good. The plant which was preyed upon, far from being weakened, grew more strong and healthy.

433

SOME REMARKABLE WAYS OF PLANTS

So in the Vegetable World, as in our world, it sometimes happens that those things which are looked upon as most sad may in the end bring about greater good.

IV—PLANT-LIFE IN GENERAL

We have seen in these pages some wonderful things about the Vegetable World. We have learnt a little of how its members live; how they breathe, how they feed, how they rest, how they seem to love sunshine. We have found how they differ in their ways and in their likings—if that word may be used for them—and in the kinds of soil and air and climate that they need.

Something we have noticed of what they have to do in our world : of the work of Roots, the work of Stems, the work of Leaves, the work of Flowers.

More than this, it has become clear how truly they *live ;* how utterly they differ from things without life; how much more nearly they are related to ourselves than perhaps we have imagined.

Also we have seen how tremendously useful they are to mankind, more than useful, absolutely necessary, since apart from the marvellous tasks which they carry out *we* could not live. So we may well look on them with gratitude : gratitude first to Him Who gave them to us; gratitude also to themselves, our faithful servants, ever busied for our benefit. We may think of them as our small brother and sister beings, to be loved and admired and cared for.

And all the while we know so little of their real nature; of how and in what manner they do the extraordinary things that we see them do.

THE GARDEN OF EARTH

Why *should* the roots rove hither and thither in search of the right food? Why *should* flowers and leaves turn persistently towards the sun? Why *should* the Vallisneria stalk act as it does—growing up to the water-surface for supplies of pollen, then bending and coiling downward, to be ready with ripened seeds for the next year? Where lies the connection between such actions and the unseen cause, the hidden controlling power? What *is* that cause—that power?

Such questions we cannot answer fully. We cannot define how far that which we call " sense " or " sensitiveness " on the part of plants is actually what we mean by the words. We only know that in many ways they behave almost as if they really had a measure of understanding.

Not of understanding like our own. Not of understanding equal to that of animals. This we cannot suppose.

But in recent years the thought has gained ground that perhaps—perhaps—in the mysterious world of plant-life a very faint measure may exist of something like " consciousness." That when they seem to shrink from a touch, when they droop and fail from lack of sunshine or of water, there may be in them the tiniest amount of something like discomfort. That when they gaze up at the sun, and appear to bask in his rays, they may have a dim sense of enjoyment, or at all events of something akin to satisfaction. We are certainly free to indulge in the fancy, and in time we may know that it is not only a fancy.

The word just used, " consciousness," needs defining. I think that what we mean by it in this connection is—

not only *being alive*, but *knowing that one is alive*. We ourselves live, and we know that we live. A plant lives; but can we contend that in the feeblest degree it *knows* that it lives? There lies the real question! And though we constantly talk of plants as if they knew, as if they understood, as if they did certain things for certain ends, knowing why they so act, it is not without a touch of reservation that we quote Wordsworth's couplet—

> " And 'tis my faith that every flower
> Enjoys the air it breathes."

Not that the words may not be perfectly true, but that perhaps we cannot yet be sure.

To return to the main question : How do these things, these growths, movements, adaptations, changes, developments, come about? By what power, through what control, are they caused?

" Nature," we are told, does this, and brings to pass that. But the answer does not satisfy. " Nature " is not a person, is not even a power. " Nature " means simply the sum of all that we see and know to be going on around us; possibly not including inanimate rocks and stones, but certainly including animal-life and plant-life of every description, *and* all human life. When we speak of " Nature " working changes in plants, we might just as well speak of their doing it themselves.

Nor would this, in a sense, be wrong. Not consciously —yet actually—they do it.

Some animals, in cold northern winters, change the colour of their coats from brown to white, a protective act, rendering them invisible against the snow. We cannot suppose that the *will* of the creature works this alteration. It is due to the subconscious Life which controls the creature's body.

When your heart beats day and night persistently, it is not *you*—not the conscious part of you—which keeps that heart going and regulates its beating. Here, again, the unconscious or subconscious Life in you does the work. Your soul controls your body; consciously in part, unconsciously in part. The " soul " or " life "[1] may be said in a manner to know what is needful for your body, and to bring about, so far as it can, what is needed, apart from any effort of your conscious will.

In like manner the life—the soul—of an animal controls its growth and developments, and does all in its power to bring about what is required for the good of the animal, quite irrespective of the latter's will. When we talk of the " healing power of Nature," as seen in a wounded body of man or animal, it is this to which in reality we are referring.

And so too, though in a much lower degree, may we not claim for the Plant a " soul " or " life " which does its utmost to obtain all that the plant craves for or needs to keep it in health? As the " life " of the coral-polype secretes and builds the solid framework on which it dwells, so the " life " or "soul " of a plant secretes and builds the framework of that plant, controls its actions, and fosters its developments.[2]

---

[1] One Greek word stands for both " soul " and " life," and may be translated by either.

[2] It may be asked—If plants and animals consist, like Man, of body and soul in even very limited degrees, are they to be regarded as in the same category with Man?—are they all more

SOME REMARKABLE WAYS OF PLANTS

But beyond and behind and throughout all this, as we well know, dwells ever ONE SUPREME, "The Lord and Giver of Life,"—

> " the Power
> That rules all action and all tides of thought,
> And all the secret courses of the Stars." [1]

One matter, much discussed during recent years, has not yet been mentioned. This is the extraordinary fulness and abundance of Vegetable Life on Earth, together with the thought of conflict, and of the incessant struggle for existence. In other words, the way in which each seed, each plantlet, has to fight for very life, and can only prevail by getting the better of others in the strife.

No portion of Earth's surface can support more than a certain amount of vegetation; and where one seed or one plant succeeds, many others are bound to fail.

To some extent such a condition of things is inevitable. Where hundreds of seeds have ripened, only a limited number of them can become healthy and well-grown plants. Many must fail, from lack of room and of food.

If we think once more of the acorns seen on a single Oak, we shall realise how few of them will ever become large trees. At any particular place only enough food is found in the soil to keep going a definite number of Oaks; and where one survives others must die.

Certain writers, seeing this vividly, have spoken in a

or less on the same level? No; for Man is not body and soul only; he is Body, Soul, and Spirit. Man alone was made " in the Image of God."

[1] Alfred Noyes.

melancholy key about plants as selfishly fighting for themselves, and ruthlessly trampling out the lives of their companions. Much has been written as to the "fierce struggle" going on, and the many that perish, neglected and forgotten failures.

That is not, however, a very happy way of looking on the matter, and it may be viewed from another standpoint.

We need not blame the plants which succeed, since we ourselves imperatively need them to work for us, to purify our atmosphere, to prepare our daily food. And they have to carry out these duties, to which they are called.

As for the seeming failures—the unused seeds, the wasted acorns, the dying plantlets—they are not really wasted or useless or failures. They have their simple tasks to perform, even though they can never add to the number of our stately forest-trees.

Sometimes they serve as food for man. Sometimes they serve as food for animals. Sometimes they help to enrich the soil in which more successful growths will find a home; and so they end by becoming food for future generations of Vegetable Life.

And if many multitudes of these—of pollen-grains, of seeds, of plantlets—have to fulfil such humble ends, have to give up their little lives for others, dying unnoticed and unknown, instead of becoming what they seemed to have been made for, and what they set out to be—neither they nor we have any right to complain. It is all part of the same great Service! Many kinds of plants, and many types of service, are needed for such a "Garden" as our Earth.

THE STORY OF A
THOUSAND-YEAR PINE

I

THE peculiar charm and fascination that trees exert over many people I had always felt from childhood, but it was that great nature-lover, John Muir, who first showed me how and where to learn their language. Few trees, however, ever held for me such an attraction as did a gigantic and

443

venerable yellow pine which I discovered one autumn day several years ago while exploring the southern Rockies. It grew within sight of the Cliff-Dwellers' Mesa Verde, which stands at the corner of four States, and as I came upon it one evening just as the sun was setting over that mysterious tableland, its character and heroic proportions made an impression upon me that I shall never forget, and which familiar acquaintance only served to deepen while it yet lived and before the axeman came. Many a time I returned to build my camp-fire by it and have a day or a night in its solitary and noble company. I learned afterwards that it had been given the name "Old Pine," and it certainly had an impressiveness quite compatible with the age and dignity which go with a thousand years of life.

When, one day, the sawmill-man at Mancos wrote, "Come, we are about to log your old pine," I started at once, regretting that a thing which seemed to me so human, as well as so noble, must be killed.

I went with the axemen who were to cut the old pine down. A grand and impressive tree he was. Never have I seen so much individuality, so much character, in a tree. Although lightning had given him a bald crown, he was still a healthy giant, and was waving evergreen banners more than one hundred and fifteen feet above the earth. His massive trunk, eight feet in diameter at the level of my breast, was covered with a thick, rough, golden-brown bark which was broken into irregular plates. Several of his arms were bent and broken. Altogether, he presented a timeworn but heroic appearance.

It is almost a marvel that trees should live to become the oldest of living things. Fastened in one place, their struggle is incessant and severe. From the moment a baby tree is born — from the instant it casts its tiny shadow upon the ground — until death, it is in danger from insects and animals. It cannot move to avoid danger. It cannot run away to escape enemies. Fixed in one spot, almost helpless, it must endure flood and drought, fire and storm, insects and earthquakes, or die.

Trees, like people, struggle for existence, and an aged tree, like an aged person, has not only a striking appearance, but an interesting biography. I have read the autobiographies of many century-old trees, and have found their life-stories strange and impressive. The yearly growth, or annual ring of wood with which trees envelop themselves, is embossed with so many of their experiences that this annual ring of growth literally forms an autobiographic diary of the tree's life.

I wanted to read Old Pine's autobiography. A veteran pine that had stood on the southern Rockies and struggled and triumphed through the changing seasons of hundreds of years must contain a rare life-story. From his stand between the Mesa and the pine-plumed mountain, he had seen the panorama of the seasons and many a strange pageant; he had beheld what scenes of animal and human strife, what storms and convulsions of nature! Many a wondrous secret he had locked within his tree soul. Yet, although he had not recorded what he had *seen*, I knew that he had kept a fairly accurate diary of his own personal experience. This I knew the saw would reveal, and this I had determined to see.

Nature matures a million conifer seeds for each one she chooses for growth, so we can only speculate as to the selection of the seed from which sprung this storied pine. It may be that the cone in which it matured was

SOME OF "OLD PINE'S" NEIGHBORS
(Western Yellow Pines)

crushed into the earth by the hoof of
a passing deer. It may have been hidden by a jay; or, as is more likely,
the tree may have grown from one of
the uneaten cones which a squirrel
had buried for winter food. Frémont
squirrels are the principal nurserymen

for all the Western pineries. Each autumn they harvest a heavy percent-
age of the cone crop and bury it for
winter. The seeds in the uneaten
cones germinate, and each year countless thousands of conifers grow from
the seeds planted by these squirrels.
It may be that the seed from which
Old Pine burst had been planted by
an ancient ancestor of the protest-
ing Frémont squirrel whom we found
that day in apparent possession of the
premises; or this seed may have been

A THOUSAND–YEAR PINE

in a cone which simply bounded or blew into a hole, where the seed found sufficient mould and moisture to give it a start in life.

II

II

Two loggers swung their axes: at the
first blow a Frémont squirrel came out
of a hole at the base of a dead limb
near the top of the tree and made an
aggressive claim of ownership, setting
up a vociferous protest against the
cutting. As his voice was unheeded,
he came scolding down the tree,

jumped off one of the lower limbs, and took refuge in a young pine that stood near by. From time to time he came out on the top of the limb nearest to us, and, with a wry face, fierce whiskers, and violent gestures, directed a torrent of abuse at the axemen who were delivering death-blows to Old Pine.

The old pine's enormous weight caused him to fall heavily, and he came to earth with tremendous force and struck on an elbow of one of his stocky arms. The force of the fall not only broke the trunk in two, but badly shattered it. The damage to the log was so general that the sawmill-man said it would not pay to saw it into lumber and that it could rot on the spot.

A THOUSAND-YEAR PINE

I had come a long distance for the express purpose of deciphering Old Pine's diary as the scroll of his life should be laid open in the sawmill. The abandonment of the shattered form compelled the adoption of another way of getting at his story. Receiving permission to do as I pleased with his remains, I at once began to cut and split both the trunk and the limbs, and to transcribe their strange records. Day after day I worked. I dug up the roots and thoroughly dissected them, and with the aid of a magnifier I studied the trunk, the roots, and the limbs.

I carefully examined the base of his stump, and in it I found ten hundred and forty-seven rings of growth! He had lived through a thousand and forty-seven memorable years. As he was cut down in 1903, his birth probably occurred in 856.

In looking over the rings of growth, I found that a few of them were much thicker than the others; and these thick rings, or coats of wood, tell of favorable seasons. There were also a few extremely thin rings of growth. In places two and even three of these were together. These were the results of unfavorable seasons, — of drought or cold. The rings of trees also show healed wounds, and tell of burns, bites, and bruises, of torn bark and broken arms. Old Pine not only received injuries in his early years, but from time to time throughout his life. The somewhat kinked condition of several of the rings of growth, beginning with

the twentieth, shows that at the age
of twenty he sustained an injury
which resulted in a severe curvature of
the spine, and that for some years he
was somewhat stooped. I was unable
to make out from his diary whether
this injury was the result of a tree or
some object falling upon him and pin-
ning him down, or whether his back
had been overweighted and bent by
wet, clinging snow. As I could find no
scars or bruises, I think that snow
must have been the cause of the injury. However, after a few years he
straightened up with youthful vitality
and seemed to outgrow and forget the
experience.

A century of tranquil life followed,
and during these years the rapid
growth tells of good seasons as well as

good soil. This rapid growth also shows that there could not have been any crowding neighbors to share the sun and the soil. The tree had grown evenly in all quarters, and the pith of the tree was in the center. But had one tree grown close, on that quarter the old pine would have grown slower than on the others and have been thinner, and the pith would thus have been away from the tree's center.

When the old pine was just completing his one hundred and thirty-fifth ring of growth, he met with an accident which I can account for only by assuming that a large tree that grew several yards away blew over, and in falling, stabbed him in the side with two dead limbs. His bark was broken and torn, but this healed in due time.

Short sections of the dead limbs broke off, however, and were embedded in the old pine. Twelve years' growth covered them, and they remained hidden from view until my splitting revealed them. Two other wounds started promptly to heal and, with one exception, did so.

A year or two later some ants and borers began excavating their deadly winding ways in the old pine. They probably started to work in one of the places injured by the falling tree. They must have had some advantage, or else something must have happened to the nuthatches and chickadees that year, for, despite the vigilance of these birds, both the borers and the ants succeeded in establishing colonies that threatened injury and possibly death.

Fortunately relief came. One day the chief surgeon of all the Southwestern pineries came along. This surgeon was the Texas woodpecker. He probably did not long explore the ridges and little furrows of the bark before he discovered the wound or heard these hidden insects working. After a brief examination, holding his ear to the bark for a moment to get the location of the tree's deadly foe beneath, he was ready to act. He made two successful operations. Not only did these require him to cut deeply into the old pine and take out the borers, but he may also have had to come back from time to time to dress the wounds by devouring the ant-colonies which may have persisted in taking possession of them. The wounds finally healed, and only the splitting of the affected parts revealed these records, all filled with pitch and preserved for nearly nine hundred years.

Following this, an even tenor marked his life for nearly three centuries. This quiet existence came to an end in the summer of 1301, when a stroke of lightning tore a limb out of his round top and badly shattered a shoulder. He had barely recovered from this injury when a violent wind tore off several of his arms. During the summer of 1348 he lost two of his largest arms. These were sound, and more than a foot in diameter at the points of breakage. As these were broken by a down-pressing weight or force, we may attribute the breaks to accumulations of snow.

The oldest, largest portion of a tree is the short section immediately above the ground, and, as this lower section is the most exposed to accidents or to injuries from enemies, it generally bears evidence of having suffered the most. Within its scroll are usually found the most extensive and interesting autobiographical impressions.

It is doubtful if there is any portion of the earth upon which there are so many deadly struggles as upon the earth around the trunk of a tree. Upon this small arena there are battles fierce and wild; here nature is "red in tooth and claw." When a tree is small and tender, countless insects come to feed upon it. Birds come to it to devour these insects. Around the tree are daily almost merciless fights for existence. These death-struggles occur not only in the daytime, but in the night. Mice, rats, and rabbits destroy millions of young trees. These bold animals often flay baby trees in the daylight, and while at their deadly feast many a time have they been surprised by hawks, and then they are at a banquet where they themselves are eaten. The owl, the faithful night-watchman of trees, often swoops down at night, and as a result some little tree is splashed with the blood of the very animal that came to feed upon it.

The lower section of Old Pine's trunk contained records which I found interesting. One of these in particular aroused my imagination. I was sawing off a section of this lower portion when the saw, with a *buzz-z-z-z*, suddenly jumped. The object struck was harder than the saw. I wondered what it could be, and, cutting the wood carefully away, laid bare a flint arrowhead. Close to this one I found another, and then with care I counted the rings of growth to find out the year that these had wounded Old Pine. The outer ring which these arrowheads had pierced was the six hundred and thirtieth, so that the year of this occurrence was 1486.

Had an Indian bent his bow and shot at a bear that had stood at bay backed up against this tree? Or was there around this tree a battle among Indian tribes? Is it possible that at this place some Cliff-Dweller scouts encountered their advancing foe from the north and opened hostilities? It

CLIFF DWELLINGS ON THE MESA VERDE

may be that around Old Pine was
fought the battle that is said to have
decided the fate of that mysterious
race, the Cliff-Dwellers. The imagination insists on speculating with these
two arrowheads, though they form a
fascinating clue that leads us to no
definite conclusion. But the fact remains that Old Pine was wounded by
two Indian arrowheads some time
during his six hundred and thirtieth
summer.

The year that Columbus discovered
America, Old Pine was a handsome
giant with a round head held more
than one hundred feet above the earth.
He was six hundred and thirty-six
years old, and with the coming of the
Spanish adventurers his lower trunk
was given new events to record. The

year 1540 was a particularly memorable one for him. This year brought the first horses and bearded men into the drama which was played around him. This year, for the first time, he felt the edge of steel and the tortures of fire. The old chronicles say that the Spanish explorers found the cliff-houses in the year 1540. I believe that during this year a Spanish exploring party may have camped beneath Old Pine and built a fire against his instep, and that some of the explorers hacked him with an axe. The old pine had distinct records of axe and fire markings during the year 1540. It was not common for the Indians of the West to burn or mutilate trees, and it was common for the Spaniards to do so, and as these hackings in the tree seemed to have been made with some edged tool sharper than any possessed by the Indians, it at least seems probable that they were made by the Spaniards. At any rate, from the year 1540 until the day of his death, Old Pine carried these scars on his instep.

As the average yearly growth of the old pine was about the same as in trees similarly situated at the present time, I suppose that climatic conditions in his early days must have been similar to the climatic conditions of to-day. His records indicate periods of even tenor of climate, a year of extremely poor conditions, occasionally a year crowned with a bountiful wood harvest. From 1540 to 1762 I found little of special interest. In 1762, however, the season was not regular. After the

ring was well started, something, perhaps a cold wave, for a time checked
his growth, and as a result the wood
for that one year resembled two years'
growth; yet the difference between
this double or false ring and a regular
one was easily detected. Old Pine's
"hard times" experience seems to
have been during the years 1804
and 1805. I think it probable that
those were years of drought. During 1804 the layer of wood was the
thinnest in his life, and for 1805 the
only wood I could find was a layer
which only partly covered the trunk
of the tree, and this was exceedingly
thin.

From time to time in the old pine's
record, I came across what seemed to
be indications of an earthquake shock;

but late in 1811 or early in 1812, I
think there is no doubt that he experi-
enced a violent shock, for he made extensive records of it. This earthquake
occurred after the sap had ceased to
flow in 1811, and before it began to
flow in the spring of 1812. In places
the wood was checked and shattered.
At one point, some distance from the
ground, there was a bad horizontal
break. Two big roots were broken in
two, and that quarter of the tree which
faced the cliffs had suffered from a rock
bombardment. I suppose the violence
of the quake displaced many rocks,
and some of these, as they came
bounding down the mountain-side,
collided with Old Pine. One, of about
five pounds' weight, struck him so
violently in the side that it remained

embedded there. After some years the wound was healed over, but this fragment remained in the tree until I released it.

During 1859 some one made an axe-mark on the old pine that may have been intended for a trail-blaze, and during the same year another fire badly burned and scarred his ankle. I wonder if some prospectors came this way in 1859 and made camp by him.

Another record of man's visits to the tree was made in the summer of 1881, when I think a hunting or outing party may have camped near here and amused themselves by shooting at a mark on Old Pine's ankle. Several modern rifle-bullets were found embedded in the wood around or just beneath a blaze which was made on the tree the same year in which the bullets had entered it. As both these marks were made during the year 1881, it is at least possible that this year the old pine was used as the background for a target during a shooting contest.

While I was working over the old pine, a Frémont squirrel who lived near by used every day to stop in his busy harvesting of pine-cones to look on and scold me. As I watched him placing his cones in a hole in the ground under the pine-needles, I often wondered if one of his buried cones would remain there uneaten, to germinate and expand ever green into the air, and become a noble giant to live as long and as useful a life as Old Pine. I found myself trying to picture the

A THOUSAND-YEAR PINE

scenes in which this tree would stand
when the birds came singing back
from the Southland in the springtime
of the year 3000.

III

III

AFTER I had finished my work of splitting, studying, and deciphering the fragments of the old pine, I went to the sawmill and arranged for the men to come over that evening after I had departed, and burn every piece and vestige of the venerable old tree. I told them I should be gone by dark on a trip to the summit of Mesa Verde, where I was to visit a gnarled old cedar. Then I went back and piled into a pyramid every fragment of root and trunk and broken branch. Seating myself upon this pyramid, I spent some time that afternoon gazing through the autumn sun-glow at the hazy Mesa Verde, while my mind rebuilt and shifted the scenes of the long, long drama in which Old Pine had played his part and of which he had given us but a few fragmentary records. I lingered there dreaming until twilight. I thought of the cycles during which he had stood patient in his appointed place, and my imagination busied itself with the countless experiences that had been recorded, and the scenes and pageants he had

THE MESA VERDE

witnessed but of which he had made
no record. I wondered if he had enjoyed the changing of seasons. I
knew that he had often boomed or
hymned in the storm or the breeze.
Many a monumental robe of snow-
flowers had he worn. More than a
thousand times he had beheld the
earth burst into bloom amid happy
songs of mating birds; hundreds of
times in summer he had worn countless crystal rain-jewels in the sunlight
of the breaking storm, while the brilliant rainbow came and vanished on
the near-by mountain-side. Ten thousand times he had stood silent in the
lonely light of the white and mystic
moon.

Twilight was fading into darkness
when I arose and started on my night

journey for the summit of Mesa Verde.
When I arrived at the top of the Mesa,
I looked back and saw a pyramid of
golden flame standing out in the
darkness.